THE CREATIVE IMPERATIVE

THE CREATIVE IMPERATIVE

School Librarians and Teachers Cultivating Curiosity Together

JAMI BILES JONES AND
LORI J. FLINT, EDITORS

LIBRARIES UNLIMITED

AN IMPRINT OF ABC-CLIO, LLC
Santa Barbara, California • Denver, Colorado • Oxford, England

Library of Congress Cataloging-in-Publication Data

The creative imperative : school librarians and teachers cultivating curiosity together / Jami Biles Jones and Lori J. Flint, editors

   pages cm
  Includes index.
   ISBN 978-1-61069-307-3 (pbk.) — ISBN 978-1-61069-308-0 (ebook)
1. Creative thinking—Study and teaching—United States.   2. Creative thinking in children—United States.   3. Creative ability—Study and teaching—United States. 4. Creative ability in children—United States.   5. Problem solving—Study and teaching—United States.   6. School librarian participation in curriculum planning. I. Jones, Jami Biles. II. Flint, Lori J.
  LB1590.5.C65   2013
  370.15'7—dc23   2013018364

ISBN: 978-1-61069-307-3
EISBN: 978-1-61069-308-0

17   16   15   14   13   1   2   3   4   5

This book is also available on the World Wide Web as an eBook.
Visit www.abc-clio.com for details.

Libraries Unlimited
An Imprint of ABC-CLIO, LLC

ABC-CLIO, LLC
130 Cremona Drive, P.O. Box 1911
Santa Barbara, California 93116-1911

This book is printed on acid-free paper ∞

Manufactured in the United States of America

We dedicate this book to those among us and
those past who have devoted their lives to doing everything
possible to make the world a more creative place, and
not just sitting and thinking about it.

Don't think. Thinking is the enemy of creativity. It's self-conscious,
and anything self-conscious is lousy. You can't try
to do things. You simply must do things.

—Ray Bradbury

CONTENTS

FOREWORD

Vera John-Steiner

No accurate cognition of reality is possible without a certain element of imagination, a certain flight from the immediate, concrete, solitary impressions in which this reality is presented. . . .

—Vygotsky (1987, p. 349)

The challenges and pleasures of creative education are carefully explored in this book. The authors recognize the roles of parents, teachers, librarians, peers, and people representing the community in the construction of stimulating and adventure-filled classrooms. They recognize the complexity of creativity, and how it is rooted in play and exploration. It is fueled by children's powerful attraction to a particular domain of their choice and possibly predisposition, amplified by the cultural practices of those who surround them, guided by their teachers, and enriched by the many new resources available for their creative projects. This book overcomes the false dichotomies between the arts and the sciences, engagement and inspiration, and teacher-centered and child-centered learning environments.

The authors draw upon the more than half-century–long exploration of psychological and educational studies of creativity. We have been learning from creativity researchers about the fortuitous combinations of novelty and usefulness through case studies (Gardner, 1993; John-Steiner, 1985); personality studies (Barron & Harrington, 1981); psychometric inventories (Torrance, 1975); experimental studies (Amabile, 1983); ethnographic studies of classrooms (Sawyer, 1997; St. John, 2010); theoretical analyses (Csikszentmihalyi, 1996; Sternberg, 1999; Gardner, 1993; John-Steiner & Moran, 2003) to name but a few sources. The chapters which follow examine this rapidly growing literature and propose a variety of ways to enrich classrooms. This is particularly urgent at a time when teachers are penalized for students' low grades on standardized tests and have limited time to stimulate creative activities in their classrooms.

The playful explorations of young children can be driven out of classrooms or they can serve as a foundation to more systematic teaching/learning. In our own work (John-Steiner & Moran, 2003; Connery, John-Steiner, & Marjanovic-Shane, 2010; Connery & John-Steiner, in press) we have built on the Russian psychologist Lev Semyonovich Vygotsky's writings. His central idea is the social origin of linguistic, cognitive, and creative processes starting in infancy when the newborn's survival is dependent on caretakers. The closeness across generations during children's early years provides the opportunity for the young learner to internalize the shared knowledge of his community. This is not a passive process, but, as envisioned by Vygotsky, it is one of play, appropriation, discovery, and collaboration.

Children create imaginary situations in play, an activity that Vygotsky saw as "the leading source of development in preschool years" (1933/1976, p. 537). In the course of play, children try to fulfill desires which are not met in their immediate lives. They explore roles inspired by adult reality as well as fantasy figures and structure their activity with the help of some rules which shape their actions within these imaginary situations. Through play children create, with the help of a more experienced other, a zone of proximal development (ZPD) between their present level of achievement and their more effective future accomplishments. Vygotsky's (1978) most widely discussed concept, the ZPD "awakens a variety of internal developmental processes that are able to operate only when the child is interacting with people in his environment and in cooperation with his peers. Once these processes are internalized, they become part of the child's independent developmental achievement" (p. 90).

This, particularly at its beginning, is a social process. The developmental researchers Larry Smolucha and Francine Smolucha (1986) found that object substitutions such as a broom becoming a dancing partner occur during children's second year of life while being engaged with their caregivers. The increased sophistication of children's play allows them to explore interpersonal situations, develop judgment and memory, and contributes to their language behavior and emotional control. They start learning the importance of asking open-ended questions which may result in multiple directions and complex answers. Their play turns into inquiry requiring classroom and library resources. The authors of this book describe in rich detail the benefits of creative activities built on play in the classroom. Most importantly, they assert that students are more actively involved in learning when given the opportunity to be co-participants in planning innovative projects.

In this volume, the authors argue powerfully that it is very difficult to sustain the wonder and excitement of young children in school. Beth Hennessey elegantly describes how grading and other extrinsic rewards depress the quality of children's innovative contributions, stifles curiosity and engagement, and undermines creative behavior. Teachers face a difficult task mobilizing children's intrinsic motivation both in their productive activities and reading. However, once a teacher identifies the different sources of children's interest and relies on them, the students engage with projects of longer duration and greater depth than the many short tasks that populate school life.

The crucial role of motivation in creative activities does not end in childhood. The contemporary writer Michael Chabon (2012) described in a recent issue of the *New York Times* how his current book was motivated by a vision of a fully integrated United States. The sources of that vision hark back to his young years when he lived in an unusual utopian community. Vygotsky (1965/1971) wrote that art "introduces the effects of passion, violates inner equilibrium, changes will in a new sense, and stirs feelings, emotions, passions and vices without which society would remain in an inert and motionless state" (p. 249). The building on wishes and desires starts with young children's poems, drawings, scientific explorations, cooking adventures, and jointly authored books. The skilled teacher and librarian know how to expand these projects and provide the knowledge in a particular creative domain to help sustain the long arc from childhood experimentation to adult achievement.

Creativity has become a major topic of discussion in education, psychology, and the mass media. In 2010, the realization that children's creativity scores have decreased contributed to an international focus on shifting public school curricula from test-dominated to more project-inclusive approaches (Kim, 2011). Such a change supports a theoretical shift from conceptualizing creativity as a set of traits to the notion of a dynamic system. The best-known systemic approach is that developed by Mihalyi Csikszentmihalyi (1996). His focus on the interaction of field, domain, and person introduced the dynamics between knowledge and creator as well as the representatives of the broader field who are responsible for the establishment and maintenance of the institutions that sustain and control entry of creative products. Vygotskian theory also approaches creativity from a systemic perspective. The dynamics of the individual and the social, of emotion and cognitive expertise, of intrinsic and extrinsic motivation, of convergent and divergent thinking all interact in complex functional systems which, once fully explored, will inspire sustained inquiry and application to creative education.

While major developments have taken place in creativity research and theories of creativity, the recognition of creativity's importance in schools and society at large is lagging behind. We are facing a world in which people are increasingly dependent on consuming entertainment during their leisure hours while losing the pleasure and rewards of creative activities.

This loss of intense engagement, so characteristic of creative activities, has many causes. One of those is the addiction to television with its concurrent material gains for the advertisers. Another is the competitive pressure in schools. As already mentioned, play is pervasive in young children's lives. Also, play, when linked with imagination, relevant research, specialized skills, persistence, curiosity, and social support develops into sustained, fulfilling activities.

The result of these frequently yields an outcome that produces pride and self-confidence in children which overflows in all domains of their being. Creative projects are also the settings in which children learn to collaborate; building on each other's strengths and encouraging each other when their motivation wanes or relevant knowledge is limited. In a frequently repetitive and laborious school life, the practice of creative endeavors brings passion to learners and the sense of possibilities that makes growing up the great adventure that it can be.

REFERENCES

Amabile, T. (1983). *The social psychology of creativity*. New York: Springer-Verlag.

Barron, F. X., & Harrington, D. M. (1981). Creativity, intelligence, and personality. *Annual Review of Psychology, 32*, 439–476.

Chabon, M. (2012, September 27). O. J. Simpson, racial utopia and the moment that inspired my novel. *New York Times Magazine* (pp. 42–44).

Connery M.C., & John-Steiner, V.P. (in press). The power of imagination. *LEARNing landscapes.* Quebec, Canada: McGill University.

Connery, M.C., John-Steiner, V.P., & Marjanovic-Shane, A. (2010). *Vygotsky and creativity: A cultural-historical approach to play, meaning making, and the arts.* New York: Peter Lang Publishing.

Csikszentmihalyi, M. (1996). *Creativity: Flow and the psychology of discovery and invention.* New York: HarperCollins.

Gardner, H. (1993). *Frames of mind: The theory of multiple intelligences.* New York: Basic Books, Inc.

John-Steiner, V. (1985). *Notebooks of the mind: Explorations in thinking.* New York: Oxford University Press.

John-Steiner, V. (2000). *Creative collaboration.* New York: Oxford University Press.

John-Steiner, V., & Moran, S. (2003). Creativity in the making: Vygotsky's contemporary contribution to the dialectic of development and creativity. In Sawyer, R.K., et al (Eds.), *Creativity and development* (pp. 61–90). New York: Oxford University Press.

Kim, K.H. (2012). The creativity crisis: The decrease in creative thinking scores on the Torrance Tests of Creative Thinking. *Creativity Research Journal,* 23, 285–295.

Sawyer, K. (1997). *Pretend play as improvisation: Conversation in the preschool classroom.* Mahwah, NJ: Erlbaum.

Smolucha, L.W., & Smolucha, F.C. (1986). L.S. Vygotsky's theory of creative imagination. *SPIEL,* 5(2), 299–308. Frankfurt, Germany: Verlag Peter Lang.

Sternberg, R. (1999). *Handbook of creativity.* New York: Cambridge University Press.

St. John, P. (2010). Crossing scripts and swapping riffs. In M. Cathrene Connery, Vera John-Steiner, & Ana Marjanovic-Shane (Eds.), *Vygotsky and creativity: A cultural-historical approach to play, meaning making, and the arts* (pp. 63–82). New York: Peter Lang Publishers.

Torrance, E.P. (1975). Creativity research in education: Still alive. In I.A. Taylor & J.W. Getzels (Eds.), *Perspectives in creativity* (pp. 278–296). Chicago: Aldine Publishing Company.

Vygotsky, L.S. (1933/1976). Play and its role in the mental development of the child. In J.S. Bruner, A. Jolly, & K. Sylva (Eds.), *Play—its role in development and evolution* (pp. 537–554). New York: Penguin Books Ltd.

Vygotsky, L.S. (1965/1971). *The psychology of art.* Cambridge, MA: MIT Press (Original work published as *Psikhologiia iskusstva,* 1965).

Vygotsky, L.S. (1978). *Mind in society: The development of higher psychological processes* (M. Cole, V. John-Steiner, & E. Souberman, Eds.) Cambridge, MA: Harvard University Press.

Vygotsky, L.S. (1987). Emotions and their development in childhood. In R.W. Rieber & A.S. Carton (Eds.), *The collected works of L.S. Vygotsky* (Vol. 1, N. Minick, Trans., pp. 325–338). New York: Plenum Press (Original work published in Voprosy Psikhologii, 3, 1959).

ACKNOWLEDGMENTS

We would like to thank Benny and Dan for putting up with us working on weekends and other odd hours to get this done, after we've finished our "real" jobs, and Chris for coming through with illustrations on demand. Thanks also to the friends and colleagues who spent hours reading and writing for this book; we couldn't have done it without you. Finally, we have to sing the praises of editors; where would we be without you?

INTRODUCTION

Jami Biles Jones and Lori J. Flint

"I am not creative." This graduate student's response to Jami's invitation to be open and creative was the genesis for this book. Other students in this online class shook their virtual heads in agreement, which began Jami's quest to study creativity with the goal of helping school librarians embrace creative practices and pass these ways of thinking and learning to their students. Teaching online classes, she moved to New York City and matriculated in a master's program at Columbia University's Teachers College that emphasized creativity. Jami developed the proposal for this book and invited Lori to collaborate.

With Lori's background in gifted and creative education, we knew that we could "do" school a lot better than we currently are and that all children deserve the kind of opportunities for creative work usually reserved for gifted children. This book schools educators in the whats, whys, and hows of creativity, but more importantly, it helps educators develop the dispositions of a creative educator, while simultaneously giving them permission to teach differently and watch their students blossom.

Everyone involved with this book understands that teaching for creativity is a daunting task, especially after decades of learning by rote and filling in the blanks, but everybody hopes it can be done. What we find alarming, however, are several newly minted mandates requiring that educators teach creativity and assess efforts with ill-defined instruments. These mandates include 21st-century skills, new professional teaching standards in several states, and the adoption of the Common Core State Standards. None of these is inherently evil, but they *are* new ways of working that come with little in the way of financial or professional support.

These mandates remind us of another largely unfunded directive: No Child Left Behind, created by legislators to impose largely unrealistic accountability on schools. How do educators move from this standardized testing mind-set to open-ended, flexible teaching and mentoring that fosters student creativity? With states considering and already adopting educational mandates, we feel that now is the perfect time for a thoughtful book to help school librarians and teachers consider creativity, in all its facets, and the environments and attitudes necessary for creativity to happen.

To meet this challenge, we assembled a team of exceptional scholars and practitioners who could help communicate the complexities of creativity and describe what is needed to successfully nurture student creators. We invite you on this journey to understand creativity in *The Creative Imperative: School Librarians and Teachers Cultivating Curiosity Together*.

Readers might be asking themselves why so much content when the journey they envision is a simplistic and easy-to-follow template for nurturing creativity—a vapid tool kit that does not upset the rigid educational apple cart. As educators, we are too used to being given 10-step plans to meet standards and initiatives that by and large have been forced on us. In this book you will learn how anticreative these practices are. Educators who ask for short guides on creativity and want to be told what to do and how to do it are missing the point—creativity is hard work that requires persistence, motivation, and expertise. Creativity is complex.

Although some educators nonchalantly bandy about the term creativity and ask students to be more creative, it is our ethical obligation to understand creativity and what we are asking of students. To do this, some educators may need to develop their own creativity as well. Each chapter in this book presents an aspect of creativity that is essential if one wants to understand what is needed to nurture student creativity or yours. Without this, understanding creativity remains a noun, a descriptor, rather than a verb, an action. It is the verb we desire for readers. We want students and educators actively involved and engaged in creating.

The Creative Imperative: School Librarians and Teachers Cultivating Curiosity Together, is an invitation to learn, beginning with a foreword by Vera John-Steiner. The book flows from the theoretical to the applied, through three sections and 15 chapters. At the end of each chapter you will find an extensive reference list that can be mined for more information.

In the first section, "Understanding the Complexity of Creativity," authors help readers to develop expertise about creativity. Expertise is an important concept in creativity because without it one cannot be creative. In chapter one, readers enter an imaginary bus and are guided on a historical tour of creativity that introduces them to the controversies in the field. In chapter two, six ideas at the heart of creativity—such as creativity is hard work—are presented and applied to the classroom. A notion presented in chapter two of creative people being difficult is explored in-depth in chapter three. As a society we say we value creativity, but if so, why does research show that teachers prefer compliant children over creative children? Why are students admonished for deviating from closed-ended assignments assessed with staid rubrics? Chapter four presents meta-analysis and content analysis research that indicates we are in the throes of a creativity crisis. Reasons for this crisis are explored, and suggestions for reversing the trend are made.

In the second section, "The Components of Creativity," authors help readers understand individual and group characteristics as well as environmental factors important for nurturing creativity. In chapter five, the notion of expertise and the 10,000 hour rule is presented. Scholars know that expertise is required for creativity, inventions, and innovations, but are students learning enough content to prepare them to "bisociate" ideas (a term presented in chapter 13), identify discrepancies, and create knowledge at the "mini-c" level (this notion is presented throughout the book). In chapter six, motivation, the wellspring of creativity, is presented. The author describes ways to immunize children against the five killers of motivation—expected rewards, expected evaluation, competition, time limits, and surveillance. In chapter seven, readers are introduced to eminent collaborative duos; the value of collaboration is discussed. In chapter eight, the habits of mind necessary for creative production are presented, along with suggestions for helping educators elicit creative responses from their students. In chapter nine, the importance of curiosity as a stepping-stone to thinking deeply is described.

In the third section, "Creativity in the Classroom and the School Library of Curious Delight," authors apply what was presented in the two previous sections to actual school library (and classroom) practice. In chapter 10, three keys to fostering student creativity—developing an environment supportive of creativity, teaching the skills and attitudes of creativity, and teaching the creative methods of the disciplines—provides a practical framework for creative practice. In chapter 11, suggestions are provided for applying the Common Core State Standards. In chapter 12, the author makes a case for video game development and technology to spur students to practice creativity. In chapter 13, inquiry is presented as the school librarian's surest way to foster creativity. In chapter 14, readers are introduced to problem-solving frameworks that are appropriate for both school librarians and teachers. Finally, in chapter 15, bibliocreativity—or fostering creativity through books, is presented.

The final section of the book includes two appendices: a tool for assessing creativity, a list of Future Problem Solving International topics, as well as an extensive list of resources, and finally, contributors' biographies.

Nurturing creativity is central to this book. A second but perhaps more difficult aspect though is strengthening children to maintain their creativity over the long haul even as they are bombarded with messages and practices destructive to creativity. E. Paul Torrance (whose import is presented throughout this book) studied creativity in children to predict whether their creative potential and achievements could be maintained as adults. For many children, potential and achievements faded away. How can we help children maintain their creativity and become even more creative? Torrance's *Manifesto for Children* is his advice synthesized from his longitudinal research and deserves memorizing by heart and posting on school library and classroom walls. As you read Torrance's *Manifesto for Children* consider if your practice supports children's fledgling creativity or is destructive of it. A Manifesto for School Librarians is presented in chapter 13.

Don't be afraid to fall in love with something and pursue it with intensity.

Know, understand, take pride in, practice, develop, exploit and enjoy your greatest strengths.

Learn to free yourself from the expectations of others and walk away from the games they impose on you. Free yourself to play your own game.

Find a teacher of mentor who will help you.

Learn the skills of interdependence.

Don't waste your time trying to be well rounded.

Do what you love and can do well.

Reprinted by permission of the Torrance Center for Creativity and Talent Development at the University of Georgia, Athens.

We hope this book whets your appetite to learn how to be more thoughtful and creative educators. Even more, we hope this primer on creativity leads you to taking permission to be the creative educator you wish to be and wish you'd had as a student.

Section I

UNDERSTANDING THE COMPLEXITY OF CREATIVITY

1

LOOKING AND LEAPING: AN INTRODUCTION TO CREATIVITY RESEARCH

Sarah E. Sumners
University of Georgia, Athens

Garrett J. Jaeger
University of Georgia, Athens

As educators, we are not merely conveyors of information, but rather facilitators of learning whose job is to guide students along the path to knowledge and understanding. Think of yourself as a travel guide who plays an integral part in the learning environment. You are there to help the tourists (students) in your group (classroom) to unlock their inborn potential. Our goal with this chapter is to help you develop the critical background information needed to facilitate the journey and make it more interesting for your students. We welcome you to join us and take in the breathtaking views as we navigate from current theories, to the island of prominent researchers, and onto our final destination of the ever-disputed state of controversies in the field and what our future travel plans might be. To this end, we must begin at the beginning, exploring the cornerstones of the modern creativity movement.

WHAT IS CREATIVITY?

Most literature on creativity begins with the proposal of a definition of creativity. It is our intention to harness your tension, as the reader, through the ambiguity of defining such a complex phenomenon. So, please be patient as we set up the historical backdrop of what the field now believes creativity to be. Along the way, this chapter will make stops and report on specific perspectives of creativity research. However, much of what is explored has been a focal point of human curiosity for millennia. It has been argued that creativity began when we acquired the capacity for metacognition—the ability to think about our own thinking (Flavell, 1976). In an effort to remain explicit, let us begin our tour of creativity research with its predecessors—those academic traditions that preceded it.

Creativity, Ideation, and Imagination

Where does creativity begin? Historically, an idea is the first step toward representing something we find appealing. Many brilliant thinkers have pondered the source of ideas, and our tour of creativity research needs to spend some time inside a dimly lit cave. Plato provided an exquisite example through his "Allegory of the Cave," in his famous dialogue in *The Republic*. The metaphor of a candle causing a shadow of the object upon a wall literally highlights the role an idea plays in creativity. The shadow symbolizes the representation of an idea or form (the object which casts the shadow) that is lit by the creative individual and his or her process.

Intelligence Tests

Currently, a prominent feature of our modern educational system is the standardized testing of intelligence. For decades, the Stanford-Binet Intelligence Scales have been the gold standard by which we assess student intelligence and educational effectiveness. However, Alfred Binet had previously investigated the importance of divergent thinking in intelligence, but found difficulty in standardizing the measurement of what has become a significant indicator of creativity (Binet & Simon, 1905). The implicit theories of many great thinkers have pointed at what the field of psychology embraced in the second half of the 20th century.

J. P. Guilford—APA Address in 1950

On our journey toward a destination of understanding the modern creativity movement, we must stop for a moment to acknowledge how creativity research, and its roots in psychology, began. Most summaries of creativity research begin with an homage to one particular event— J. P. Guilford's American Psychology Association (APA) presidential address in 1949 (Guilford, 1950). The position of APA president is obviously a prestigious one, and the organization's annual conference provides an opportunity to address current and potential zeitgeist in the field of psychology. Guilford took to the stage and led the field of psychology into what he declared an appallingly neglected investigation of creativity. At the time of his address, Guilford reported that "less than two-tenths of one percent of the books and articles indexed in the [*Psychological*] *Abstracts* for the past quarter century bear directly on this subject" (p. 34).

Process

With Guilford's emphasis on creativity research in our rear-view mirror, let us now embark on an exploration of the definition of creativity. We will start by examining the creative process as outlined by Mel Rhodes's "Four Ps" framework (1961). Undertaking an analysis of creativity may seem a somewhat daunting task to those who consider themselves creative because they may find their own process to be very personal and often difficult to understand. However, the Four Ps of Person, Process, Product, and Press provide an alliterative, mnemonic device for separating creativity research into conceptual categories. The first "P," Person, furthers the initial investigations that Guilford conducted on investigating creativity as the behavior of creative individuals. Subsequent sections of this chapter will address all Four Ps of Rhodes's framework, but we would like to begin with how well it elaborates upon the creative Process.

In his book, *The Art of Thought*, Graham Wallas (1926) described the creative process as having four stages: preparation, incubation, illumination, and verification. Preparation lives up to its title, such that the individual collects and interprets information. Once someone is "prepared," then they often need time away from the process so that he or she can allow their subconscious to incubate. This release of focus allows a person to reduce constraints and consider a wider range of options. The end of the incubation is marked by the romantic insight, or aha moment, of the illumination phase. While this appearance is not as sudden as often suggested, it is the culmination of what can often be a long period of incubation.

Now, it is not uncommon for an insight to be a bit of a false alarm due to it violating the creativity criteria of originality or effectiveness. The verification phase provides the reflection necessary to determine whether our insight is indeed creative. We find it important to explain how difficult it is to determine originality and propose that it be viewed as a construct of relativity. In other words, original ideas consistently emerge in two locations, often around the same time frame, unbeknownst to the parties involved. These occurrences do not make either idea less original, but how they are historically reported does cast a more favorable light on one or the other. For an excellent example, consider how Charles Darwin and Alfred Russell Wallace (1858) both independently developed the idea of natural selection, then collaborated their data and presented them to the Linnean Society of London, yet Darwin's publication of *Origin of Species* established his position as the father of evolutionary theory.

Product

Establishing an overview of the creative process is important, yet including how we assess a creative product is vital when providing a comprehensive description of creativity. There have been various adjectives used by researchers to define creativity. As proposed by Runco and Jaeger (2012), there is a long-standing standard definition of creativity that researchers agree upon: in order for something to be creative, it must be both original and effective. Most of the alternative definitions of creativity involve synonyms for either of these two definitional terms. Something can be original or unique, but not be appropriate for its context, thus being perceived simply as weird. Please take note that appropriateness or effectiveness can be subject to historical interpretation; for example, Vincent Van Gogh was seen as an outcast during his life, only to have his work and artistic perspective posthumously revered. Such is an all-too-familiar tale about the misunderstood creative individual. On the other hand, a product (or process) can be extremely effective, but not be original and becomes the established convention (i.e., the traditional form for the transmission of that knowledge) of its domain (e.g., Google was not the first search engine developed for the World Wide Web). Accommodation of both criteria allows for a consistently accurate definition of creativity. To sum up our definition, for something to be considered creative, it must be both original and effective in some way.

Historiometry

Now that we understand what we mean when we say creativity, let's take a look at the most current perspective of how to go about researching it. Over the past 30 years, research in creativity has employed historiometric techniques toward the investigation of prominent (eminent) people and events in history. Defined as "the application of quantitative methods to archival data about historic personalities and events to test nomothetic (generalized) hypotheses about human thought, feeling, and action" (Simonton, 1999a, p. 815), this method is considered by some to be one of the most hopeful approaches in the study of creativity (Runco, 2007). Put simply, historiometry uses statistics to evaluate eminent people and events in the past in an effort to test theories about people and events in the future. The first known historiometric study was Quetelet's (1835/1968) longitudinal investigation of age and creative productivity of eminent dramatists (Simonton, 1999b).

CREATIVITY THEORIES

Intelligence

Having a base understanding of creativity, let's continue along our journey into the land of creativity theories and prominent researchers. Early explorations into the relationship between creativity and intelligence found an association between the two, suggesting that creativity could not be separated from the cognitive facilities (Getzels & Jackson, 1962). However, subsequent studies found that the types of tasks and environmental conditions for creativity differ greatly from that of intelligence (Wallach & Kogan, 1965). Research on this delicate relationship has been highlighted by a threshold theory, suggesting that creativity requires a minimum amount of intelligence, beyond mere experience alone (Runco, Dow, & Smith, 2006).

Toward the end of this chapter we will revisit the relationship between creativity and intelligence because it is one of the more controversial topics in creativity literature. In order to provide a more detailed map of our travels toward those controversies, two more models of intelligence will help orient you. So, off to the right we have Guilford's Structure of Intellect (SOI) model and to the left is Robert Sternberg's Triarchic Model—both of which rely on tripartite distinctions.

How we process information is what drives the incredibly sophisticated model that Guilford presented. Similar to Howard Gardner's Multiple Intelligences, the SOI model reduces such processes into more distinctive abilities. The current chapter cannot detail the individual ability, but let us at least outline the main structures; if you desire more in-depth knowledge, visit Guilford's book *The Nature of Human Intelligence* (1967). He suggested that intellect can be divided into three categories (with their own subcategories): content (visual, auditory, symbolic, semantic, and behavioral); products (units, classes, relations, systems, transformation, and implications); and operations (cognition, memory, divergent production, convergent production, and evaluation).

The Triarchic Theory of human intelligence is another model that outlines potential correlates with creativity. Of course, when summarizing a theory about intelligence, brevity merely provides conceptual landmarks to guide the reader. Each of Sternberg's three subtheories is best clarified with interrogative words. The first subtheory, contextual, provides the where and what of intellectual behaviors. The second subtheory, experiential, maps when behavior is intelligent. The third subtheory completes the triarchic theory by how intelligent behavior is generated within the individual. Again, for further details of this intricate theory, use your librarian prowess to check out Sternberg's *Beyond IQ: A Triarchic Theory of Human Intelligence* (1985).

Associations

Along our journey to better understand creativity, we must take a few moments to stretch our legs and our minds to consider the ideas of problem-solving and problem-finding. Some definitions of creativity include problem-solving, but part of the creative process involves the need for self-expression without the need to solve a specific problem. Therefore, creative skills may involve more than problem-solving (Runco & Sumners, in press).

When trying to plan one's trip around the world, potential problems (tire blow-out, detours, etc.) are not always predictable or obvious and oftentimes require further identification, definition, and preparation. The quality of the problem can greatly impact the quality of the solution to the problem (Getzels, 1975). For instance, have you ever taken your car to the mechanic to fix a problem, only to have the same issue a week later? Here, the mechanic fixed what she thought was the problem, only to find out ($400 later) that the real problem was something completely different. There are those who possess problem-finding skills and those who are better at problem-solving (hopefully your mechanic has both!). Important is the recognition of both problem-solving and problem-finding as aspects of the creative process and their worth in the classroom.

While problem-solving and problem-finding are both important to the creative process, so too are the connections between seemingly unrelated ideas known as associative thinking. Empirical studies of these associative processes have developed methods to map the cognitive transitions between ideas (Mednick, 1962). There are common associative strategies that can be readily implemented in the classroom to encourage creative output such as the Remote Associates Test.

Another strategy that can help facilitate creative output is the use of divergent thinking. Divergent Thinking (DT) tasks ask students to produce as many responses to a given assignment as possible (e.g., name things that are round). Responses are then assessed on multiple criteria: (a) fluency (a numerical count of ideas given); (b) originality (i.e., uniqueness, often established by their statistical infrequency); and (c) flexibility (determined by lexical categories, or themes, established by common responses). Ideational fluency may be high for some students simply because they have had more experiences. For an extensive tour of DT, read Mark Runco's book aptly titled, *Divergent Thinking* (1991).

When students are asked to apply divergent thinking to a task, they commonly give ideas in order of their proximity to the student (i.e., experiential bias). A students' classroom environment can provide stimuli for the production of their ideas. For example, when asked for things that are round, if there is a clock in the classroom it will most certainly be given as a response. Next, students' responses will be derived directly from previous experiences (proximal) with round objects. After both of these repositories of ideas have been exhausted, divergent responses emerge from associations that are not experience-based (distal). These responses are often considered the most creative, and generally qualify as original. These transitions from proximal to distal associations are captured by flexibility criteria, such that the ability to shift from one category of ideas to another indicates higher levels of creativity. When students exhaust categorical solutions to the task, they find another.

Behavioral

Let us get back on the bus and travel to our next point of interest—behavioral and developmental perspectives of creativity. First, the understanding of social influences might be the most valued (Runco, 1999)—while not necessary—contribution to the journey into the investigation of creativity. The evaluation of creativity through socially validated (i.e., a method that establishes agreement) measures focus on the end product, but lacks attention toward the intrapersonal processes that occurs during the interaction with a social reward structure.

When considering how social environments influence a student's creativity, it is important to acknowledge how unsubstantiated support and unfounded positive feedback (unconditional positive regard) actually limits creative potential. Put simply, giving students an "A" for creativity when their product was not original limits their creative potential. The integrity of social feedback is dependent upon responses that consistently and accurately assess creativity. Students' individual creative processes should be supported by means other than a *status quo* of across-the-board approval, based on an equality-based reward system within the classroom.

Developmental

Second, we are not born with the implied knowledge of the society of which we will become a part. Through rearing by family, society, and culture, we assimilate conventional knowledge that eases our acceptance into these social groups. School is often the first venue for consistent social interactions (outside of our own family), thus delineating the onset of adulterated creative potential (Rosenblatt & Winner, 1988). The use of conventional terms and concepts facilitate functioning within a society and therefore takes precedent in our social and educational systems. The assimilation of these common methods becomes the dominant paradigm through which we interact in the world, but often creates obstacles to generating original ideas. Young children lack conventions whereas adults can reject them, allowing us to think outside the commonly held and often contradictory parameters (e.g., aesthetic sensibilities and debates on gay marriage and capital punishment). These conundrums are quite personal but question the accepted conventions of the society.

Across the life span, we are naive to experiences outside of our own. We remain oblivious to, and are challenged by unfamiliar situations, perspectives, and beliefs. Jean Piaget suggested that the transitions between developmental stages may be more important foci than the stages themselves (Flavell, 1963). The disequilibrium we encounter—when previously held abilities (or stages) interface new ones—become threatening and require more than awareness of their existence in order to be accommodated. It is only through the direct experience of these transitions that we progress to the next stage.

The disequilibrium that occurs when convention appears inappropriate is a bifurcation point for the creative process. A novel approach is by definition, both a challenge to the norm and a necessary component of creativity (Runco & Jaeger, 2012). The need to subjugate conventions is often the motive for the second definitional component of creativity, effectiveness. The disequilibrium caused by facing the decision to do what everyone else does, or to forge your own resolution is frequently what many of us intuitively identify as the act of a creative individual.

Personality and Motivation

Our next stop affords us the chance to visit one of the most historical and influential organizations in creativity research, the Institute for Personality and Assessment Research (IPAR) at the University of California, Berkeley. As a groundbreaking place for seminal research and prolific theorists of creativity (e.g., Eric Erikson, Frank Barron, James MacKinnon, etc.), IPAR investigations brought to light some common traits between creative individuals (for a comprehensive list of personality traits, see Tardif & Sternberg, 1988), while also addressing domain-specific differences. Of particular interest, MacKinnon (1965) found that defensiveness was negatively correlated with creativity, suggesting that self-actualization—the honest acceptance of one's own personality and preferences (Runco, 1993)—is an important personal attainment when achieving greater heights of creative feats.

However, sometimes on road trips we encounter odd highway attractions such as the world's largest ball of twine. So too are history (and our classrooms) filled with examples of creative people who did not fit the mold of common society such as Vincent van Gogh and Andy Warhol. These eccentric and marginal attractions, students, and creators often lie outside the usual and operate along the fringes of society. Research indicates that there does exist an optimal level of marginality (McLaughlin, 2000). Inside this optimal spectrum lies the potential of marginal individuals to enhance creative production and enrich the lives of others, while outside of it there is often insufferable behavior that does not benefit anyone. It is important to us as educators to consider how many creative individuals feel marginalized by society and therefore are more comfortable working alone or in small groups.

Moving along from personality to motivation, there is a misnomer that creativity is only extrinsic because it is easier to assess than intrinsic motivation. A commonly held understanding of creativity is based on a process-oriented perspective that implies that intrinsic motivation is more important, which in some ways conflicts with the current product-oriented creativity assessments. Both sources of motivation are required in creativity, but one is more product-based and the other is process-based.

It is important for us to recognize the role motivation plays during your students' educational journey through the creative process. However, first, our students must want to take the journey with us. Motivated both by external pressures, such as grades or peer pressure, and intrinsic forces, such as a love of learning, student motivation to express themselves creatively is important for us to understand as a significant contributor to the creative process. As such, Amabile's Consensual Product Assessment (CPA) method (1982) was developed in order to evaluate creative products in a subjective matter by using judges to determine the creativity of a product. While the CPA speaks to extrinsic motivation, it does not adequately address the intrinsic motivation to be creative. While extrinsic motivation is useful for sparking student interests and participation, ultimately, it is the lack of external rewards that result in a more prolonged and sustained engagement with a task. Most creative individuals create because they love it, not because they seek rewards or recognition from others. How often does the term "starving artist" come to mind when searching for anecdotes about creative individuals?

Climate and Organizational

Speaking of creative individuals, in order to maximize the creative potential of all our students, we must first create a school and classroom climate that fosters creativity and allows each student to enhance his or her own creative abilities. This is because the climate in which we teach and learn has a tremendous impact on the creative processes occurring within that climate. One key element we must have to create a climate conducive to creativity is tolerance. In his study of the creative class, Florida (2004) noted that creative individuals are often unconventional and need a more tolerant and permissive classroom. It is this tolerance and appreciation for diversity in the classroom that helps to increase overall opportunities for creative endeavors.

In an effort toward a tolerant classroom climate, we must also make a commitment to remove social blocks to creativity, which may be the most negatively influential factor affecting creativity. Davis (1999) refers to these blocks as idea squelchers, or things that we say internally and to others that stifle creative thinking. Some common idea squelchers that we hear in the classroom and sometimes say to ourselves are, "I'm just not very creative," "we've always done it this way," or "see, I told you it wouldn't work!" Teachers and other educators must be aware that rigid rules, policies, regulations, and traditions in the classroom can squelch creativity as well. Classrooms that are free of squelchers are inherently more tolerant and therefore more creative environments.

Furthermore, a tolerance of culture opens us up to new categories of creativity. A tolerant classroom is led by a teacher able to take into account the varied cultural contexts from which her students come. In order to enhance creative efforts of our students, we must first understand the impact that values have on creativity and how they are perceived across distinct cultures. This is important because differences in the economic and political plights of a student's culture thereby influence the assumptions they have about creativity. Much like using classroom differentiation to address learning styles and ability levels, an appreciation and understanding of the cultural values students bring with them into the classroom allows teachers to capitalize on the diversity of the student population. In this way, we can further maximize creative potential by providing opportunities for creative production tailored specifically toward what students value. If we are more tolerant of these cultural differences, we can use these differences to further our creative output. In essence, a tolerance of diversity provides greater fluency of ideas in the classroom.

On a larger scale, school and district wide climate are an integral part of fostering creative potentials in our students. This is because creativity has the potential to benefit all aspects of an organization's functions (Amabile, 1998). One way to understand the interplay between creativity and organizations is through the lens of organizational climate, or the patterns of behavior, attitudes, and feelings that exist within an organization. The concepts and ideas of creating an organizational climate of creativity can help maximize creative potentials in students. An organization can benefit from taking a stance of tolerance in an effort to develop a climate of creativity.

Humanistic

As the name implies, a focus on the importance of what it is to be human is profoundly impacted by our creative endeavors. Within the trajectory toward self-actualization, creativity allows an individual to become aware of social conventions so that they can subjugate them in an effort to attain their idiosyncratic and individual health and well-being (Maslow, 1971; Rogers, 1995). Creative potential is an important individual need that can be deterred by many of the social constructions mentioned throughout this chapter. Humanistic theories suggest that many of the social support systems that provide basic needs later become antiquated and encroach upon creative processes. In other words, structure can provide stability for unorthodox behaviors often required for creativity.

Systems Approaches

As many of the theories above suggest, there is a confluence of variables that both support and assess creativity. The application of systems theories onto creativity research helps to provide a comprehensive map of interactions among the field, the domain, and the individual (Csikszentmihalyi, 1988). The effectiveness of a creative endeavor often requires an interaction among the subjective feedbacks of an audience, along with originality that the domain requires (Gruber, 1988). The individual struggle to accommodate these acknowledgments often leads to some of the most creative individuals to abandon their creative field. Such attrition also suggests that the judgment of what is creative has a biased sample to select from. The evaluation of creativity also holds a bias of the personal experiences, preferences, and other influences that diminish their objectivity. The systems approach to creativity attempts to integrate these biases in an effort to triangulate the internal and external influences on creative process and creativity itself. (For further introduction, read the collaborative efforts of Feldman, Csikszentmihalyi, & Gardner, 1994.)

CREATIVE CONTROVERSIES

Definition of Creativity

As you may have intuited throughout the reading of this chapter, the definition of creativity itself has been, and may still remain, a controversial declaration. The standard definition of creativity has majority support in its proclamation that creativity requires originality and effectiveness, but those two words spawn many synonyms and interpretations (Runco & Jaeger, 2012). The most significant speed bump in adopting these criteria is the relativity in which the moment of creativity occurs. Furthermore, if an individual is unaware that his brilliant idea has been discovered in a remote time or place, does that make it less original? The subjective evaluation of useful is also a decision to be made by others whose experience and context may find the acts of a creative endeavor as simply weird.

Cognition of Creativity versus Cognition of Intelligence

During the pioneering research of creativity, there were significant efforts to separate creative thinking from the thinking commonly associated with intelligence.

As we alluded earlier in the chapter, there has been significant conjecture around whether creativity is a type of intelligence as well. Despite a trend toward equating divergent thinking with creativity, an academic stand has been made to avoid such an assumption—broadening the field of creative process to include both divergent and convergent thinking. In other words, the production of myriad ideas inevitably requires a selection of the appropriately creative idea.

However, the experiential bias of knowledge may have a negative effect on intelligence. The balance of intelligence and creativity has raised questions about how the conventional influence of intelligence can hinder the openness to experience commonly associated with creative cognition (i.e., if one knows what works, why would one try a different approach just for the sake of its potential?). A threshold has been discovered that intelligence at the ends of the spectrum are negatively correlated with creativity (Runco & Albert, 1986). If creativity were a type of intelligence, there would be no need to study creativity as it could be inferred from intelligence testing.

General versus Domain

Like the debate of where to eat dinner on our trip, there exists a conjecture within the field of creativity research, about whether creativity has a structure similar to Charles Spearman's "g" theory of intelligence (1907), which posits that intelligence is distributed across both general-specific and domain-specific resources. The theory of general creativity relies on the premise that there are some people who are just more creative than others; the medium of creativity is secondary. Meanwhile, domain-specific theorists find that there are cognitive (linguistic, musical, spatial, etc.) and also task/content (e.g., poetry, singing, painting, etc.) domains in which individuals can excel in creatively (Baer, 1988). Now, it doesn't seem too difficult to think of people, whether famous or close friends, whose creative lives fall into one of those categories.

However, we seek an integration of both perspectives. Oftentimes, students are initially perceived as creative, and only later in life find the specific area where their creativity blossoms. Conversely, there are abundant anecdotal examples of individuals prolific in one area who later find expression in different (e.g., Leonardo da Vinci gained distinction for myriad inventions and techniques after being identified as a master painter; Jean Piaget received a PhD in zoology before he made a profound effect on the field of psychology, etc.), often contextually remote media, which suggests the transferability of general creativity in their process. Additionally, some research suggests that analogical thinking (the application of a prior approach within a seemingly unrelated context; Weisberg, 1995) contributes to the effective use of unconventional approaches toward gaining insight on either unfamiliar or unsolved problems.

Big "C" and Little "c"

There may be a correlation between the activities, behaviors, and personalities of prolifically creative individuals and those students we hope to encourage in their creativity. An important, and extremely practical, distinction to make is that between "Big C" creativity and "little c" creativity—that of groundbreaking and that of everyday creativity, respectively (Richards, 1993). It might seem impossible to write sonnets all day long and not have to work, but that shouldn't stop our students from engaging in little "c" along the way. Put simply, most creativity has a developmental trajectory and need not parallel the biographies of eminent artists, scholars, or any other creative endeavors. Further categories have been developed by Kaufmann and Beghetto (2009), of "mini-c" for creativity inherent to learning, and "Pro-c" that exists in prolifically creative individuals who have not achieved eminence yet.

Potential versus Product

Another polarizing dialogue in creativity research is one that imparts value upon whether creative potential or product is more relevant when determining individual creativity. From a product-based perspective, creativity is measured by socially validated rules, often a profitable approach toward empirical research. However, a focus on creative production often overshadows the individual creative process, thereby de-emphasizing one's potential for creative production in the future.

The importance of product in creativity has much to do with the denotation— creativity implies that something has been created. For an empirical investigation, there is a desire for a physical manifestation to assess for its creativity. Without the product, individuals may be perceived as creative, when they may be expressing pseudo- or quasi-creativity (Cropley & Cropley, 2010). Respectively, the nonconformist or weird-for-the-sake-of-weird behaviors do not result in the effectiveness needed for creativity. The subjective assessment of creative product measures an outcome, yet lacks the sensitivity to identify in individuals who may not have found the domain that fulfills their creative potential. In our journey toward a better understanding of creativity, we must recognize the value of both approaches to creativity research.

Brainstorming

The increasing value of brainstorming (ideation) in educational, institutional, and corporate business models has encouraged deeper investigations into the effectiveness of brainstorming. Long-held is the notion that as the number and diversity of those participating in brainstorming meetings increases, the greater the quality of contributions. Although the number of relevant ideas (ideational fluency) may be increased, the qualitative value of a prolifically creative individual can only be squelched by a competitive social structure—and social loafing (Diehl & Stroebe, 1987). Permitting individuals to work independently, before contributing ideas for a suggested problem-to-be-solved can increase both quantity and quality of those disinclined to contribute in an extroverted climate. Support of both introverted and extroverted personalities accommodates the contributions of a broader stakeholder consensus.

Brainstorming involves more than just the divergent production of ideas. Unfettered ideation is invaluable, but is often undermined by the subsequent evaluation of those ideas (see Campbell's Blind Variation and Selective Retention model, 1960). For example, if a team of teachers brainstorm ideas on how to increase creativity in the classroom and those ideas are either ignored or usurped by an administrator as their own, future brainstorming efforts will suffer from a lack of positive reinforcement. Often, our production of ideas accommodate those who evaluate them, resulting in the editing of ideas during their production. Please consider these contributions to the fragile social environment when using brainstorming in an educational context.

Mental Illness

If we are to fully understand creativity, we must venture into the world of mental illness and its connections with creativity research. One common assumption of creativity is that it has a close connection with that of mental illnesses such as manic depression, attention deficit disorder, and schizophrenia. While it is true that several research studies have documented a greater prevalence of mental illness in highly creative people, others suggest that the processes attributed to people with mental illness are also essential parts of the creative process. The shared characteristics of mental illness and creativity can be both detrimental to some and beneficial to others, suggesting a threshold effect where traits of both exist along a continuum. However, like that of the overrepresentation of men in historiometric research on eminence, so too may there be a disproportionate number of occurrences of mental illness in historical records. For more information, see Simonton (2010).

Assessment

Kasof (1995) noted that, historically, researchers in the field of creativity have attributed creative behavior to those dispositional (cognitive and personal processes) abilities of creative individuals. However, the propensity to attribute creative behaviors to external influences is less prevalent in the research literature, but has gained attention in recent years. The tendency to use objective tests to measure creativity ignores the subjective aspects of creative products that rely on judgment of whether or not they are novel and useful. As such, attributional theories of creativity rely heavily on situational elements such that "creativity is not inherent in any idea or product but is instead attributed by some social group" (Runco, 2007, p. 156). This theory challenges the notion of traditional approaches to understanding creativity that concentrate on dispositional factors of individuals rather than groups.

Education

On our last stop through the world of creativity research, we must address the controversies that exist in education. In the broadest sense, there is an inherent disconnect between the theories identified in creativity research and the practices utilized in the educational arena. This disconnect is illustrated by controversial questions such as "Can creativity be taught?" "Can creativity be used to identify giftedness?" and "Can creativity be standardized like that of math and science or does such standardization squelch creativity?" While we cannot expect to know the answers to these questions, we can offer them as jumping off points for exploration into how we utilize creativity research to inform educational practice and vice versa. A discussion focused on the fulfillment of creative potentials in the classroom is a starting point with which to reconcile this disconnect.

As we strive to increase creativity and innovation in our students, we must recognize the importance of placing an emphasis on maximization of creative potential in the classroom. The fulfillment of potential is relevant to studies of positive psychology and optimal development and also related to both psychological and physical health—areas that seem to benefit from creative self-expression. Although creativity takes many forms, the best way to address creativity in the classroom is through the fulfillment of potential (Runco & Sumners, in press).

To this end, teachers must be trained in how to foster creativity in their classroom. Mark Runco (1991) suggested that there are—at minimum—three things educators should do in order to support creative endeavors and maximize potential in their students, including (1) create opportunities in the classroom for students to practice creative thinking, (2) value and appreciate these creative efforts, (3) and model creative behaviors.

Likewise, there are several pedagogical practices, models, and strategies that have been shown to effectively enhance creative potential in the classroom. Torrance's Incubation Model of Teaching (1979) focuses on collaborative learning in a three-stage process: (1) heightening anticipation and awareness of real-world issues along with their expectations for learning, (2) understanding and knowledge assimilation, and (3) incorporating the new knowledge into existing schemas and the momentum of its application. Several strategies within the model are also purposed to facilitate creativity at each step.

Other various tactics teachers can use to improve creative thinking in their classrooms include visualization, changing your perspective, using analogies and "thinking big" just to name a few examples of many that exist. Quite possibly the most widely used model for incorporating creativity into the classroom is the Creative Problem Solving model (CPS), developed by Alex Osborne and Sidney Parnes in the 1950s. CPS is a six-step method for addressing a problem or task from a creative stance. Other programs such as the Future Problem Solving (FPS) Program were developed based on the Osborn–Parnes CPS Model. Founded in 1974 by Dr. E. Paul Torrance and his wife Pansy, FPS is a future-oriented, extracurricular program designed to stimulate critical and creative thinking skills.

SUMMARY

We hope you have enjoyed our excursion into the world of understanding creativity research. While we aimed to provide you with a comprehensive summary of creativity research, we in no way want to portray these efforts as complete. With the advent of advancing technologies, be aware of investigations by the fields of neuroscience, along with the influence of digital interfaces and their creative products. As you depart to the next chapter, use what you have learned here as a guide with which to frame your future reading.

REFERENCES

Amabile, T. M. (1982). Social psychology of creativity: A consensual assessment technique. *Journal of Personality and Social Psychology, 43*(5), 997–1013.

Amabile, T. M. (1998). How to kill creativity. *Harvard Business Review, 76,* 76–87.

Baer, J. (1988). The case for domain specificity of creativity. *Creativity Research Journal, 11,* 173–177.

Binet, A., & Simon, T. (1905). The development of intelligence in children. *L'Annee Psychologique, 11,* 163–191.

Campbell, D. T. (1960). Blind variation and selective retention in creative thought as in other knowledge processes. *Psychological Review, 67,* 380–400.

Cropley, D. H., & Cropley, A. J. (2010). Functional creativity: "Products" and the generation of effective novelty. In R. J. Sternberg & J. C. Kaufmann (Eds.), *The Cambridge handbook of creativity,* 301–317. New York: Cambridge University Press.

Csikszentmihalyi, M. (1988). Society, culture, and person: A systems view of creativity. In R. Sternberg (Ed.), *The nature of creativity* (pp. 325–339). New York: Cambridge University Press.

Darwin, C. R., & Wallace, A. R. (1858). On the tendency of species to form varieties and on the perpetuation of varieties and species by natural means of selection. *Journal of the Proceedings of the Linnean Society of London. Zoology, 3*(9), 45–62.

Davis, G. (1999). Barriers to creativity and creative attitudes. In M. A. Runco & S. Pritzker (Eds.), *Encyclopedia of creativity,* 165–174. San Diego, CA: Academic Press.

Diehl, M., & Stroebe, W. (1987). Productivity loss in brainstorming groups: Toward the solution of a riddle. *Journal of Personality and Social Psychology, 53*(3), 497–509.

Feldman, D. H., Csikszentmihalyi, M., & Gardner, H. (1994). *Changing the world: A framework for the study of creativity.* Westport, CT: Praeger Publishers.

Flavell, J. H. (1963). *The developmental psychology of Jean Piaget.* Princeton, NJ: D. Van Nostrand Company.

Flavell, J. H. (1976). Metacognitive aspects of problem solving. In L. B. Resnick (Ed.), *The nature of intelligence* (pp. 231–236). Hillsdale, NJ: Erlbaum.

Florida, R. (2004). The great creative class debate: Revenge of the squelchers. The next American city, disposable cities. Issue 5, July 2004, pp. 1–7. Retrieved from http://creativeclass.com/rfcgdb/articles/Revenge%20of%20the%20Squelchers.pdf.

Getzels, J. W. (1975). Problem finding and the inventiveness of solutions. *Journal of Creative Behavior, 9,* 12–18.

Getzels, J. W., & Jackson, P. W. (1962). *Creativity and intelligence: Explorations with gifted students.* New York: Wiley.

Gruber, H. E. (1988). The evolving systems approach to creative work. *Creativity Research Journal, 1,* 27–51.

Guilford, J. P. (1950). Creativity. *American Psychologist, 5,* 444–454.

Guilford, J. P. (1967). *The nature of human intelligence.* New York: McGraw-Hill.

Kasof, J. (1995). Explaining creativity: The attributional perspective. *Creativity Research Journal, 8*(4), 311–366.

Kaufmann, J. C., & Beghetto, R. A. (2009). Beyond big and little: The Four C Model of creativity. *Review of General Psychology, 13*(1), 1–12.

MacKinnon, D. W. (1965). Personality and the realization of creative potential. *American Psychologist, 20,* 273–281.

Maslow, A. (1971). *The farther reaches of human nature.* New York: Viking.

McLaughlin, N. (2000). Book review of the sociology of philosophies: A global theory of intellectual change. *Journal of the History of the Behavioral Sciences, 36*(2), 171–175.

Mednick, S. A. (1962). The associative basis of the creative process. *Psychological Review, 69,* 220–232.

Quetelet, A. (1968). *A treatise on man and the development of his faculties.* New York: Franklin. (Original work published in 1835).

Rhodes, M. (1961). An analysis of creativity. *Phi Delta Kappan, 42,* 305–310.

Richards, R. (1993). Everyday creativity, eminent creativity, and pscyhopathology. *Psychological Inquiry, 4*(3), 212.

Rogers, C. R. (1995). *On becoming a person: A therapist's view of psychotherapy.* Boston, MA: Houghton Mifflin (Original work published in 1961).

Rosenblatt, E., & Winner, E. (1988). The art of children's drawings. *Journal of Aesthetic Education, 22,* 3–15.

Runco, M.A. (1991). *Divergent thinking.* Norwood, NJ: Ablex Publishing Corporation.

Runco, M.A. (1993). Operant theories of insight, originality, and creativity. *American Behavioral Scientist, 37*(1), 54–67.

Runco, M.A. (1999). Creativity need not be social. In A. Montuori & R.E. Purser (Eds.), *Social Creativity Vol. 1* (pp. 237–264). Cresskill, NJ: Hampton Press.

Runco, M.A. (2007). *Creativity theories and themes: Research, development, and practice.* New York: Elsevier.

Runco, M.A., & Albert, R.S. (1986). Exceptional giftedness in early adolescence and intrafamilial divergent thinking. *Journal of Youth and Adolescence, 15,* 333–342.

Runco, M.A., & Jaeger, G.J. (2012). The standard definition of creativity. *Creativity Research Journal, 21,* 92–96.

Runco, M.A., & Sumners, S.E. (in press). Creativity training. In N. J. Smelser & P.B. Baltes (Eds.), *International encyclopedia of the social and behavioral sciences,* Vol. 2. New York: Elsevier.

Runco, M.A., Dow, G., & Smith, W.R. (2006). Information, experience, and divergent thinking: An empirical test. *Creativity Research Journal, 18,* 269–277.

Simonton, D.K. (1999a). Historiometry. In M.A. Runco & S. Pritzker (Eds.), *Encyclopedia of creativity* (pp. 815–822). San Diego, CA: Academic.

Simonton, D.K. (1999b). Significant samples: The psychological study of eminent individuals. *Psychological Methods, 4*(4), 425–451.

Simonton, D.K. (2010). So you want to become a creative genius? You must be crazy! In: D.H. Cropley, A.J. Cropley, J.C. Kaufman, & M.A. Runco (Eds.), *The dark side of creativity* (pp. 218–234). Cambridge, UK: Cambridge University Press.

Spearman, C. (1907). Demonstration of formulae for true measurement of correlation. *The American Journal of Psychology, 18*(2), 161–169.

Sternberg, R.J. (1985). *Beyond IQ: A triarchic theory of human intelligence.* Cambridge, UK: Cambridge University Press.

Tardif, T.Z., & Sternberg, R.J. (1988). What do we know about creativity? In R.J. Sternberg (Ed.), *The nature of creativity: Contemporary psychological perspectives* (pp. 429–440). Cambridge, UK: Cambridge University Press.

Torrance, E.P. (1979). An instructional model for enhancing incubation. *Journal of Creative Behavior, 13*(1), 23–35

Wallach, M.A., & Kogan, N. (1965). *Modes of thinking in young children.* New York: Holt, Rinehart, & Winston.

Wallas, G. (1926). *The art of thought.* New York: Harcourt Brace Jovanovich.

Watson, J.D. (1968). *The double helix: A personal account of the discovery of the structure of DNA.* New York: American Library.

Weisberg, R.W. (1995). Prolegomena to theories of insight in problem solving: Definition of terms and a taxonomy of problems. In R.J. Sternberg, & J.E. Davidson (Eds.), *The nature of insight* (pp. 157–196). Cambridge: MIT Press.

2

CREATIVITY THEORY AND EDUCATIONAL PRACTICE: WHY ALL THE FUSS?

Michael Hanchett Hanson
Teachers College, Columbia University

For some time now, psychologists and other social scientists have argued that people must learn to be more creative. Overcoming humanity's greatest challenges (e.g., Gruber, 1989a; Hennessey, 2010), serving economic growth (e.g., Florida, 2005; Sawyer, 2007), producing flourishing cultures (Csikszentmihalyi, 1999; Simonton, 1999) and having successful, meaningful lives (e.g., Csikszentmihalyi, 1997; Sternberg, 2002), it seems, depend on creativity. Many of these theorists invoke education as the means to assure that today's young people have the creativity necessary to take on these Promethean tasks.

What, then, should be the relation of education and creativity? Various theories of creativity differ on the answer to that question. Almost all of the theories derive from a basic concept of creativity as producing something novel and valuable, appropriate or adaptive (Amabile et al., 1996; Feist, 1999; Gruber, 1989b; Simonton, 1999). However, even that simple notion is challenging. Can educators *teach* students to do things that are novel—not yet defined? From the opposite direction, does education not already include creativity? Planning novelty may be difficult, if possible, but novelty comes up all of the time. Teaching students how to conduct an experiment or mix colors or solve a math problem involves prescribed steps. Each can also include surprises, discoveries, and improvisation. If creativity is already—and inevitably—present in the classroom, why all the fuss?

CREATIVITY AND GOOD EDUCATION

This chapter argues that there is ample reason for a fuss, but it is often misplaced. Teaching creativity is neither new nor exotic. The challenge is the hard work of providing good education, and creativity research brings some new perspectives and opportunities to that much older, but still challenging, enterprise.

Techniques

Most of what creativity researchers propose for education can already be found in teaching. Some of the often cited guidelines include encouraging sensible risk-taking, questioning assumptions, using open-ended assignments, encouraging tolerance of ambiguity, building motivation, stimulating idea generation, and modeling all of these behaviors. For example, see Nickerson (1999); Piirto (2004); Starko (2005); Sternberg (2003); Sternberg and Williams (1996). All of these guidelines also have their place as part of traditional education. For example, questioning assumptions is key to critical thinking as well as creativity, and Fairweather and Cramond (2010) have argued that critical thinking is necessary for the development of creative products and ideas. Testing a hypothesis through experimental method is risky, especially if the hypothesis is also a cherished belief or the experiment has to be elaborate. Even idea generation happens in almost every assignment, including the most conventional.

Furthermore, as with all education, there is no one-size-fits-all approach for the development of creativity. Students who are unmotivated and not doing their schoolwork may need to focus more on the motivational side of creativity lessons and the idea of creativity as work. High-achieving students who insist on the certainty of one answer may need to focus on exploring different ways of thinking. In other words, as is generally true of education, teaching creativity requires knowledge, preparation, sensitivity, and flexibility.

Outcomes

Moreover, many—if not most—of the outcomes of the methods advocated for creativity will fall in the bailiwick of traditional education: more knowledge, deeper understanding, better skills, and the excitement of learning. Other outcomes will be more distinctly aligned with creativity, such as appreciation of novelty and greater understanding of how novelty can be integrated into social, economic, and personal life. Through education, students' personal goals for changing their worlds can also emerge.

The Work for Educators

From this perspective, creativity theories are resources that contribute to the toolboxes of teachers and educational policy makers. Integrating the idea of creativity and educational practices cannot be a passive application of psychological theories, however. By necessity, educators are active participants in this enterprise, not only in defining educational practices, but also in the ongoing construction of the idea of creativity itself.

AN EVOLVING CONCEPT

Romantic and Growing Root

The idea of creativity as a force within people and groups arose not so long ago in Western Europe (Mason, 2003; Pope, 2005; Weiner, 2000). The word creativity was coined in 1875 and did not appear in most English-language dictionaries until after World War II (Weiner, 2000). The ancient Greeks did not have an equivalent idea. For them inspiration came from outside the self, the Muses. Even so, the Greeks emphasized values that are linked to creativity today, such as the importance of intrinsic motivation and the ideals of beauty and art. In the Middle Ages, for the most part, the Church reserved the Latin verb *creare* for divine creation. Humans *made* things. In the Renaissance the adjective creative started being applied to human work, as a dim reflection of divine creation. Throughout the Romantic era, the importance of imagination, individuality, and market economics grew in how people conceived of change, value, and truth. On the heels of those ideas, arose the concept of creativity as a force within people, groups, or societies—a force that can be nurtured or squelched.

1950 to the Present: A Wealth of Theories

As the word "creativity" began appearing in English-language dictionaries, J. P. Guilford (1950), outgoing president of the American Psychological Association, called for the psychological study of creativity. That speech began a broad range of research and theory development that continues today, starting with Guilford's definition of divergent thinking. Cognitive psychologists (e.g., Hanchett Hanson, 2004; Gruber & Wallace, 1999; Sternberg & Lubart, 1991; Weisberg, 2006) have studied how people think when they are creative. Personality researchers (e.g., MacKinnon, 1962; Feist, 1999) have identified social personality traits that seemed to differentiate more from less creative people. Gestalt theorists (e.g., Kohler, 1925; Wertheimer, 1945/1982) built on their existing work in examining how insight occurred. Humanist and existential psychologists (e.g., May 1974; Rogers, 1954) saw creativity as a critical part of the development of a fulfilling human life. Then social psychologists (e.g., Amabile et al., 1996; Hennessey, 2003) began looking at environmental factors that could facilitate or diminish creative output, and sociocultural theorists (e.g., Csikszentmihalyi, 1999) moved the focus away from individuals to group dynamics and social systems.

Amid this Cambrian period of creativity theory development, educational techniques initially focused on idea generation, the key component of divergent thinking. In recent years, the push to link education more directly to a wide array of creativity theories has gained momentum (e.g., Beghetto & Kaufman, 2010; Smith & Smith, 2010; Starko, 2005). The potential of this broader approach is a richer and more integrated view of the roles of creativity within education, as well as more nuanced use of the tools creativity theorists have advocated.

SIX IDEAS FOR EDUCATORS

As examples of how various creativity theories can apply to the classroom, six ideas that may help educators are listed in the following text. The teaching techniques suggested in these ideas reflect current literature on fostering creativity in education (e.g., Beghetto & Kaufman, 2010; Craft, 2005; Piirto, 2004; Runco, 2007; Sawyer, 2011; Starko, 2005), educational standards that explicitly aim at development of creativity, as well as the sections of the standards that do not (e.g., Common Core State Standards Initiative, 2010; Partnership for 21st-Century Skills, 2009). Above all, these ideas emphasize the relation of a broad range of creativity theories to good educational practices.

Some may object that different theories of creativity are not commensurate. They do not mix and match. Actually, they often do. The guidelines for promoting creativity in education, discussed earlier, come from an array of theories, not just one or two, and many theories are, themselves, confluence models that take into account multiple factors. When theories sharply disagree, they reflect important debates—issues that educators and students should consider. For example, is creativity present in the individual as trait theories assume or in the dynamic of the individual and society as sociocultural theories assert? That is an important issue for educators to consider, as well as a relevant topic for exploration in the classroom.

THE FIRST IDEA

Divergent Thinking Is Not Enough—and May Not Even Be Necessary

The Theory and Tools

Guilford (1950) originally proposed divergent thinking as a trait, something that differentiates individuals. Unlike eye color, however, Guildford proposed that creativity was a soft trait, in that it could probably be enhanced through education. Guilford was a test designer, and from the beginning he envisioned that divergent thinking as a trait could be tested. A number of psychologists followed his suggestion and developed divergent thinking tests (e.g., Wallach & Kogan, 1965): the most widely used being the Torrance Tests of Creative Thinking (TTCT), (Torrance, 1966, 2008). Divergent thinking tests examine a number of cognitive abilities: most centrally, fluency (the ability to produce many different ideas); flexibility (not staying within a limited number of categories when producing ideas); originality (producing ideas other people do not produce—statistically improbable ideas); and elaboration (producing detailed ideas).

Many tools for education have been designed to facilitate divergent thinking or include similar assumptions in a broader process. These include, for example, questions to ask oneself, such as Substitute, Combine, Adapt, Modify/Magnify/Minify, Put to other uses, Eliminate, Reverse/Rearrange (SCAMPER) (Eberle, 2008) or morphological synthesis (Starko, 2005)—identifying the aspects of various phenomena and mixing them. Examples of the more complex, structured approaches include brainstorming and the Creative Problem Solving Model (Osborn, 1963; Parnes, 1981) that has six steps, each including a divergent and convergent (evaluative) component—objective-finding (sometimes referred to as mess-finding), data-finding, problem-finding, idea-finding, solution-finding, and acceptance-finding.

Caveats

Even the staunchest advocates of divergent thinking claim only that the tests measure one aspect of creative potential (Kaufman, Plucker, & Baer, 2008; Plucker, 1999; Runco, 2007). Longitudinal studies, correlating childhood divergent thinking test scores to later creative achievement have shown mixed results (Plucker, 1999), most ranging from disappointing (Torrance, 2002, p. xi) to moderate predictive validity. In a reanalysis of 22-year longitudinal data of the original TTCT test groups, Plucker (1999) found that the verbal form of the test accounted for slightly less than half of the variability in creative work later in life. The correlations for the figural form of the test (drawing only), however, were not strong enough to factor into the statistical model. A 50-year follow-up to the same study (Runco, Millar, Selcuk, & Cramond, 2010) found that the childhood TTCT scores of the group, now in their 50s, did not correlate with public creative achievements, but did show moderate correlation to everyday creative activities and personal creativity (p. 366).

Other controversies concerning divergent thinking are even more important to educational practice. First, there is controversy about whether divergent thinking is really distinct from intelligence. Some studies indicate that it is, and others that it is not. (For review of research, see Weisberg, 2006.) Second, there is a question of face validity—does the theory appear correct on its face? Guilford hypothesized that being able to think of lots of ideas would increase the chances of thinking of good ideas. It seemed logical, but was not based on empirical research. Case study research does not show that people doing creative work necessarily try to think of lots of different ideas as part of their work (Gruber, 1989b; Wallace & Gruber, 1989; Weisberg, 2006; Weisberg, 2011). Some may brainstorm with themselves or others sometimes, but the case evidence does not point to divergent thinking as essential to creative work. Analyses of the predictive validity of divergent thinking tests do not address the face validity of divergent thinking as part of the creative work. Many factors can predict behaviors without being essential to those behaviors. (Products people buy may be fair predictors of their political views.)

Of course, the divergent thinking processes may occur at unconscious levels (Simonton, 1999) or just may not show up in the evidence case studies use (sketches, lab notebooks, diaries, letters, etc.). In other words, controversies about the relation of divergent thinking to creativity persist. Finally, after decades of research, the jury is out as to whether divergent thinking can be taught (Nickerson, 1999, 2010).

Domain Specificity and the Creativity Crisis

Kim (2011)—see also chapter four—synthesized studies published between 1965 and 2005 about the relationship between creativity and intelligence and found through meta-analysis a decline in the TTCT-Figural scores from 1966 to 2008. She argued that these declines indicated a creativity crisis in American education. According to the tests, children have become less creative over the last few decades. This conclusion is based, not just on decline in divergent thinking, but also on aspects of the TTCT-Figural form that Kim sees as testing emergent (elaborative, integrated, and applied) thinking, as well as creative attitudes. For example, scores for elaboration of details in the test drawings and scores for abstractness of titles people assign to their drawings test for emergent thinking.

Here, again, there is plenty of controversy. Remember that the Figural TTCT—the form of the test analyzed by Kim—was the form for which Plucker (1999) did not find predictive validity in his reanalysis of longitudinal data. In addition to that and other controversies concerning divergent thinking, already discussed, Kim's analysis highlights a controversial, underlying assumption of all divergent thinking tests: creative thinking is a cognitive ability independent of content that is not domain-specific. The divergent—or convergent or emergent—thinker in music has the same creative potential for thinking in art or science or literature. Here, specifically, the types of detail children draw in a timed, pencil-and-paper test and the titles they give to those drawings indicate how well they will ultimately be able to refine and implement ideas (emergent thinking) in fields where they have gained expertise and want to do creative work.

That is a basic assumption, not only of divergent thinking tests and some other creativity assessment tools (see discussion in idea number five in text that follows), but also of intelligence testing and many educational goals (e.g., critical thinking). Even Gardner's theory of multiple intelligences (1993) has large groupings of types of thinking, such as linguistic intelligence.

There is, however, a large body of research on the *lack* of transfer of knowledge and skills across domains; for reviews, see Feltovich, Prietula, and Ericsson (2006); Weisberg, 2006. Research has tended to show that creativity is domain-specific even when people do not have specific expertise. For example, Baer (1998) requested that judges rate ordinary people's creative work in a variety of domains, such as poetry, short stories, collages, and mathematical puzzles. He found that people who were creative in one domain were not particularly creative in other domains. Baer also provided divergent thinking training relating to poetry to seventh graders and found that the training did improve their poetry, but not their short stories.

It may be, then, that the decline in TTCT-Figural form scores reflect an overall reduction in creativity, or the decline may reflect changes in the specific pencil-and-paper drawing and labeling tasks required by the figural test.

Implications for Education

So much controversy: what are educators to do? Remember that the goal is good education, not just producing lists of ideas. Whatever the strengths or weaknesses of Kim's claim of a creativity crisis (2011), her conclusions call for a return to educational practices that engage and motivate students in multiple ways of thinking.

Furthermore, even assuming that the most severe critics are right about lack of validity for divergent thinking as part of creative work, the educational tools developed for divergent thinking can still be useful. Each technique has its own educational strengths, apart from thinking up lots of ideas. For example, SCAMPER accentuates the point that there are different ways to approach a topic. The Creative Problem Solving model, on the other hand, emphasizes that thinking through new ideas is a process. In using these tools, however, students need to understand that each technique is one way to engage *specific* fields of study, and none represent *the* way to be creative. Furthermore, thinking up lots of ideas is, at best, a step toward more serious work.

Example

Brainstorming is a popular practice, based on the goals of divergent thinking. In classic brainstorming the group free associates, coming up with lots of ideas, but does not evaluate them until after the ideas are generated. Decades of research have shown that this practice usually produces no more good ideas than the individuals would have, working alone. For review of research, see Nijstad, Diehl, and

Stroebe (2003). Although it may not serve the goals of divergent thinking so well, group brainstorming can serve other educational purposes. For example, Baer and Garrett (2010) used the example of introducing a lesson on President Lincoln by brainstorming what students know about Lincoln. In that process the students activated their background knowledge about the subject. They did not come to class with 19th-century presidents in mind, but did have relevant knowledge. Students learned facts from one another, and the teacher got a quick read on both the students' knowledge and misconceptions. Finally, Baer and Garrett noted that, to whatever extent it is helpful, the students practice divergent thinking. In addition to these outcomes, such a discussion could encourage students to build on each other's ideas (team building) and produce questions that the students can then research.

THE SECOND IDEA

Creativity Is work

Evolving Systems

Creativity cannot be reduced to a single way of thinking or studied as a norm (Gruber, 1989b; Gruber & Wallace, 1999). It is, by definition, new and unexpected. Each case will be a unique circumstance where the creative person may deploy a surprising combination of thinking strategies. Gruber and his associates conducted case studies of exceptionally creative people—those whose work has been publicly recognized, many of whom made major contributions to their fields. These case studies examined, not people's traits, but their behaviors; how they did their creative work. This research found that creative people organized their thinking, activities, and feelings—their lives—around their long-term creative purposes. Creativity, then, is work and commitment according to Gruber. People commit to the long, challenging, and often isolating work of creative endeavors in order to change their fields, sometimes in big ways. In the process, they purposefully develop unique points of view.

Ordinary Expertise

Other theories also emphasize creativity as work toward creative goals. Weisberg (2006, 2011) has contended that creativity is the application of expertise to creative goals. Indeed, what appears to be outside-the-box thinking to others is usually *inside* the well-studied and interesting boxes of the people who do the work. (See further discussion in chapter five.)

Investment Theory and Propulsion Theory

Sternberg and Lubart (1991) developed the investment theory of creativity, emphasizing the conscious choices people make in deciding to invest their time, energy, and other resources. In other words, they buy low, investing in unproven ideas, in hopes of selling high (success). In addition to this decision to be creative, people also decide how they want to change their fields. For propulsion theory, see Sternberg (2003).

Caveats

These theories emphasize conscious, purposeful decisions, but purposes emerge, sometimes slowly, and can change over the course of people's lives. Furthermore, all thinking is not conscious. For thousands of years people have described the aha experience, where inspiration seems to come from nowhere. Thus, the Muses! Wallas (1926) codified self-reflections from the physicist Hermann von Helmholtz and the mathematician and philosopher Henri Poincaré, into the well-known four-step process of creativity: preparation, incubation, illumination, and verification. Here, incubation is an undefined, unconscious process. None of the purpose-oriented theories already discussed deny the roles of unconscious processes, but the emphasis on conscious decisions can be misleading.

Implications for Education

Gruber's emphasis on how thinking is organized led him to research (1962) supporting use of open-ended, self-directed projects, specifically in science education. He found that this kind of classic constructivist educational approach had greater impact on *how* students thought, as opposed to simply teaching them what to think.

In addition, all of these theories contend that at some points in creative work people make conscious decisions to be creative. As a result, metacognition—helping students develop awareness of how they think—is important. Metacognition is already part of many curricula and educational standards (e.g., Common Core State Standards Initiative, 2010). These theories specifically imply the need for reflection on the students' creative goals, how they are gaining knowledge, and how they are organizing resources to meet those goals.

Example

Even if, as Gruber contended, each case of creative work is unique, learning about how people who have done serious creative work, organized their lives, and persisted in the face of obstacles can be both instructive and inspiring. Learning about the long hours of practice of great musicians, the bad early works of many great writers or about the thousands of combinations of filaments Thomas Edison tried in inventing the light bulb brings the idea of creativity as work to life. Examining the decisions made in such cases can then link to discussions of the students' goals and decisions, enhancing metacognitive skills.

THE THIRD IDEA

Creative People Can Be Difficult

Social Personality Traits

Researchers have also examined personality traits that differentiate extraordinarily creative people form less creative people in a variety of fields—for overview, see Feist (1999, 2010). Overall, the research has found correlations that are somewhat different for scientists versus those who work in arts and literature. The more creative people in both science and the arts tend to be open to new experiences and have high levels of drive and ambition. The scientists tend to be flexible thinkers, autonomous, introverted, and independent. They also tend to be self-confident, dominant, arrogant, and socially hostile. The artists tend to be oriented to fantasy and imagination, be impulsive and lack conscientiousness. They are more likely to be emotionally sensitive, be anxious and have mood disorders. Socially, they tend to be nonconforming, aloof, and unfriendly. For review of the findings of social trait research, see Feist (1999).

Caveats

The studies that have led to these findings are correlational and not causal. Therefore, the relationships between personality characteristics and creative achievement found in those studies are open to multiple interpretations. Being aloof may help lead people to creative work, or doing creative work may lead to the need to be aloof, protecting one's unusual ideas from early criticism and protecting the time needed for difficult work. There may also be a complex relationship among the various social characteristics, or different factors, such as particular kinds of life experience that may lead someone to be both aloof and creative —for review, see Weisberg (2006).

Openness to New Experience

In addition to the research specifically on creativity, overall personality research has tended to consolidate definitions of personality traits into "the big five" (Feist, 2010, p. 120): openness to new experience, extraversion, neuroticism, conscientiousness, and agreeableness. Of these, openness to new experience includes factors that directly relate to creativity, such as preference for variety of experiences and intellectual curiosity. Ratings of openness to new experience correlate positively with divergent thinking scores and some other creative personality measures (McCrae, 1987; Dollinger, Urban, & James, 2004). The same is not true for the other four traits. The correlation between the openness to new experience trait and creative performance also seems to be mediated by intrinsic motivation and how open-ended the activity is (Feist, 2010).

Educational Implications

The general point of research on creative personalities is that creative people can have unusual personalities. Although much of the discussion about creativity and education is about nurturing creativity in all students, those already on their own creative fast track can pose equally daunting challenges. In reviewing a longitudinal study of children who had taken the TTCT, Torrance profiled a young man who had gone on to become a successful novelist. Mack Jamison (pseudonym) was a very imaginative and talented child. "Even by second grade, his drawings approached the expertness of a professional illustrator . . . he drew dinosaurs and space creatures on everything, including his desk" (Torrance, 2002, p. 8). He also drew during all classes, whatever the agenda of the teacher. As Torrance noted, accommodating, supporting, and guiding a student like Mack would not be easy in many classrooms.

In addition to fitting some of the characteristics of artists found in the personality research, Mack would fit Renzulli's category of "creative productive giftedness"

(Renzulli & De Wet, 2010, p. 27), as opposed to "schoolhouse ability" (p. 25). Students like Mack seem to profit most from learning experiences that take their interests and learning styles into account and from work where they apply knowledge, actively participating in the construction of meaning. For more complete reviews of these curricular and teaching approaches, see Renzulli and De Wet (2010) and also Renzulli, Gentry, and Reis (2003). Daniels and Piechowsky (2010) recommend similar approaches, as well as particular ways of talking to creatively gifted children to help them regulate and constructively use psychomotor, sensual, intellectual, imaginational, and emotional over-excitability. (Mack, as described by Torrance, had a very easily excited imagination.)

Example

Every assignment will not fit the interests of a creatively gifted child like Mack, but many assignments can allow room for integrating students' interests, including opportunities for independent work. Mack's passion for imagined worlds could fit into literature, art, science, and even math (story problems). Also, teachers have to remember that, as previously discussed, creative purpose and abilities develop over the long term. Success or failure can be hard to measure in grade school. Mack's fourth-grade teacher remembered being tolerant of the student's lack of cooperation, but disappointed. Years later, as a successful novelist, Mack remembered that teacher as his mentor in his development: "Fourth grade ended but his [the teacher's] influence has been permanent" (in Torrance, 2002, p. 6).

THE FOURTH IDEA

Everyone Participates

Sociocultural Theory

Csikszentmihalyi (1997, 1999) suggested changing the question of "What is creativity?" to "Where is creativity?" His answer was that creativity lies in the tension between individuals, domains (symbol systems as in music, math, art, literature, history), and the fields that integrate new ideas into those domains (gatekeepers). Creativity then becomes long-term impact of a new idea on a domain, with the field holding much of the power as gatekeepers. Note: generally children do not make such long-term impacts on culture, prodigies notwithstanding. As a result, Csikszentmihalyi et al. (2003) has argued that children are not creative *per se*.

Improvisation

Inspired by improvisational theater and jazz, Sawyer and his associates (Sawyer, 2010a, 2010b; Sawyer & DeZutter, 2009) have analyzed small group interactions and found that creativity does not necessarily reside in any one participant, but in the overall group dynamic. The group members build on the contributions of each other. Looking at the history of the big thinkers who have changed their domains forever—the ones critical to Csikszentmihalyi's theory—Sawyer (2007) has noted that they too built on each other's work. The lone creator is a myth.

Educational Implications

On a general level, the improvisational aspects of creativity require cooperation, collaboration, and teamwork, recognizing the value of others' work and building on it. These are familiar goals for 21st-century teachers. Within the classroom, Sawyer (2010b) conceptualizes these ideas as paradoxical relationships between structures and improvisation. In the curricula, in the teacher's plans or scripts and scaffolding for the learners—the help the teacher provides to assure students can succeed—Sawyer has argued that the structure can actually facilitate improvisation. Through that process learning emerges collaboratively.

Even though Csikszentmihalyi's cultural systems theory is not supposed to apply to children, the kinds of dynamics for integrating new ideas that he has analyzed occur in classrooms. New ideas are also reviewed and integrated in educational institutions and local governments—all of which can be studied, while learning traditional social science methods. In addition, helping students analyze the ways in which they participate in fields can help them understand the process by which new ideas are diffused. Examples might include, editing school publications, using websites, recommending music to one another, and, of course, being consumers.

Examples

In a unit on modern history, explore, not just the invention of new technologies, but also their adoption and diffusion. In a science unit, discuss when key scientific principles were discovered, how they were verified, and how long it took before they were broadly accepted. What factors affected adoption? Were there special equipment or financial constraints? Who were the key promoters, and who were the detractors?

THE FIFTH IDEA

For the Perilous Tasks of Assessment and Grading—Context, Context, Context

Much has been written about assessment of student creativity (e.g., Kaufman, Plucker, & Baer, 2008; Plucker & Makel, 2010; Starko, 2005). The approach to linking creativity theory and overall quality education advocated in this chapter calls for some additional comment on both assessment of students' overall creativity and grading of creative work.

First Decision: Whether or Not to Deploy the Concept

The famous preschool program Reggio Emilia eventually comes up in most conversations about creativity in education. That program is known for free expression across modalities (visual, verbal, kinesthetic), as well as highly motivated, engaged, in-depth learning demonstrated by very young children: the stuff of creativity. Reggio Emilia, however, seldom talks about creativity. Instead, it focuses on the possibilities of multimodal learning, "the 100 languages of children" (Katz, 1998, p. 37). Just as the ancient Greeks did not need a psychological idea of creativity to produce a civilization unlike anything the world had seen, schools do not have to use the idea of creativity to promote it.

On the other hand, this chapter has argued that the concept of creativity can help promote good overall education because it is so salient to today's world and brings with it a wealth of research and theory. Indeed, to improve educational practices in some—and possibly many—instances, a powerful idea like creativity may be necessary. Once educators decide that creativity is a desired outcome, it will need to be assessed and graded.

Assessment

As is evident from the wealth of theories, the idea of creativity resists reduction to one or two factors, and some researchers recommend using more than one form of assessment (e.g., Kaufman, Plucker, & Baer, 2008). The most commonly used tools for assessment of creativity include divergent thinking tests, personality assessments, and self-report inventories. Some tests, like the Evaluation of Potential Creativity (EPoC) (Barbot, Besançon, & Lubart, 2011) and the Structure of Intellect Model (SOI) (Guilford, 1967, 1988), include divergent and convergent-integrative thinking along with assessment of other factors. Given the number of traditional education outcomes that also relate to creativity (critical thinking, teamwork, and so on), school programs may also choose to include assessment of some of those outcomes, depending on the particular use of the assessment.

Examples

An assessment for acceptance to an advanced arts program may need to include assessment of interests, demonstrated behaviors, and experience that would not apply to an assessment for acceptance to many high schools. Pre/post testing for evaluation of a creativity curriculum might need to include teamwork, along with more traditional creativity measures, if that is one of the components of the curriculum.

Grading

Research on motivation has found that when students are asked to complete creative tasks, expected concrete rewards tend to shift the students' motivation from intrinsic (make up the stories for the fun of it) to extrinsic (do it for the reward). Furthermore, the shift to extrinsic motivation leads to less creative products. As a result some researchers have concluded that the expected rewards or evaluations are killers of creativity (Hennessey, 2003, p. 183).

Importance of Instructions

On the other hand, the rewards provided in the motivation research were not grades *for creativity*. Research has also consistently shown that people score higher on flexibility and originality in divergent thinking tests when they are specifically instructed to be creative, flexible, or original (Harrington, 1975; Plucker & Makel, 2010). In other words, when trying to be creative, people can modulate at least some potentially creative behaviors in the explicitly evaluative context of a test.

Other Caveats

This divergent thinking test research addresses instructions and behaviors, not motivation. The motivational issues are also complex. In one experiment (Hennessey, Amabile, & Martinage, 1989), students who saw a video of youth of their own age talking about maintaining their motivation in spite of grades seemed to be immunized (p. 212) against losing their intrinsic motivation. They maintained their intrinsic motivation more than a control group who saw a different video that did not discuss maintaining intrinsic interests. Apparently, the difference was just being exposed to the idea, presented by peers, that their intrinsic interests could be maintained even when there were extrinsic rewards.

Furthermore, adult creative work—for which education on creativity should be preparing students—almost always includes extrinsic rewards, from status to hard cash. For creative professionals extrinsic rewards, like commissions for artwork, can have a dampening effect on creativity (Amabile et al., 1996). There are, however, striking exceptions. In their race to discover the structure of DNA, after all, Crick and Watson wanted to *win* (Weisberg, 2006), which brought them fame. Indeed, case studies (e.g., Wallace & Gruber, 1989; Weisberg, 2006) and creative people's own accounts (e.g., Barron, Montuori, & Barron, 1997) show that people develop a variety of *creative* strategies for managing their motivations. Examples of such strategies include consciously focusing on play rather than rewards (Feynman in Barron, Montuori, & Barron, 1997), keeping sexy, creative, and pay-the-bills work separate (MacLeod, 2004 p. 13), and self-consciously attributing the inspiration of genius to forces outside the self (Gilbert, 2009).

Implications for Education

In other words, context is crucial. The warnings: do not rush to assess or grade; when assessing, use multiple measures, and be aware that no perfect evaluation of creativity exists. In addition, make students aware that maintaining intrinsic motivation is an important goal.

Example

Over the course of the year, the teacher has emphasized the informative, rather than evaluative, function of grades. The teacher has also led discussions with the students about valuing creativity, the different factors that may contribute to creativity, the importance of maintaining intrinsic motivation, and different ways creative people maintain their motivation. When possible, students have self-directed time to explore issues of interest to them, producing work that can be presented, but not graded. Then, as part of a larger portfolio assignment, students include a project of particular interest to them. For this self-directed project students are told to think creatively about the issues they are studying (the larger portfolio). In presenting their portfolios the students talk about the creativity of their self-directed project. A grade for creativity may be part of the overall portfolio grade.

THE SIXTH IDEA

Creativity Alone Is Not Enough

The Dark Side of Creativity

Remember today's Promethean tasks that creativity is supposed to solve: overcoming humanity's great challenges, serving economic growth, and giving people successful, meaningful lives. Many causes of those challenges and obstacles to resolutions have also come from creativity. The sources of greenhouse gases and the inventive investment products that contributed to the economic collapse of 2008 are just a couple of prominent examples.

Scholars who have looked at the history and use of the idea of creativity have noted as much—this idea has a dark side (Cropley, Cropley, Kaufman, & Runco, 2010). For example, Mason (2003) analyzed two strands of thought contributing to the idea of creativity as it emerged in the 19th century: one where creativity was seen as purely positive and one where it was seen as dangerous and disruptive. He noted that we have lost the sense of the danger of creativity. In looking at more recent history, Weiner (2000) has analyzed the ways in which the idea of creativity has been used as a smoke screen for oppression of non-Western cultures. Individuals within market economies can also be oppressed by the rhetoric of creativity as they are told to recreate themselves continually.

These cultural trends in conceiving of creativity are reflected in the classroom. Teachers tend to say that the ideal student is creative but may also define that student as smart, polite, punctual, and conventional (Runco, 2007)—not the James Mackey type who is highly self-motivated and independent to the point of being uncooperative. Cropley (2010) has further observed that student responses to assignments that are far from the expected outcomes (radical creativity as opposed to orthodox creativity, p. 309) can challenge the underlying assumptions of the assignments and pose difficulties for teachers. In addition, students and parents are often uncomfortable with the uncertainty of creative work as they compete for places and success in the educational system. All of these are educational examples of the disruptive nature of creativity that Mason described in the culture at large.

Implications for Education

Appreciation of the challenging, unintended, and negative consequences of creativity adds dimension to students' awareness of decisions to be creative (metacognition). That decision cannot be treated as a no-brainer. It carries true risks and all kinds of intended and unintended consequences (critical thinking). To help students think through these issues, teachers need to present material in ways that help explore the perspectives from which different changes are seen as positive and negative.

More broadly, educators' attention to the varied consequences of change includes the changes that come with promoting creativity. For example, in Torrance's longitudinal study (2002), everyone was not like James Mackey. One young woman who had an IQ of 141 as a child, had earned a PhD and was pursuing a career in science as an adult, wrote that the divergent thinking tests had been so frustrating for her as a child that they had left a lasting impression. As an adult, even with her achievements, she did not consider herself to be creative, and expectations that she should produce more ideas left her feeling insecure. Torrance speculated that somehow, outside forces had "caused her to sacrifice her creativity at a young age" (p. 3), evidently before her low scores on the Torrance divergent thinking tests. He also believed that her accomplishments and interests indicated that she was more creative than she thought (once again, bringing the relation of divergent thinking and creativity into question). But what if the theory underlying Torrance's test is right, and one's degree of divergent or convergent thinking is a *trait*, and, at least in some cases, a relatively fixed trait?

Ironically, divergent-thinking heuristics, like SCAMPER, may be even more useful to such students who are frustrated with demands to come up with new ideas than for divergent thinkers. The heuristics can provide a back-pocket trick for coming up with ideas when necessary for people who do not naturally think divergently.

More generally, though, education needs to provide a place for all students. Any task has some dimension of creativity involved, but the primary work in many fields involves following well-established protocols to produce valuable outcomes. Examples include science as practiced by the young woman in Torrance's study, much scholarship, and many instances of musical performance. Teaching creativity is not the answer for every social question or for every student. That is why educators need to think of using theories of creativity to enhance good, overall education more than using education simply to produce creativity.

CONCLUSION

Why all the fuss? Making innovative, artistic, and useful things, coming up with new ideas, and developing new ways of making sense of the world—these phenomena—are as old as humanity. Attributing those phenomena to creativity as a force within individuals and groups, however, is a relatively new idea and one that continues to take form. Today, education is playing an ever-greater role in defining the construct of creativity by using the idea in ways that improve education. In taking on that opportunity and responsibility, educators can profit from understanding the research, debates, and theories to date.

Applying creativity theories to the classroom has rich potential. Understanding the theories is a starting place, an expertise that is useful, maybe even critical, for educators in today's world. The theories and techniques do not, however, demand an entirely new approach to education. Instead, they can contribute to the longstanding, and still far from complete, struggle to advance good education. From that perspective, creativity research offers fresh ways of seeing, and enhancing, the value of well-known practices. This will be hard work—a creative endeavor—just as producing good education has always been.

REFERENCES

Amabile, T.M., Colins, M.A., Conti, R., Philllips, E., Picariello, M., Ruscio, J., & Whitney, D. (1996). *Creativity in context*. Boulder, CO: Westview Press/Persius Books Group.

Baer, J. (1998). The case for domain specificity in creativity. *Creativity Research Journal, 11*, 173–177.

Baer, J., & Garrett, T. (2010). Teaching for creativity in an era of content standards and accountability. In R. A. Beghetto & J. C. Kaufman (Eds.), *Nurturing creativity in the classroom* (pp. 6–23). New York: Cambridge University Press.

Barbot, B., Besançon, M., & Lubart, T. I. (2011). Assessing creativity in the classroom. *The Open Educational Journal, 4* (Suppl 1: M5), 58–66.

Barron, F., Montuori, A., & Barron, A. (1997). *Creators on creating: Awakening and cultivating the imaginative mind.* New York: Jeremy P. Tarcher/Penguin.

Beghetto, R. A., & Kaufman, J. C. (2010). *Nurturing creativity in the classroom.* Cambridge, UK: Cambridge University Press.

Center for Creative Learning (2012). Common Core State Standards Initiative (2010). *Common core standards for English language arts & literacy in history/social studies, science, and technical studies.* Council of Chief School State Officers (CCSSO) and National Governors Association (NGA). Retrieved from http://www.corestandards .org/the-standards.

Craft, A. (2005). *Creativity in schools: Tensions and dilemmas.* New York: Routledge.

Cropley, A. J. (2010). Creativity in the classroom: The dark side. In D. H. Cropley, A. J. Cropley, J. C. Kaufman, & M. A. Runco (Eds.), *The dark side of creativity* (pp. 297–315). Cambridge, UK: Cambridge University Press.

Cropley, D. H., Cropley, A. J., Kaufman, J. C., & Runco, M. A. (Eds.) (2010). *The dark side of creativity.* Cambridge, UK: Cambridge University Press.

Csikszentmihalyi, M. (1997). *Creativity: Flow and the psychology of discovery and invention.* New York: Harper Perennial.

Csikszentmihalyi, M. (1999). Implications of a systems perspective for the study of creativity. In R. J. Sternberg (Ed.), *Handbook of creativity* (pp. 313–335). New York: Cambridge University Press.

Csikszentmihalyi et al. (2003). Key issues in creativity and development. In K. Sawyer (Ed.), *Creativity and development* (pp. 217–242). Oxford, UK: Oxford University Press.

Daniels, S., & Piechowski, M. M. (2010). When intensity goes to school: Overexcitabilities, creativity, and the gifted child. In R. A. Beghetto & J. C. Kaufman (Eds.), *Nurturing creativity in the classroom* (pp. 313–328). New York: Cambridge University Press.

Dollinger, S. J., Urban, K. K., & James, T. A. (2004). Creativity and openness: Further validation of two creative product measures. *Creativity Research Journal, 16,* 35–47.

Eberle, R. F. (2008). SCAMPER: Creative games and activities for imagination development. Waco, TX: Prufrock Press.

Fairweather, E., & Cramond, B. (2010). Infusing creative and critical thinking into the curriculum together. In R. A. Beghetto & J. C. Kaufman (Eds.), *Nurturing creativity in the classroom* (pp. 113–141). New York: Cambridge University Press.

Feist, G. J. (1999). The influence of personality on artistic and scientific creativity. In R. J. Sternberg (Ed.), *Handbook of creativity* (pp. 273–296). Cambridge, UK: Cambridge University Press.

Feist, G. J. (2010). The function of personality in creativity: The nature and nurture of creative personality. In J. C. Kaufman & R. J. Sternberg (Eds.), *The Cambridge handbook of creativity* (pp. 113–130). New York: Cambridge University Press.

Feltovich, P. J., Prietula, M. J., & Ericsson, K. A. (2006). Studies of expertise from psychological perspectives. In K. A. Ericsson, N. Charness, P. J. Feltovich, & R. R. Hoffman (Eds.), *The Cambridge handbook of expertise and expert performance* (pp. 41–67). Cambridge, UK: Cambridge University Press.

Florida, R. (2005). *The flight of the creative class: The new global competition for talent.* New York: HarperBusiness.

Gardner, H. (1993). *Creating minds: An anatomy of creativity seen through the lives of Freud, Einstein, Picasso, Stravinsky, Eliot, Graham, and Gandhi.* New York: Basic Books.

Gilbert, E. (2009). On nurturing creativity. *TED Talks.* Podcast retrieved from http:// www.ted.com/talks/lang/eng/elizabeth_gilbert_on_genius.html.

Gruber, H.E. (1962). The process of science education. *Teachers College Record, 63,* 367–376.

Gruber, H.E. (1989a). Creativity and human survival. In D.B. Wallace & H.E. Gruber (Eds.), *Creative people at work* (pp. 278–287). New York: Oxford University Press.

Gruber, H.E. (1989b). The evolving systems approach to creative work. In D.B. Wallace & H.E. Gruber (Eds.), *Creative people at work* (pp. 3–24). New York: Oxford University Press.

Gruber, H.E., & Wallace, D.B. (1999). The case study method and evolving systems approach for understanding unique creative people at work. In R.J. Sternberg (Ed.), *Handbook of creativity* (pp. 93–115). Cambridge, UK: Cambridge University Press.

Guilford, J.P. (1950). Creativity. *American Psychologist, 5,* 444–454.

Guilford, J.P. (1967). *The nature of human intelligence.* New York: McGraw-Hill.

Guilford, J.P. (1988). Some changes in the Structure of Intellect Model. *Educational and Psychological Measurement, 48*(1), 1–4.

Hanchett Hanson, M. (2004). Dialogue with history: Roles of irony in thinking about new kinds of war. *Metaphor and Symbol, 19*(3), 191–212.

Harrington, D.M. (1975). Effects of explicit instructions to "be creative" on the psychological meaning of divergent thinking test scores. *Journal of Personality, 43,* 434–454.

Hennessey, B.A. (2003). Is the social psychology of creativity really social? Moving beyond a focus on the individual. In P.B. Paulus & B.A. Nijstad (Eds.), *Group creativity: Innovation through collaboration.* Oxford, UK: Oxford University Press.

Hennessey, B.A. (2010). Intrinsic motivation and creativity in the classroom: Have we come full circle? In R.A. Beghetto & J.C. Kaufman (Eds.), *Nurturing creativity in the classroom* (pp. 329–361). Cambridge, UK: Cambridge University Press.

Hennessey, B.A., Amabile, T.M., & Martinage, M. (1989). Immunizing children against the negative effects of reward. *Contemporary Educational Psychology, 14,* 212–227.

Katz, L.G. (1998). What can we learn from Reggio Emilia? In C. Edwards, L. Gandini, & G. Forman (Eds.), *The hundred languages of children: The Reggio Emilia approach—advanced reflections* (2nd ed.) (pp. 27–45). Westport, CT: Ablex Publishing.

Kaufman, J.C., Plucker J.A., & Baer, J. (2008) *Essentials of creativity assessment.* Hoboken, NJ: John Wiley & Sons.

Kim, K.H. (2011). The creativity crisis: The decrease in creative thinking scores on the Torrance Tests of Creative Thinking. *Creativity Research Journal, 23*(4), 285–295.

Kohler, W. (1925). *The mentality of apes.* New York: Harcourt, Brace.

MacKinnon, D.W. (1962). The personality correlates of creativity: A study of American architects. In G.S. Neilsen (Ed.), *Proceedings of the 14th International Congress of Applied Psychology* (pp. 11–39). Copenhagen, DK: Munksgaard.

MacLeod, H. (2004). *How to be creative.* Retrieved from http://changethis.com/manifesto/show/6.HowToBeCreative.

Mason, J.H. (2003). *The value of creativity: The origins and emergence of a modern belief.* Hampshire, UK: Ashgate Publishing Ltd.

May, R. (1974). *The courage to create.* New York: W.W. Norton & Company.

McCrae, R.R. (June 1987). Creativity, divergent thinking, and openness to experience. *Journal of Personality and Social Psychology, 52*(6), 1258–1265.

Nickerson, R.S. (1999). Enhancing Creativity. In R.J. Sternberg (Ed.), *Handbook of creativity* (pp. 392–430). Cambridge, UK: Cambridge University Press.

Nickerson, R.S. (2010). How to discourage creative thinking in the classroom. In R.A. Beghetto & J.C. Kauman (Eds.), *Nurturing creativity in the classroom* (pp. 1–5). Cambridge, UK: Cambridge University Press.

Nijstad, B A., Diehl, M., Stroebe, W. (2003). Cognitive stimulation and interference in idea-generating groups. In P.B. Paulus & B.A. Nijstad (Eds.), *Group creativity: Innovation through collaboration* (pp. 137–159). Oxford, UK: Oxford University Press.

Osborn, A. (1963). *Applied imagination: Principles and procedures of creative thinking*. New York: Scribner.

Parnes, S. J. (1981). *Magic of your mind*. Buffalo, NY: Bearly.

Partnership for 21st-century skills (P21) (December 2009). P21 Framework Definitions. Retrieved from http://www.p21.org/overview/skills-framework.

Piirto, J. (2004). *Understanding creativity*. Scottsdale, AZ: Great Potential Press.

Plucker, J. A. (1999). Is the proof in the pudding? Reanalyses of Torrance's (1958–present) longitudinal data. *Creativity Research Journal, 12*(2), 103–114.

Plucker, J. A., & Makel, M. C. (2010). Assessment of creativity. In J. C. Kaufman & R. J. Sternberg (Eds.), *The Cambridge handbook of creativity* (pp. 48–73). New York: Cambridge University Press.

Pope, R. (2005). *Creativity: Theory, history, practice*. New York: Routledge.

Renzulli, J. S., & De Wet, C. S. (2010). Developing creativity in young people through pursuit of idea acts of learning. In R. A. Beghetto & J. C. Kaufman (Eds.), *Nurturing creativity in the classroom* (pp. 24–72). Cambridge, UK: Cambridge University Press.

Renzulli, J. S., Gentry, M., & Reis, S. M. (2003). *Enrichment clusters: A practical plan for real-world, student-driven learning*. Mansfield Center, CT: Creative Learning Press.

Rogers, C. (1954). Toward a theory of creativity. *ETC: A Review of General Semantics, 11*(4), 249–260.

Runco, M. A. (2007). *Creativity theories and themes: Research, development and practice*. Burlington, MA: Elsevier Academic Press.

Runco, M. A., Millar, G., Selcuk, A., & Cramond, B. (2010). Torrance Tests of Creative Thinking as predictors of personal and public achievement: A fifty-year follow-up. *Creativity Research Journal, 22*(4), 361–368.

Sawyer, R. K. (2007). *Group genius: The creative power of collaboration*. New York: Basic Books.

Sawyer, R. K. (2010a). Learning for creativity. In R. A. Beghetto & J. C. Kaufman (Eds.), *Nurturing creativity in the classroom* (pp. 172–190). Cambridge, UK: Cambridge University Press.

Sawyer, R. K. (2010b). *Structure and improvisation in creative teaching*. New York: Cambridge University Press.

Sawyer, R. K. (2011). What makes good teachers great? The artful balance of structure and improvisation. In R. K. Sawyer (Ed.), *Structure and improvisation in creative teaching* (pp. 1–24). New York: Cambridge University Press.

Sawyer, R. K., DeZutter, S. (2009). Distributed creativity: How collective creations emerge from collaboration. *Psychology of Aesthetics, Creativity, and the Arts, 3*(2), 81–92.

Simonton, D. K. (1999). *Origins of genius: Darwinian perspectives on creativity*. Oxford, UK: Oxford University Press.

Smith, J. K., & Smith, L. F. (2010). Educational creativity. In J. C. Kaufman & R. J. Sternberg (Eds.), *The Cambridge handbook of creativity* (pp. 250–264). New York: Cambridge University Press.

Starko, A. J. (2005). *Creativity in the classroom: Schools of curious delight*. Mahway, NJ: Lawrence Erlbaum.

Sternberg, R. J. (2002). Raising the achievement of all students: Teaching for successful intelligence. *Educational Psychology Review, 14*, 383–393.

Sternberg, R. J. (2003). The development of creativity as a decision-making process. In K. Sawyer (Ed.), *Creativity and development* (pp. 91–138). Oxford, UK: Oxford University Press.

Sternberg, R. J., & Lubart, T. I. (1991). An investment theory of creativity and its development. *Human Development, 34*, 1–31.

Sternberg, R. J., & Williams, W. M. (1996). *How to develop student creativity*. Baltimore, MD: Association for Supervision and Curriculum Development.

Torrance, E. P. (1966). *The Torrance Tests of creative thinking: Norms-technical manual research edition*. Princeton, NJ: Personnel Press.

Torrance, E. P. (2002). *The manifesto: A guide to developing a creative career*. Westport, CT: Ablex Publishing.

Torrance, E. P. (2008). *The Torrance Tests of creative thinking: Norms-technical manual figural (streamlined) forms A & B*. Bensonville, IL: Scholastic Testing Service.

Wallace, D. B., & Gruber, H. E. (1989). *Creative people at work*. New York: Oxford University Press.

Wallach, M. A., & Kogan, N. (1965). *Modes of thinking in young children: A study of the creativity-intelligence distinction*. New York: Holt, Rinehart & Winston.

Wallas, G. (1926). *The art of thought*. London, UK: Cape.

Weiner, R. P. (2000). *Creativity and beyond: Cultures, values and change*. Albany, NY: State University of New York.

Weisberg, R. W. (2006). *Creativity: Understanding innovation in problem solving, science, invention and the arts*. Hoboken, NJ: John Wiley & Sons.

Weisberg, R. W. (2011). Frank Lloyd Wright's Fallingwater: A case study in inside-the-box creativity. *Creativity Research Journal, 23*(4), 296–311.

Wertheimer, M. (1982). *Productive thinking*. Chicago, IL: University of Chicago Press. Original published 1945.

3

THE DARK SIDE OF CREATIVITY IN THE CLASSROOM: THE PARADOX OF CLASSROOM TEACHING

Arthur Cropley
University of Hamburg

David Cropley
University of South Australia

It has become almost a truism in modern society that creativity is a good thing. Kampylis and Valtanen (2010) reviewed 42 modern definitions and no fewer than 120 terms typically associated with creativity (collocations) and concluded that the vast majority of definitions and collocations do not take any account whatsoever of negative aspects of creativity. As the Nobel Prize winner Herbert Simon (1990, p. 11) put it: "Creativity is thinking. *It just happens to be thinking we think is great*" [emphasis added]. Gora (2009) reviewed the general thrust of discussions of this greatness of creativity. At the broad societal level it derives from its contribution to national prosperity, social justice, health and welfare, the quality of cultural life, and similar aspects of the life of the nation. At a more everyday level, creativity is seen as enhancing the convenience and comfort of day-to-day life through technology, appliances, or systems for interacting with other people; and at the level of the individual it is seen as contributing to mental health, personal well-being, and satisfaction with life.

DISLIKE OF CREATIVITY

Despite what has just been said, the fact is that in real life, teachers not infrequently express disapproval or even dislike of the students in their classes who are most creative (Dawson, D'Andrea, Affito, & Westby, 1999) and do little to foster creativity. As Westby and Dawson (1995) showed, many teachers who claimed to have a favorable view of creative children almost bizarrely described them as "conforming," something that Brady (1970) had already reported early in the modern creativity era. When the teachers in the Westby and Dawson study were given adjectives describing traits typical of what creative children are really like (e.g., risk-taking, curious), they said they *disliked* such youngsters; see also Aljughaiman and Mowrer-Reynolds (2005). As Smith and Carlsson (2006, p. 222) put it, " . . . teachers seem to have a confused picture of what is a favourite pupil and what is a creative pupil."

This finding is not new. Early studies (e.g., Getzels & Jackson, 1962; Holland, 1959; Torrance, 1959) concluded that highly creative children tended to be less well known and less well liked by teachers than children with a high IQ. The finding is also not confined to the United States. In an early study in the United States, Germany, India, Greece, and the Philippines, Torrance (1965) showed that there was near unanimous disapproval of creative schoolchildren across countries. In fact, right up until today similar findings have consistently been reported in a number of different countries and regions; Cropley (2009) listed studies in Africa, Australia, Chinese societies such as Singapore, Europe, the Middle East, and North America, which all supported this conclusion.

The paradox is also not confined to teachers. For instance, DeFillippi, Grabher, and Jones (2007) discussed the paradoxical role of creativity in business and organizations, where it is simultaneously desired and rejected. In fact, recent research has shown that there is widespread unease about creativity in the broader society, despite almost fawning emphasis on creativity and its offspring, innovation, as something like a universal panacea. Staw (1995) asked why, when the truth is told, no one really wants creativity, and Mueller, Melwani, and Goncalo (2012) concluded that the widespread social aversion to it (in practice as against lip service) results from the fact that creativity involves *uncertainty*, a state that makes most people uncomfortable. From the point of view of teachers, the problem seems indeed to arise from uncertainty at both the conceptual and practical levels, including:

- failure to appreciate what creativity is good for (especially in the classroom)
- lack of a clear idea of what creativity is
- misunderstanding of what creative students are actually like
- lack of information on how to promote it and benefit from it in the classroom.

We turn now to an examination of the failures and lacuna just outlined in order to close the gaps in teachers' knowledge and understanding.

UNDERSTANDING CREATIVITY

What Is Creativity Good for in the Classroom?

Turning specifically to education, Cropley (2012) gave a long list of benefits that researchers have shown to be related to emphasis on creativity in classroom instruction. These include *process benefits* such as more active involvement in learning, reduced inattention, improved planning and goal setting, ability to make and accept constructive criticism, use of the imagination and production of ideas, improved questioning skill, generation of multiple solutions, recognition of patterns, and problem-solving. *Personal benefits* listed by Cropley include, among numerous others, improved self-esteem, better expression of emotions, more positive self-concept, greater openness to the new, greater spontaneity, increased desire to understand things, and increased willingness to develop new skills. These benefits seem so overwhelming that it would be expected that teachers would be universally enthusiastic about creativity.

What Is Creativity?

Creativity is not exclusively a personal property, a specific talent or a unitary trait, or the unique possession of a small band of chosen ones. It is not an event such as the reception of a bolt from the blue or a divine inspiration and is not a specific object or product. It is a *process* that is possible for everybody, and that ultimately leads to a *product*. The process is influenced by characteristics of the *person* such as personal properties, motivation, and feelings. The surrounding environment provides environmental support or lack thereof (referred to as environmental *press*) for the mental actions and personal factors involved in the process and decides whether the product is creative or not.

This way of looking at creativity is encapsulated in the "Four Ps" approach of Barron (1955), Rhodes (1961), and in Csikszentmihalyi's (1996) systems approach. It is consistent with the definition of creativity of Plucker, Beghetto, and Dow (2004) as "the interaction among aptitude, process, and environment by which an individual or group produces a perceptible product that is both novel and useful as defined within a social context" (p. 90). According to Csikszentmihalyi, the easiest thing to change in this system is press—in the present case, the classroom environment—a fact, which places great responsibility on teachers. The management of this press in a favorable way is the teacher's main contribution to fostering the process of creativity.

The Product

At least since Morgan (1953) it has been widely accepted that the essential core of creativity—its *sine qua non*—is *novel products*. However, novelty alone is not sufficient for a product to be creative. It may involve mere pseudocreativity, which is novel only in the sense of nonconformity, lack of discipline, blind rejection of what already exists or simply letting oneself go—often manifesting itself in the classroom as disruptive behavior. These properties may be confused with creativity, but they are not actually an inherent part of it. Consequently, there is widespread, almost universal agreement among creativity theorists that in order to be creative a product must not just display novelty but must also be helpful in some way and appropriate to the task at hand—it must be useful. These two definitive elements—novelty and usefulness—have been stressed by many authors over the years (e.g., Barron, 1955; Kozbelt, Beghetto, & Runco, 2010; Stein, 1953; Sternberg, Kaufman, & Pretz, 2002).

Using Bruner's terminology (1962), creative products must—in addition to displaying novelty—be *effective* and *relevant*. Otherwise, every far-fetched, outrageous or preposterous idea or every act of nonconformity would, by virtue of being novel, be creative. In the classroom this means that mindless defiance, failure to fulfill requirements, sheer unruliness, disobedience and the like are not, on their own, creative unless they lead to some kind of useful solution. In general life, the product of a creative process can be earthshaking (curing cancer or establishing world peace, let us say) or mundane and everyday (filing office records more efficiently or making a stew more tasty with a limited range of ingredients). Researchers, therefore, distinguish among "eminent accomplishments" or "Big-C" creativity; "professional expertise" or "Pro-C" creativity; "everyday innovation" or "little-c" creativity; and "transformational learning" or "mini-c" creativity (Kaufman & Beghetto, 2009). The latter two classifications seem to be most applicable to the classroom context.

A Hierarchy of Creativity in Products

Relevance and Effectiveness

Relevance and effectiveness define the minimum profile of a useful product. A product, which does not go beyond these is merely "routine"; it may be very useful for solving some problem or fulfilling a task (and therefore praiseworthy), but it is not creative because it lacks novelty. Relevance and effectiveness accompanied by novelty lead to an original product that, by virtue of its novelty, goes beyond a routine one and is in fact creative, although at a mundane level.

Elegance

However, in addition to being novel, relevant, and effective, and thus original, a product can go further: It can look the part, fit together well, make an impression of being complete, be obviously what is needed, or make sense. In other words, it can be elegant. Elegance is often readily recognizable simply by looking at the product: As Rechtin and Maier (2000) put it, citing Wernher von Braun, "The eye is a fine architect. Believe it!"

Elegance encapsulates concepts of aesthetics and ergonomics—factors that determine how a product looks and feels, and the interaction between the product, the user, and the environment. Visual aesthetics—the recognition of the functionality or utility of a design—draws on the intuitive associations that we make between, for example, symmetrical shapes with broad bases and concepts like *stability* and *inertness*. In the same manner, visual patterns that show a separation of an object from a base tend to suggest *mobility* and *action*. In simple terms, this is why a concrete bridge will almost certainly look stronger, safer, and better than a bridge made from bamboo.

Genesis

Finally, comes "genesis": this is the property of a relevant, effective, and novel product that makes it transferable to different (quite possibly unanticipated) situations (transferability), opens up new ways of looking at known problems (seminality), or draws attention to the existence of previously unnoticed problems (germinality).

Winglets on commercial aircraft—the small, vertical extensions on the wingtips of commercial airliners—are a good example. Originally designed and implemented to address the problem of reducing fuel consumption (by reducing drag), winglets also solved other, unanticipated problems. The reduction in drag, for example, means that aircraft can take off and land with reduced power, making them quieter. Thus, the problem of noise pollution near airports is mitigated. The saving in fuel not only makes the cost of flying cheaper, but also solves another unanticipated problem—how to reduce the carbon footprint of air travel. Less fuel burned means less carbon emissions, so that winglets also become a solution to the problem of reducing the environmental impact of air travel (or in some countries, like Australia, a means for airlines to reduce their carbon tax obligations). Generic solutions solve more than one problem. Generic creativity is most usually associated with "Big-C" creativity that opens up new ways of understanding the world. These five manifestations of a product—three of them involving creativity—are shown in table 3.1. The hierarchy of creativity in products is discussed more fully in, for instance, Cropley, Kaufman, and Cropley (2011).

Creative Thinking

Guilford (1950) laid the groundwork for a relatively down-to-earth and systematic way of conceptualizing creative thinking. He argued that people can apply their intelligence by working as fast as possible, sticking to the tried and trusted, playing it safe, looking at the new in terms of the old, putting everything in its proper place, using everything as it was intended to be used, always being right, and so on. This can produce a useful routine product (see table 3.1), but it does not generate novelty. Guilford called this "convergent" thinking. He then pointed out that people are capable of applying their intellect in a different way, which involves branching out from the given to envisage previously unknown possibilities and arrive at unexpected or even surprising answers: "divergent" thinking. According to Boden (1994) such thinking involves three basic processes:

- Exploring known ideas
- Making unfamiliar combinations of familiar ideas
- Transforming existing ideas.

In order to explore, combine, or transform ideas, a student must first of all be familiar with them, that is, know that they exist. This implies a link between knowledge and creativity, since the more a person knows the richer the store of ideas that can be drawn on, while it is impossible to expand or transform knowledge you do not possess. Numerous authors have emphasized the importance of this link—Scott (1999) listed Albert, Amabile, Campbell, Chi, Feldhusen, Gardner, Gruber, Mednick, Simonton, Wallas, and Weisberg, whereas Csikszentmihalyi (1996) gave great emphasis to knowledge of a field. Thus, *creativity also requires convergent thinking* (the process that leads to acquisition of accurate and plentiful information). This may help to explain why teachers struggle with creativity in the classroom. It is not merely a case of teaching students to think divergently. Rather, the teacher must not only understand which type of thinking is required at any given point but must also be able to help students switch from convergent to divergent thinking according to the situation's demands.

Table 3.1   The Hierarchical Organization of Creative Products

	KIND OF PRODUCT				
CRITERION	PSEUDO- OR QUASI-CREATIVE	ROUTINE	ORIGINAL	ELEGANT	GENERIC
Effectiveness	–	+	+	+	+
Novelty	+	–	+	+	+
Elegance	–	–	–	+	+
Genesis	–	–	–	–	+

The Person

Although views diverge, most writers in the area agree that personality is involved in creativity, and various authors have published reviews of the personal characteristics that are of particular importance; for an overview, see Cropley and Cropley (2009). The creative person possesses special personal properties such as independence, openness, flexibility, curiosity, willingness to take risks or pleasure in uncertainty, experiencing positive feelings/moods such as optimism in the face of a challenge, and satisfaction in doing something differently. Such a person is in a good position to acquire and apply skills such as coming up with the unexpected, seeing things differently from most people, or linking ideas not usually regarded as belonging together (process).

In a comprehensive review Silvia, Kaufman, Reiter-Palmon, and Wigert (2011) showed that the only one of the Big Five personality dimensions on which there is unanimity about the existence of a link to creativity is *openness*. Some people like to go beyond the conventional and enjoy (are open to) the unexpected, whereas others consistently display caution, preferring to stick to the tried and trusted. Some studies have also reported that there are also undesirable traits associated with creativity, such as self-centeredness, self-justification, lack of concern about others, arrogance, dishonesty, willingness to lie and greater skill at lying, hostility, and even destructiveness (Gino & Ariely, 2012; Silvia, Kaufman, Reiter-Palmon, & Wigert, 2011). The favorable personal properties, personal motivation, and personal feelings/mood, which promote creativity, are summarized in table 3.2. The entries in the right-hand column are not meant to be exhaustive, but merely to give an idea of what is meant by the reference to creativity-facilitating processes, personal properties, personal motives, and personal feelings.

Table 3.2   Creativity-Facilitating Aspects of Person

ASPECT OF PERSON	EXAMPLES OF ASPECTS FAVORABLE FOR CREATIVITY
Personal properties	High-ego strength Openness Acceptance of fantasy Independence Flexibility
Personal motivation	Curiosity Willingness to take risks Tolerance of ambiguity Being excited by conflicts/contradictions Being spurred on by risk/uncertainty Having the courage of one's convictions
Personal feelings/mood	Atypical values High self-esteem Positive feelings in contact with uncertainty Feeling of satisfaction upon doing something differently Enjoyment of being challenged

Coupled with thinking skills a simple dichotomization of each of these three areas (personal properties, motivation, and feelings/mood) into favorable/unfavorable for creativity (+/−), plus a dichotomization of thinking, yields $2^4 = 16$ possible combinations. These are shown in table 3.3. A plus sign indicates a favorable state for creativity, a minus sign an unfavorable one. This table shows that there are many combinations of circumstances in which students might possess some (or even most) of the characteristics necessary for creativity (although some combinations are harder to imagine than others in practice), but lack others, with the result that their creativity is blocked or inhibited.

Table 3.3   Possible Combinations of Personal Prerequisites for Creativity

	1	2	3	4	5	6	7	8	9	10	11	12	13	14	15	16
Personal properties	+	+	+	+	−	−	−	−	+	+	+	+	−	−	−	−
Motivation	+	+	+	−	+	+	−	−	−	−	−	+	+	+	−	−
Thinking	+	+	−	+	+	−	+	−	−	+	−	−	+	−	+	−
Feelings	+	−	+	+	+	+	+	+	−	−	+	−	−	−	−	−

Column one depicts a person in whom all four elements are favorably developed, and represents "fully realized" creativity; column two describes a person in whom the personal properties, thinking skills, and motivation are favorable, but the feelings are unfavorable (stifled creativity, blocked by negative feelings or mood). In column three the person lacks the ability to get unusual ideas, make atypical links, or explore ideas, despite the desire to be creative, a good feeling about being exposed to novelty, and openness, flexibility, and the like (frustrated creativity). The person depicted in column four could be creative, but the motivation is missing (abandoned creativity). The various incomplete combinations could all be given similar labels. Gabora (2002, p. 170) gave the amusing analogy of the "beer can theory": A person who is good at some aspects but lacks something is like the cans of beer in a six pack, where all the elements of a whole are present but "the plastic thingy holding them all together is missing." One task for teachers—and another possible reason why teachers may struggle with creativity in the classroom—can be seen as identifying the "thingy" that is missing more specifically (diagnosing creativity), and taking appropriate action. The teacher's role, therefore, goes well beyond merely passing on the requisite skills and includes their management and synthesis into the students' entire educational experience.

PRESS—THE ROLE OF THE CLASSROOM ENVIRONMENT

The original discussion of press by Rhodes (1961) focused on education, and press was seen as involving the level of support (or lack thereof) for creativity in the classroom or the facilitatory or inhibitory influence of the classroom climate or atmosphere on creative activities. A favorable environment can be said to be congenial.

The Phase Approach to Creativity

One problem with developing a congenial classroom climate is that promoting creativity involves fostering both convergent and divergent thinking, tolerating intolerable personal traits such as arrogance, and evaluating products that simultaneously preserve and attack the already known. A high level of skepticism is scarcely surprising. Cropley and Cropley (2009) argued that a *phase approach* to understanding the process of production of relevant and effective novelty is what is needed. They drew on Wallas's (1926) well-known four-phase model and proposed seven phases, which they labeled "Preparation," "Activation," "Generation," "Illumination," "Verification," "Communication," and "Validation." In the phase of Preparation a person becomes familiar with a field; Activation involves the emergence of problem awareness or indeed of problem invention; Generation involves the production of possible solutions; Illumination involves identification of a promising candidate solution; Verification involves confirmation of the value of a solution; Communication involves the passing on of the solution to other people (such as teachers); and Validation involves acceptance by other people of the solution's worth (through for instance, positive feedback or the awarding of a good grade). (See chapter 13 for application of the seven-phase model to inquiry.)

The first five phases involve generation of effective novelty whereas the last two involve communicating the novelty and receiving feedback: They are, in a sense, the phases where creativity fuses with the real world. In the classroom, Communication involves, for instance, handing in an assignment, and Validation is contained in the teacher's feedback, often evaluation. These phases do not necessarily form a lockstep progression of completely distinct stages. There may well be false starts, early breakups, restarts, and jumps over a particular phase, or various interactions such as the result of one phase forcing a return to an earlier one but with a different starting point derived from the now abandoned phase. Shaw (1989) referred to these involving "loops."

What this means is that there is no such thing as a unitary, one-size-fits-all congenial environment. For instance, to give just two examples, teaching that promotes careful acquisition of accurate knowledge (the core of Preparation) may inhibit becoming aware of previously unnoticed problems (Activation) or making unexpected links among elements of existing knowledge (Generation), or the need for Verification may intimidate students when it comes to Communication. Thus, different combinations of cognitive processes, personal characteristics, motivation, and feelings are ideal for creativity in different phases; for a more detailed discussion, see A. J. Cropley and Cropley (2010). This means that it is important for teachers to understand what phase in the generation of effective novelty is currently active and optimize the congeniality of the classroom for that phase. For instance, in the phase of Preparation, learning by heart (intuitively anathema to creativity enthusiasts) may be extremely facilitatory: Acquiring knowledge of irregular verbs by means of rote exercises may be very helpful for developing mastery of a foreign language.

The different possible combinations of psychological factors outlined in table 3.3 indicate that creativity may be blocked in the individual for differing reasons: It can, for instance, be "stifled," "frustrated," or "abandoned" (see the discussion of table 3.3). What this means, in turn, is that teachers, among other things, need to be able to diagnose students' work by identifying where their strengths and weaknesses lie and reacting accordingly (i.e., providing appropriate press): Thus, the congenial classroom environment needs to be highly differentiated according to phase on the one hand and the strengths and weaknesses of individual learners on the other.

WHAT IS NEEDED IN THE CLASSROOM?

Assessment—Diagnosing Products

D. H. Cropley and Cropley (2010) proposed a system for rating the creativity of classroom products, which they later (Cropley, Kaufman, & Cropley, 2011) refer to as the Creative Solution Diagnosis Scale (CSDS). The CSDS involves five dimensions of the creativity of a product: Relevance and Effectiveness; Novelty; Problematization; Elegance; Genesis. Cropley and Cropley identified *indicators* of these characteristics, which can be applied to a wide range of products such as artworks, essays, designs, models, sporting moves, or solutions to mathematics problems. Examples of indicators are: "The solution accurately reflects conventional knowledge and/or techniques"; "The solution draws attention to shortcomings in other existing solutions"; "The solution shows how to extend the known in a new direction"; "The beholder sees at once that the solution makes sense"; or "The solution draws attention to previously unnoticed problems" (Cropley, Kaufman, & Cropley, 2011).

Cropley, Kaufman, and Cropley (2011) showed that raters are perfectly capable of recognizing the presence or absence of the CSDS's indicators and that there is a high degree of agreement among them on whether they are present or absent. Scores on the scale yield a differentiated assessment of the creativity of a product (e.g., a particular product shows, let us say, a high level of originality but is poorly worked out and unconvincing—i.e., it lacks elegance), and students are capable of understanding the feedback they receive, as shown by Cropley and Cropley (2000). In summary, it is possible to specify what makes a product creative, identify this in real products, communicate strengths and weaknesses of their product to students, and indicate what needs to be done to make products more creative. (See appendix for the CSDS that is described by Arthur Cropley and David Cropley in the previous paragraphs as a helpful tool for teachers to assess products of creativity.)

Diagnosing Teachers

Cropley (2012) proposed looking at differential diagnosis of creativity from a different perspective. Different disciplines may offer more congenial environments for different phases or different combinations of personal properties as outlined in table 3.3. He speculated, for instance, that modern languages or mathematics may promote reapplication of the known to produce small amounts of conventional novelty, thus being very supportive of Preparation, Activation, and Validation, but less supportive of Generation and Illumination, whereas, let us say modern dance may promote radical departures from the tried and trusted (Generation) and Communication, but neglect Preparation and Activation.

Cropley (2012) took this line of argument further and speculated that there may be different teacher types who provide a congenial environment for different phases of creativity. Using a framework based on type of creativity (e.g., focused on process versus focused on product; involving radical novelty versus conventional novelty; involving large amounts of novelty versus small increments), he described eight stereotypical teacher types and gave them labels such as the "stickler," the "avant-gardist," the "Bohemian," or the "innovator" (see table 3.4). This classification system is essentially intuitive at present (i.e., the types have not been strictly defined and objectively determined to exist).

Table 3.4   Different Kinds of Teachers and Some Dimensions of Creativity

LEVEL OF NOVELTY	KIND OF NOVELTY	PRODUCT/ PROCESS ORIENTED	LABEL
High	Radical	Product	Innovator
High	Radical	Process	Individualist
High	Orthodox	Product	Adaptor
High	Orthodox	Process	Pathfinder
Low	Radical	Product	Avant-gardist
Low	Radical	Process	Bohemian
Low	Orthodox	Product	Stickler
Low	Orthodox	Process	Traditionalist

An "innovator" may be particularly effective at promoting Generation and Communication but weak at promoting Verification, whereas an "adapter" may promote Preparation, Verification, and Validation, but do little to support Generation or Illumination. Even the stickler and the traditionalist—bearers of labels, which intuitively seem anticreative—would support Preparation, Verification, and Validation, but not Activation, Generation, or Illumination. Thus, it seems that the establishment of a congenial environment would involve all disciplines and all teachers, that is, it is a general principle that should infuse the entire curriculum. This, in turn, implies the need for highly differentiated teacher training. For instance, different trainee teachers would require sensitization to different aspects of their disciplines and of their own preferred ways of promoting familiarity with them.[1]

Examples from Classroom Practice

McWilliam (2009) gives an example involving three approaches to teaching a lesson on Shakespeare's *Macbeth*. One pedagogical approach is for the teacher to read and explain the text, drawing attention to the big issues that the play touches upon. Students are passive and follow the text in copies of the play in their books, absorbing the explanations of the teacher, who is the acknowledged expert and leader of learning. A second approach involves trying to engage the students by, for instance, showing them a film of the play and guiding the focus of their attention by asking them to fill out a worksheet while watching the film. After the film they could form groups and discuss their responses to the worksheet, then report back to the entire class in a plenary session. These approaches focus on Preparation, Communication, and Validation.

By contrast with both of these approaches, it is possible to ask students to process information actively, theorize, and solve puzzles. In the case of teaching *Macbeth* this could involve dividing the class into six-person "detective agencies" with the task of solving the murder of Duncan. Initially, they would not be allowed to look at the actual text of the play, but only be told that someone had been murdered and given a list of characters. They would be permitted to question any characters they chose—the teacher would play all characters and answer questions accurately (in terms of the play). The students' task would be to work out motive, opportunity, and means, and formulate a theory of the crime. Subsequently, they would check out their theory against the actual text of the play. McWilliam (2009) made the point that this approach is not laissez-faire and does not involve the teacher becoming passive. She also emphasized that it involves rigor, system, and purpose: Among other things, the teacher has to be thoroughly familiar with the play.

The students would be expected to understand the historical and psychological context of the events described in the play, analyze the way Shakespeare presented events, such as organization of material or dramatic effects, and identify the more general lessons about life to be learned from Macbeth's ultimate fate, such as the destruction of his personality by guilt. In addition to gaining understanding of Shakespeare's literary art, the teacher wanted the students to obtain experience in working through problems (as against receiving factual information), taking a mental risk, assembling, and editing knowledge rather than passively listening, or evaluating information; that is, the approach emphasizes not only Preparation, Communication, and Validation but also Activation, Generation, Illumination, and Verification.

Williams (2007) also gave a detailed and practical example of creative pedagogy: in her case, however, in teaching mathematics to primary school students, that is, not in an arts-type discipline, as above, but in a more scientific one. Her aim was to promote, among others, "cognitive autonomy," "autonomous access," and "spontaneous pursuit," close to what we call "Activation" and "Generation." The children were given various numbers of small cubes (initially 24) and asked to make as many different boxes (rectangular cuboids) as they could, by *using all the cubes every time*. Working in groups of four they were then asked to find a way of proving mathematically that they had built all possible boxes involving exactly 24 cubes. The students worked out for themselves that the volume of a rectangular cuboid is the product of length x breadth x depth and then that the number 24 has a fixed number of sets of three smaller whole numbers (length, breadth, and depth), which when multiplied yield 24 (e.g., $2 \times 3 \times 4 = 24$; $2 \times 2 \times 6 = 24$; $12 \times 1 \times 2 = 24$). Finally, they developed the concept of "factor" (e.g., it is impossible to build a box with one dimension equal to 5, because 5 "won't go" into 24, that is, it is not a factor of 24).

Cropley and Cropley (2000) adopted a creativity-facilitating approach in a university class on engineering design. Part of the course assessment involved building "a wheeled vehicle powered by the energy stored in a mousetrap and capable of moving at least 1 metre under its own power." Although a passing grade was guaranteed if the vehicle proved to be capable of moving at least one meter under its own power, assessment emphasized the importance for obtaining a high grade of novelty, elegance, and genesis (see table 3.1), all of which had been explained to the students in class and demonstrated in a practical form through case studies. If students asked for an elaboration of the assignment, they were told that the problem had been sufficiently defined by the words, "Design and build a wheeled vehicle powered by the energy stored in a mousetrap."

The vehicles the students eventually built were rated on four dimensions: Relevance and Effectiveness (whether or not they travelled the required distance); Novelty (whether or not they differed from the usual idea of a wheeled vehicle); Elegance (understandability and workmanlike finish); and Genesis (ability to make people reconsider concepts like "wheeled vehicle," "powered by," ability to open up new perspectives, etc). Again, emphasis was expanded from Preparation and Activation to encompass Generation, Illumination, Verification, and Communication.

Closing Remarks

The paradox of creativity in the classroom is characterized by the "Four Ps" framework: person, product, process, and press. While universally acclaimed for its benefits across each of the Ps, creativity in the classroom nevertheless comes with a heavy price tag. To achieve, for example, the reduced inattention, or improved self-esteem, as well as the ability to generate outcomes that successfully combine both novelty and effectiveness, the price demanded is that teachers must develop a deep understanding of a construct—creativity—that has traditionally been poorly understood. Resolving this paradox will require that teachers are helped to develop a clear understanding of what creativity is; that they have available to them a stable profile describing what creative students are actually like; that they understand what creativity offers in the classroom; that they have the knowledge of how to promote it and benefit from it in the classroom. The responsibility for resolving this paradox must lie with creativity researchers, teacher trainers, and the teachers themselves.

NOTE

1. Readers may find it interesting to ask themselves which type most closely resembles them.

REFERENCES

Aljughaiman, A., & Mowrer-Reynolds, E. (2005). Teachers' conceptions of creativity and creative students. *Journal of Creative Behaviour, 39*, 17–34.

Barron, F.X. (1955). The disposition towards originality. *Journal of Abnormal and Social Psychology, 51*, 478–485.

Boden, M.A. (1994). Introduction. In M.A. Boden (Ed.), *Dimensions of creativity* (pp. 1–12). Cambridge, MA: MIT Press.

Brady, E.B. (1970). The effects of creativity and intelligence on teacher ratings. *British Journal of Educational Psychology, 40*, 342–344.

Bruner, J.S. (1962). The conditions of creativity. In H. Gruber, G. Terrell, & M. Wertheimer (Eds.), *Contemporary approaches to cognition* (pp. 1–30). New York: Atherton.

Cropley, A.J. (2009). Teachers' antipathy to creative students: Some implications for teacher training. *Baltic Journal of Psychology, 10*, 86–93.

Cropley, A. J. (2012). Creativity and education: An Australian perspective. *International Journal of Creativity and Problem Solving, 22*, 9–25.

Cropley, A. J., & Cropley, D. H. (2009). *Fostering creativity: A diagnostic approach for higher education and organizations.* Cresskill, NJ: Hampton Press.

Cropley, A. J., & Cropley, D. H. (2010). The innovative institutional environment: Theoretical insights from psychology. *Baltic Journal of Psychology, 11*, 73–87.

Cropley, D. H., & Cropley, A. J. (2000). Fostering creativity in engineering undergraduates. *High Ability Studies, 11*, 207–219.

Cropley, D. H., & Cropley, A. J. (2010). Recognizing and fostering creativity in design education. *International Journal of Technology and Design Education, 20*, 345–358.

Cropley, D. H., Kaufman, J. C., & Cropley, A. J. (2011). Measuring creativity for innovation management. *Journal of Technology Management and Innovation, 6*(3), 13–30.

Csikszentmihalyi, M. (1996). *Creativity: Flow and the psychology of discovery and invention.* New York: Harper Collins.

Dawson, V. L., D'Andrea, T., Affito, R., & Westby, E. L. (1999). Predicting creative behaviour: A reexamination of the divergence between traditional and teacher-defined concepts of creativity. *Creativity Research Journal, 12*, 57–66.

DeFillippi, R., Grabher, G., & Jones, C. (2007). Introduction to paradoxes of creativity: Managerial and organizational challenges in the cultural economy. *Journal of Organizational Behavior, 28*(5), pp. 511–521.

Gabora, L. (2002). Cognitive mechanisms underlying the creative process. In T. Hewett & T. Kavanagh (Eds.), *Proceedings of the fourth international conference on creativity and cognition* (pp. 126–135). Loughborough, UK: Loughborough University Press.

Getzels, J. W, & Jackson, P. W. (1962). *Creativity and intelligence.* New York: Wiley.

Gino, F., & Ariely, D. (2012). The dark side of creativity: Original thinkers can be more dishonest. *Journal of Personality and Social Psychology, 102*, 445–459.

Gora, P. (2009). "I don't have a creative bone in my body": Awakening creativity in educators. *Theses and dissertations.* Paper 566. http://digitalcommons.ryerson.ca/dissertations/566.

Guilford, J. P. (1950). Creativity. *American Psychologist, 5*, 444–454.

Holland, J. L. (1959). Some limitations of teacher ratings as predictors of creativity. *Journal of Educational Psychology, 50*, 219–223.

Kampylis, P. G., & Valtanen, J. (2010). Redefining creativity: Analysing definitions, collocations, and consequences. *Journal of Creative Behavior, 44*, 191–214.

Kaufman, J. C., & Beghetto, R. A. (2009). Beyond big and little: The Four C Model of Creativity. *Review of General Psychology, 13*, 1–12.

Kozbelt, A. R., Beghetto, R. A., & Runco, M. A. (2010). Theories of creativity. In R. J. Sternberg & J. C. Kaufman (Eds.), *The Cambridge handbook of creativity* (pp. 20–47). New York: Cambridge University Press.

McWilliam, E. (2009). Teaching for creativity: From sage to guide to meddler. *Asia Pacific Journal of Education, 29*, 281–293.

Morgan, D. N. (1953). Creativity today. *Journal of Aesthetics, 12*, 1–24.

Mueller, J. S., Melwani, S., & Goncalo, J. A. (2012). The bias against creativity: Why people desire but reject creativity. *Psychological Science, 23*, 13–17

Plucker, J. A., Beghetto, R. A., & Dow, G. T. (2004). Why isn't creativity more important to educational psychologists? Potentials, pitfalls, and future directions in creativity research. *Educational Psychologist, 39*(2), 83–96.

Rechtin, E., & Maier, M. (2000). *The art of systems architecting.* Boca Raton, FL: CRC Press.

Rhodes, M. (1961). An analysis of creativity. *Phi Delta Kappan, 42*, 305–310.

Scott, C. L. (1999). Teachers' biases toward creative children. *Creativity Research Journal, 12*, 321–328.

Shaw, M. P. (1989). The Eureka process: A structure for the creative experience in science and engineering. *Creativity Research Journal, 2,* 286–298.

Silvia, P. J., Kaufman, J. C., Reiter-Palmon, R., & Wigert, B. (2011). Cantankerous creativity: Honesty–Humility, Agreeableness, and the HEXACO structure of creative achievement. *Personality and Individual Differences, 51,* 687–689.

Simon, H. (1990). Interview. *Carnegie-Mellon University Magazine,* Fall, 1990.

Smith, G.J.W., & Carlsson, I. (2006). Creativity under the Northern Lights: Perspectives from Scandinavia. In J.C. Kaufman & R. J. Sternberg (Eds.), *International handbook of creativity* (pp. 202–234). New York: Cambridge University Press.

Staw, B. M. (1995). Why no one really wants creativity. In C. Ford & D. Gioia (Eds.), *Creative action in organizations, ivory tower visions and real voices* (pp. 161–166). Los Angeles, CA: Sage.

Stein, M. I. (1953). Creativity and culture. *Journal of Psychology, 36,* 311–322.

Sternberg, R. J., Kaufman, J. C., & Pretz, J. E. (2002). *The creativity conundrum: A propulsion model of kinds of creative contributions.* New York: Psychology Press.

Torrance, E. P. (1959). *Explorations in creative thinking in the early school years: VIII. IQ and creativity in school achievement.* Minneapolis, MN: Bureau of Educational Research, University of Minnesota.

Torrance, E. P. (1965). *Rewarding creative behavior.* Englewood Cliffs, NJ: Prentice Hall.

Wallas, G. (1926). *The art of thought.* New York: Harcourt Brace.

Westby, E. L., & Dawson, V. L. (1995). Creativity: Asset or burden in the classroom? *Creativity Research Journal, 8,* 1–10.

Williams, G. (2007). Classroom teaching experiment: Eliciting creative mathematical thinking. In J. Woo, H. Lew, K. Park, & D. Seo (Eds.), *Proceedings of the 31st Conference of the International Group for the Psychology of Mathematics Education,* Vol. 4 (pp. 257–364). Seoul, KR: PME.

4

THE CREATIVITY CRISIS, POSSIBLE CAUSES, AND WHAT SCHOOLS CAN DO

Kyung Hee Kim
The College of William and Mary

Stephen V. Coxon
Maryville University

Intelligence as measured by IQ has increased worldwide consistently since several decades ago, a trend known as the Flynn Effect (Flynn, 1984, 2007). If intelligence and creativity are related, then creativity should also have increased over the same period, but it has not (Kim, 2011b). Kim (2005a) conducted a meta-analysis synthesizing studies published between 1965 and 2005 regarding the relationship between creativity and intelligence. One finding was that there is only a negligible relationship between creativity and intelligence, meaning that high IQ is not necessary for high creativity, and it might indicate that creativity can occur with mastery of the knowledge and skills in a specific domain. Findings of Kim's (2011b) are presented in this chapter, and suggestions are made for how to increase creativity.

WHAT IS CREATIVITY?

Creativity as defined in this chapter is making or doing something useful that is original or better. It improves every facet of life by bringing change and development in the arts, scientific innovation, economic development, and every other endeavor. Creativity requires creative climate, creative attitude, and creative thinking. As figure 4.1 shows, CAT, denoting the Creative Climate (C), Creative Attitude (A), and Creative Thinking (T), must be present for successful creativity to occur (Kim, 2011a). Only in a creative school climate can there be students' expressions of creative attitudes, which may then result in creative thinking. The stronger the foundational creative school climate, the more students' creative attitudes can be expressed, and the more likely their successful creativity will result.

Measuring Creative Thinking

The Torrance Tests of Creative Thinking (TTCT)-Figural creativity test is the most widely accepted measure of creativity in the world. It is also the most

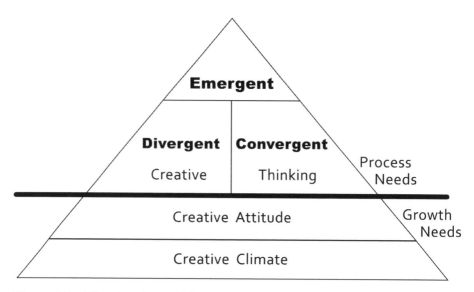

Figure 4.1   The Creative CAT's Cradle: Creative Climate, Creative Attitude, and Creative Thinking (Kin, 2011)

researched, reliable, and valid creativity test to date. It has been translated into almost 40 languages. Kim (2011b) considers the TTCT scores to be the most accurate measure of creative thinking available. Torrance developed the test in the 1950s, and the TTCT has been updated six times. It measures how creative a test subject is and also identifies the specific strengths and weaknesses of the test takers in creative thinking and display of creative attitudes; see Kim (2006) for more detailed information.

The TTCT measures the thought processes of divergent thinking, convergent thinking, and emergent thinking, as well as the expression of the different creative attitudes typical of creative people. Divergent thinking means having lots of diverse ideas, and the TTCT tests for each of the divergent thinking skills of fluency, originality, and flexibility. Convergent thinking is the process of drawing diverse ideas together and arriving at a decision or solution. The TTCT does not directly test convergent thinking as does the IQ test, for example, but the TTCT does test convergent thinking indirectly through its measure of emergent thinking. Emergent thinking is the process of transferring ideas into a final product. It requires shifting between divergent and convergent thinking as the creator deals with the reality of making the thought a reality. The TTCT measures the skills of abstract mindset, persistence, and elaboration, and integration, which are required for emergent thinking to occur. The TTCT also tests for each of the creative attitudes typically expressed by creative people. The creative attitudes measured by the TTCT are listed and defined in table 4.1.

The Creativity Crisis study (Kim, 2011b) included 272,599 TTCT scores from kindergartners through adults, including the following: 3,150 from 1966; 19,111 from 1974; 37,814 from 1984; 88,355 from 1990; 54,151 from 1998; and 70,018 from 2008. These participants represented all regions of the United States. See Kim (2011a, 2011b) for more detailed information. The diminishing trends

Table 4.1   Descriptions of the TTCT Measures in Relation to Creative Thinking and Attitudes

	CREATIVE THINKING AND CREATIVE ATTITUDE	*NAME* OF THE TTCT MEASURE/DESCRIPTION
Divergent thinking	Fluency (generating many ideas)	*Fluency*—the number of ideas generated
	Originality (generating unusual ideas)	*Originality*—the number of unique ideas generated
	Flexibility (having another perspective or using another sense)	**Unusual visualization*—looking with another angle **Internal visualization*—conceptualizing the invisible **Colorfulness of imagery*—using the five senses **Movement or action*—using body movement
Emergent thinking	Abstract mindset (enjoying the complex and ambiguous)	*Abstractness of titles*—thinking beyond what is seen
	Persistence and elaboration (working on details or describing with imagination)	*Elaboration*—The degree of detail and persistence **Storytelling articulateness*—the skill to tell a story **Expressiveness of titles*—the skill to be expressive **Richness of imagery*—the skill to visualize
	Integration (unconventional and connecting between the seemingly irrelevant)	**Extending or breaking boundaries*—nonconforming **Synthesis of lines or circles*—reorganizing **Synthesis of incomplete figures*—connecting the different
Creative attitude	Open-mindedness	*Resistance to premature closure*—deferring judgment
	Emotional sensitivity	**Emotional expressiveness*—emotional and sensitive
	Humor	*Humor—playful, childlike, and humorous
	Fantasy	*Fantasy—future-oriented and enjoying fantasy, daydreaming, and the unknown
✓Convergent thinking	Logical	✓ *Analytical/evaluative logical thinking*—part of intelligence

in emergent and divergent thinking, and the decreasing expression of creative attitudes, are described in the following text.

Decrease in Emergent Thinking

Emergent thinking decreased the most, followed by divergent thinking. The creative attitude had less of a decline, but expression of the creative attitudes, and tolerance of creative people, have decreased since 1990. The divergent thinking skill of *Elaboration* decreased the earliest, starting in 1984, which indicates that individuals are less able to elaborate ideas with imagination, think reflectively, and persevere to be creative. Some component of Elaboration generally correlates with IQ scores, which have steadily increased. Despite the buoying effect of rising IQ scores, elaboration skills have continued to drop.

In another area of emergent thinking, *Abstractness of Titles*, scores have decreased since 1998. Abstractness of titles refers to thinking beyond the obvious, which allows some people to recognize patterns and the essence of problems without distorting the information. Despite decades of rising IQ scores, these scores have continued to diminish.

Decrease in Divergent Thinking

Divergent thinking skills have also decreased. *Fluency* scores have decreased since 1990, indicating that individuals are less able to come up with ideas. The best way to generate an unusual and unique idea is by generating as many ideas as possible; therefore, if individuals cannot generate a lot of ideas, then they are less likely to come up with good ideas.

Originality scores have also decreased since 1990, indicating that individuals are less able to generate unique or unusual ideas. Originality is one of the most essential components of creative thinking. A decrease in originality might result from a climate that is continually growing less tolerant of creative individuals and their expressions (Kim, 2011b). In order for thinkers to present unusual and wild ideas, the climate needs to be receptive, or at least not hostile, to expression and consideration of these ideas. The proponent of an original idea starts out as a *minority of one*. A creative climate respects original ideas for the possibilities they offer and considers how new ideas may work, instead of dismissing ideas because of reasons they will not work. The decrease in originality scores might be an indirect measure of growing social pressures toward conformity and status quo and an increasing intolerance for new ideas.

Decrease in Creative Attitudes

Creative attitudes have also decreased. *Resistance to Premature Closure* scores have decreased since 1998. The decrease in Resistance to Premature Closure scores indicates that individuals are less able to defer judgment and are less open-minded. Better solutions to problems require keeping an open mind and deferring quick judgment in order to take the time to understand a problem and consider all potential solutions to that problem. Despite decades of rising IQ scores, these scores have continued to diminish.

It is especially troubling that this decrease is most prevalent in young children who should be encouraged and enabled to develop their creative instincts the most. Based on the decrease of the combined scores, children displayed fewer *emergent* thinking skills, and they display reduced elaboration skills in storytelling, expressiveness, or visualization. They displayed less integration, which is seen in reduced ability to think unconventionally, reorganize and synthesize, or connect between seemingly irrelevant things or concepts. Reduced *divergent* thinking skills present as less flexibility: that is, failing to look at things from different perspectives; failing to see beyond the hidden aspects of a problem or a situation; or failing to use the five senses including body expressions. Children have lowered creative *attitudes*, displaying less emotion, displaying less playful and humorous attitude, displaying less fantastical thinking, daydreaming, or embrace of the unknown. Creativity requires CAT: creative Climate, creative Attitude, and creative Thinking. Displaying students' creative attitudes requires an encouraging creative school climate. As the school climate becomes progressively more antagonistic to students' creative expression, their creative attitudes will diminish; creative thinking will diminish; and creative potential will be lost.

LIKELY SUSPECTS AND REMEDIES FOR THE CREATIVITY CRISIS

Why creativity is on the decline remains unknown, but there are some likely suspects. Since the large scale and pace of decline in the United States started in the 1980s, it seems logical to focus our attention on changes in the ways children have spent their time since then in both school and home.

School and the Standards

The standards movement, beginning with the national report, *A Nation at Risk* (National Commission on Excellence in Education, 1983), and increasing dramatically with the *No Child Left Behind* Act (NCLB, 2001) has pushed schools toward increasing time spent on rote learning—the exact opposite of what is needed for creative climates, attitudes, and thinking (CAT). Since *A Nation at Risk*, higher academic standards, rather than more learning, are emphasized; schools are held accountable for ensuring that all students achieve minimum proficiency by 2013–2014 on state-constructed standards. The NCLB received enough strong political and public support to change the entire public school system to focus on achievement on minimum proficiency tests (Crocker, 2003).

Most studies indicated that state-mandated standardized tests tend to sample lower-level standards (Gandal & McGiffert, 2003) and measure lower-order thinking skills (Hillocks, 2002), meaning a decreased focus on creativity and student-led activities that hold the highest potential for creative talent development in favor of lower-levels of thinking. Further, Kohn (1993, 2000) argued that the state-mandated standardized testing system decreases students' natural curiosity and the joy for learning in its own right, which increases extrinsic motivation at the expense of intrinsic motivation. Increasing children's intrinsic motivation is essential to encourage children's creativity.

> ## WAYS TO INCREASE INTRINSIC MOTIVATION FOR LEARNING IN SCHOOL
>
> - Give children choices about what work to accomplish, and how to accomplish it
> - Encourage students to take pride in their work, not to work for external rewards
> - Allow children to explore a variety of topics and build new skills
> - Teach students to pursue topics of strong interest
> - Provide the time necessary for in-depth exploration
> - Develop curriculum that appeals to the imagination
> - Create opportunities for engagement with fantasy
> - Demonstrate value for creative endeavors by exposing children to intrinsically motivated adults who enjoy thinking creatively (Kim, 2008).

Flake et al. (2006) expressed concern that NCLB forces education to focus on tests—education designed just to pass tests does not develop students' appreciation for knowledge or learning. Further, Flake is concerned that NCLB stifles creative teachers by pressuring them to focus on covering the standards required for the tests, at the expense of the creative application of classroom learning to real-life situations. Proponents of NCLB do not appear to value teachers' creative skills in encouraging personal growth, but, instead, favor turning teachers from professionals to educational technicians (Duffy, Giordano, Farrell, Paneque, & Crump, 2008).

The high-stakes testing environment created by NCLB has led to the elimination of content areas and activities including electives, the arts, enrichment, elementary science, foreign language, gifted programs, elementary recess, and a decreased emphasis on school libraries, which leaves little room for imagination, scholarship, critical thinking, creative thinking, and problem-solving. The NCLB might have stifled interest in developing individual differences, creative thinking, innovation, or individual potentials, which were the strengths that helped to make the United States a great nation (Gentry, 2006).

Europe and Asia have focused their educational systems on fostering creativity lately to follow the previous American education that had fostered creative thinking in students. The intense competition for scarce educational resources in these countries had previously fostered a system of standardized testing and rote memorization for demonstrated achievement on standard testing at a very early age, which is known to stifle creativity (Kim, 2009). Conversely, as already noted, the American educational system has implemented standardized testing and is even moving toward adopting national educational standards (Lewin, 2010) through the Common Core State Standards (CCSS). Many fear that if such standards are implemented with limited resources, this could exacerbate the demise of creativity in American children (Kim, 2004, 2009).

Integrating Creativity within the Standards-Based Classroom

Some teachers no longer use creative activities in the classroom because of the intense focus on high-stakes testing. We argue that tests are not good indicators of preparation for the 21st century. Although standards are important, these should focus on conceptual development, using learning processes such as research and the scientific method, critical thinking, and creativity—and not merely memorized knowledge and low-level skills. While the CCSS seem to be a start, it is still possible for teachers to meld the current standards with creative activities. Coxon (2012a) described several ways in which teachers can do this, including combining art and science, developing problem-solving curricula, and encouraging computer programming and robotics.

RENZULLI'S SCHOOLWIDE ENRICHMENT MODEL: WAYS TO CREATE STUDENT ENGAGEMENT

Type I Activities: Expose students to ideas and/or topics not usually taught in the standard curriculum, through speakers, enrichment activities, courses, or tasks.

Type II Activities: Help students to understand and develop their strengths and experience success by the use of their thinking and feeling processes, including self-regulation, communication, and metacognitive activities.

Type III Activities: Teach and apply research and problem-solving skills to authentic problems, using real tools of the trade.

Source: Dr. Joseph Renzulli, University of Connecticut. For more information and resources see http://www.gifted.uconn.edu/sem/semres.html.

Art and Science

Many consider these fields as polar opposites, but they are linked through creativity. Artists, including Michelangelo and Rembrandt, conducting early anatomy studies were also scientists. Botany and zoology studies in previous centuries often required artistic skill, such as the drawings of flora and fauna created by Darwin and his collaborators on the second voyage of the HMS Beagle. However, while these activities eventually lead to original ideas, they were not in themselves creative, but merely involved the development of representational artifacts. Creativity coupled with these artifacts helped Darwin formulate his theory of evolution and anatomical models aided new surgical techniques. Creativity occurred when task demands are open-ended or require unique solutions such as in these examples: newly discovered animals, toy improvement, and architecture.

Creating "newly discovered animals" is one way to combine art and science in open-ended ways that foster creative thinking. Teachers identify standards such as habitat, animal kingdom, predator and prey relationships and provide opportunities for students to create an animal new to science. Students become creators by designing these new animals and using common craft materials and repurposed items to build them.

One of Torrance's (1966) creativity tasks was to have children suggest improvements to a toy. It is possible for many toys to be created with craft sticks, building toys, note cards, paper, and other common classroom materials. For example, students wishing to improve an action figure or toy car could create it with LEGO, K'Nex, or craft materials. Teachers can bring this creative activity into the standards-based classroom with the added dimension of having students write persuasive arguments for their improved toy that meets language arts standards. Students can meet math standards by identifying and justifying the cost to produce these toys, or designing the cheapest but hardiest containers to ship these objects.

There are other opportunities to combine art and science in architecture that meet standards in social studies, math, science, and history by having students work cooperatively to create a replica of Jamestown or another place in history using note cards to create buildings and other structures. Upper grade students may use balsa wood or software, such as Google Sketch, to create unique buildings. Math standards are incorporated as students determine the scale of their models. Toothpick bridges are another example. Here, math standards can again be incorporated by determining the weight each structure can support before breaking. Associated with these designs would be authentic problems to solve such as a limited budget for materials, handicap accessibility, and environmental concerns.

Problem-Solving

There are many ways to incorporate problem-solving into the standards-based classroom to push students creatively. Problem-based learning (PBL) and Creative Problem-Solving (CPS) (Treffinger, Isaksen, & Dorval, 2006) incorporate both standards and creative opportunities for students.

In PBL units, students work toward solutions to real-world problems using research, the scientific method, critical thinking, and creativity. For example, The Center for Gifted Education's Project Clarion series of primary science units involves some opportunities for PBL. In particular, *Invitation to Invent* (2010) provides students with the opportunity to find and design solutions to problems within their cafeterias. In such problems, students usually work in groups to determine what they already know, what they need to learn, and how they plan to research and find solutions (such as through scientific experimentation). Students then design and conduct their own research and experiments—a significant and potentially creative leap from merely following directions in teacher-led experiments (Coxon, 2012b; VanTassel-Baska, Avery, Hughes, & Little, 2000). Teachers can take their existing standards-based units, especially in science, and reorganize them into PBL units that allow both for retention of the standards and creativity. Start by writing real-world problems relevant to students based on those units and then have students determine how they will go about solving aspects of the problem. By taking away canned experiments and letting students design their own with opportunities for reflection, discussion, and presentations, creativity is fostered. While teachers may find such units challenging to conduct at first, the rewards for students are large (VanTassel-Baska et al., 2000).

CPS can be integrated into existing units, including PBL units. It is a useful process in solving open-ended problems within all disciplines, including the arts, science, social studies, math, and language arts. Students should act as problem-solvers and seek to solve problems with no single, simple solution such as measuring the volume of an oddly shaped puddle or researching the best-tasting cereal. Students are taught to explore the problem and gather relevant data, generate ideas, and implement solutions (Treffinger et al., 2006).

Computer Programming

While this may seem something only for adults with computer science degrees, an array of options exist for children and adolescents to create games and other programs. Two examples are *Scratch*, a free download from Massachusetts Institute of Technology's Lifelong Kindergarten, and *Alice*, a free download from Carnegie Mellon. Scratch is aimed at young children and Alice at high school students, though highly able children are capable of using Alice at earlier ages. Both languages are easy to use but have very high ceilings in terms of the possibilities for complexity. Both allow for the creation of animations and video games. Animations can easily incorporate the arts, language arts standards, and social studies standards. While video games generally do not allow for creativity, video game creation is a creatively demanding activity. In both languages, math exists in both the drag-and-drop block language as well as in the use of operators. Scratch is also based on a coordinate grid, allowing for teaching about the x-axes and y-axes.

Robotics

Coxon (2012c) reported on the use of robotics to increase talents needed for science, technology, engineering, and math (STEM) and raised the question of robotics' potential to improve creativity. With kits such as the LEGO WeDo (suggested for ages six to 11) and LEGO MINDSTORMS Education NXT (suggested for ages nine and up), children and adolescents can design, build, and program robots to solve unique problems. This is a creatively demanding activity with no limit to creative possibilities. This is related to science content in the For Inspiration and Recognition in Science and Technology (FIRST) competitions, including the Junior FIRST LEGO League (ages six to nine) and FIRST LEGO League (ages nine to 14). For example, in 2012, participants studied multiple aspects of food including agriculture, transportation, safety, and environmental aspects. Teachers can look at past competitions to help find relevant ties to science curriculum in particular.

While the ability of robotics use in the classroom or competition to increase the creativity of children and adolescents remains an open question, two studies are underway and may provide evidence. Three Junior FIRST LEGO League teams were started at high-poverty schools in a Midwestern urban setting. While the number of participants (10) who completed all elements and took both pre- and post-assessments with the TTCT-Figural forms A and B was small, early analysis suggests a significant improvement for participants (Coxon, 2012d). A much larger study with nearly 100 children and adolescents ages five to 15 was conducted using the TTCT-Figural forms A and B as pre- and post-assessments over the course of 15-hour robotics courses. Assessments have not yet been scored as of this writing, but may further support robotics as a means to increase creativity.

Teachers face a challenging environment in which to incorporate creativity, to foster a creative climate, creative attitudes, and creative thinking. Using the above methods and activities as guides, it is possible to make standards-focused classrooms creative environments as well. However, children's home environments have a large influence on creativity as well. While teachers have little control here, parents may heed their recommendations. In the next section, we make a case for limiting television and video game time for children and adolescents.

Screen Time at Home

Two activities outside of school meet the criteria of changes in the ways the majority of children spend their time that began or were amplified in the 1980s and 1990s and deserve further consideration: television and video games. Both appear to be largely uncreative activities, and evidence suggests a dramatic shift in children's discretionary time away from potentially creative activities toward television and video games (Rideout, Foehr, & Roberts, 2010). While television has been widespread in American homes since the 1950s, a sharp increase in the number and around-the-clock availability of children's programming began in the 1980s and continues through the present. Likewise, although video games came into homes in the 1970s, time spent playing seems to have been limited until the advent of Nintendo's Super Mario Brothers in 1985 and the many, much more time-consuming games that followed. Subsequent games have grown in intensity, and the time children spend playing has grown concurrently. We consider both technologies suspects in the creativity crisis.

Television

The American Academy of Pediatrics (2001) issued a statement recommending that children under two years have no screen time and children over two years have no more than one to two hours of educational screen time per day. This is widely unheeded for American children: Nearly half of children under two years watch television daily, and 26 percent have televisions in their bedrooms (Rideout, Vandewater, & Wartella, 2003). A survey of over 1,000 parents found that children between two and five years watch screens an average of 32 hours per week of which 97 percent was television (McDonough, 2009). School alleviates the amount to a small degree: Children between six and 12 years watch an average of 28 hours per week (McDonough, 2009). It would be hard not to watch for many. The television is on during meals in 64 percent of households and is on nearly all waking hours in more than one-third of households (Rideout et al., 2010). At age 70, the average American will have spent nearly a decade of life watching television (American Academy of Pediatrics, 2001).

What is the effect of all this television consumption? Research on television generally suggests harm to children. School performance decreases with television viewing and health problems increase (American Academy of Pediatrics, 2001). Young children in homes where the television is on most of the time are less likely to read daily than their peers in homes where the television time is limited (59% versus 68%) and less likely to be able to read at all (34% versus 64% among ages between four and six years) (Rideout et al., 2003). Lillard and Peterson (2011) reported on their study of four-year-olds assigned to watch Sponge Bob, educational television, or simply to draw. Children in the Sponge Bob group scored lower on a measure of attention than the other two groups. In another notable study, Tomopoulos et al. (2010) followed families with infants and found that those that watched more than an hour of television per day at six months of age had significantly lower scores on measures of language development at age 14 months. Health is negatively impacted as well. The American Academy of Pediatrics (2001) concluded in their literature review of children, adolescents, and television that television viewing was related to obesity, poor body image, substance abuse, and violent behavior. Rideout et al. (2003) found that *heavy* television watchers spent an average of 30 minutes less time playing actively per day than their moderated peers.

What of creativity? While little research on television's influence on creativity has thus far been conducted, what results exist suggest that television viewing may hamper all aspects of CAT, with the possible exception of some educational programming. A study of more than 1,700 children 12 years and under found that television time is negatively related to time spent in creative play (Vandewater, Bickham, & Lee, 2006). This finding was especially strong among children under five years. Similarly, in one of the more thorough reviews of research on television and creativity, Anderson et al. (2001) found that television watching was related to lower divergent thinking levels and diminished creative play. However, the same study found that watching educational programming in preschool predicted higher participation in creative activities in adolescence. In particular, watching *Mister Rogers' Neighborhood* in preschool resulted in higher ideational fluency in adolescence. Viewing *Sesame Street*, on the other hand, was a better predictor of academic achievement and was not consistently related to creativity. It seems that both quantity and content matter. We suspect that the high exposure to commercials also has a harmful impact on all aspects of CAT.

Video Games

As with television and other screen devices such as cell phones, video games have increasingly consumed the time of children and adolescents (Rideout et al., 2010). With cell phones, handheld Internet devices, DVD players, and hundreds of channels available on ever-increasing numbers of screens, our children are wired into a wealth of entertainment and information. Gentile (2011) recommends a nuanced view of video game usage: Increased time playing video games reduces school performance, and violent video games may increase violent behavior and thoughts, but benefits may include increased spatial skills, hand–eye coordination, and in some games teamwork skills. Regardless of the apparent benefits, we argue that the volume of time children and adolescents spend with video games is hurting them overall. We speculate that all of this time is distracting children; therefore, they are unable to focus and consider such valuable information as they may receive, and they have less time to engage in creative activities. For many, the volume of time spent with screens has reached the level of addiction. Video games likely negatively affect all aspects of CAT.

In a three-year study of more than 3,000 children and adolescents in Singapore, total time spent playing video games increased impulsiveness and attention problems among participants (Gentile, Swing, Lim, & Khoo, 2012). Likewise, those who were impulsive or had attention problems spent more time playing video games, which the researchers suggest as evidence for bidirectional causality. Impulsiveness and attention problems disrupt the CAT model for children and adolescents at home and in school, making creativity less likely.

VIDEO GAMES AND CREATIVITY

Though there is very little research on video games' impact on creativity in children and adolescents, the influence of video games on creativity is debated with research supporting a positive relationship with creativity (Jackson et al., 2012) as well as research suggesting no effect (Hamlen, 2009). However, creativity arises from domain-specific knowledge, coupled with a creative need and personality. With regard to video games, however, the deeper the player's knowledge of the program, the less relevant and less productive is creative thinking in playing it. Children are born with creative potential, and the time spent playing video games is time wasted insofar as developing and preserving that potential. It is also time spent learning how to avoid being creative and practicing the low-level skill of operating without being creative. Creative thinking is like a muscle; it needs to be stretched and flexed, or it will atrophy.

Video Games and Addiction

In a study of almost 1,200 American youth of ages between eight and 18 years, eight percent exhibited pathological behaviors (Gentile, 2009). These addicted players performed poorly in school and exhibited more attention problems. Addicted players in this study reported skipping household chores and homework to play games as well as using games to escape bad feelings or problems. Twenty-four percent reported unsuccessfully attempting to use video games less (Gentile, 2009). Addictive behaviors disrupt CAT. Addiction severely hampers creativity. A healthy creative climate requires the public be educated about the effects of addictive behavior.

This does not mean that video games must be eliminated from the lives of children and adolescents, but care should be taken both in limiting the quantity of time spent on games as well as choosing games based on their potential for creativity. Some programs can be used creatively, such as Scratch and Alice (discussed here) as well as others that allow for creation. Time spent by children and adolescents operating most video games takes away from time spent exercising creative potential and abilities. When children are engaged in imagination games, reading books, building with blocks, or making art, their brains create images and gives meaning to the work. When children watch a television show or play a video game, all of the work of imagination is done for them.

CONCLUSION

Creativity is essential to improving our quality of life through the arts, scientific innovation, and economic improvement. Creativity scores have declined in the United States though the exact causes of this decline are unknown. It is essential that this trend be reversed for continued aesthetic, scientific, and economic health and advancement. The movement toward low-level learning with minimum competency standards and testing in schools as well as a large increase in time spent using some technologies are likely suspects. Teachers and school librarians should work to integrate the standards within creative activities and encourage both children and their parents or guardians to severely limit or eliminate television time and video game usage in favor of more creative activities.

REFERENCES

American Academy of Pediatrics. (2001). *Pediatrics, 107*(2), 423–426. Retrieved from http://pediatrics.aappublications.org/content/107/2/423.full.pdf+html.

Anderson, D.R., Huston, A.C., Schmitt, K.L., Linebarger, D.L., Wright, & Larson, R. (2001). Early childhood television viewing and adolescent behavior: The recontact study. *Monographs of the Society for Research in Child Development, 66*(1), i–viii, 1–154.

Center for Gifted Education. (2010). *Invitation to invent.* Waco, TX: Prufrock.

Coxon, S.V. (2012a). Innovative allies: Spatial and creative abilities. *Gifted Child Today, 35*(4), 277–284.

Coxon, S.V. (2012b). Scientifically speaking: Science is a verb. *Teaching for high potential,* Spring, 4.

Coxon, S.V. (2012c). The malleability of spatial ability under treatment of a FIRST LEGO League simulation. *Journal for the Education of the Gifted, 35*(3), 291–316.

Coxon, S.V. (2012d, September). Developing creativity for future STEM innovation in young children. American Creativity Association Innovation by Design Conference. Drexel University, Philadelphia, PA.

Crocker, L. (2003). Teaching for the test: Validity, fairness, and moral action. *Educational Measurement: Issues and Practice, 22*(3), 5–11.

Duffy, M., Giordano, V.A., Farrell, J.B., Paneque, O.M., & Crump, G.B. (2008). No child left behind: Values and research issues in high-stakes assessments. *Counseling and Values, 53,* 53–66.

Flake, M.A., Benefield, T.C., Schwarts, S.E., Bassett, R., Archer, B., Etter, F., et al. (2006). A firsthand look at NCLB. *Educational Leadership, 64,* 48–52.

Flynn, J.R. (1984). The mean IQ of Americans-Massive gains 1932 to 1978. *Psychological Bulletin, 95,* 29–51.

Flynn, J.R. (2007). *What is Intelligence? Beyond the Flynn Effect.* New York: Cambridge University Press.

Gackenbach, J., Kuruvilla, B., & Dopko, R. (2009). Video game play and dream bizarreness. *Dreaming, 19*(4), 218–231.

Gandal, M., & McGiffert, L. (2003). The power of testing. *Educational Leadership, 60*(5), 39–42.

Gentile, D.A. (2009). Pathological video-game use among youth ages 8–18: A national study. *Pathological Science, 20*(5), 594–602.

Gentile, D.A. (2011). The multiple dimensions of video game effects. *Child Development Perspectives, 5*(2), 75–81.

Gentile, D.A., Swing, E.L., Lim, C.G., & Khoo, A. (2012). Video game playing, attention problems, and impulsiveness: Evidence of bidirectional causality. *Psychology of Popular Media Culture, 1*(1), 62–70.

Gentry, M. (2006). No Child Left Behind: Neglecting excellence. *Roeper Review, 29,* 24–27.

Guilford, J.P. (1956). Structure of intellect. *Psychological Bulletin, 53,* 267–293.

Guilford, J.P. (1959). *Personality.* New York: McGraw-Hill.

Guilford, J.P. (1960). Basic conceptual problems of the psychology of thinking. *Proceedings of the New York Academy of Science, 91,* 6–21.

Guilford, J. P. (1967). The *nature of human intelligence.* New York: McGraw-Hill.

Guilford, J. P. (1986). *Creative talents: Their nature, uses, and development.* Buffalo, NY: Bearly Limited.

Hamlen, K. R. (2009). Relationships between computer and video game play and creativity among upper elementary school students. *Journal of Educational Computing Research, 40*(1), 1–21.

Hillocks, G. Jr. (2002). *The testing trap: How state writing assessments control learning.* New York: Teachers College, Columbia University.

Huang, T-Y. (2005) Fostering creativity: A meta-analytic inquiry into the variability of effects, *Dissertation Abstracts International,* 66 (04A), 2348A.

Hutton, E., & Sundar, S. S. (2010). Can video games enhance creativity? Effects of emotion generated by Dance, Dance, Revolution. *Creativity Research Journal, 22*(3), 294–303.

Jackson, L. A., Witt, E. A., Games, A. I., Fitzgerald, H. E., von Eye, A., & Zhao, Y. (2012). Information technology use and creativity: Findings from the Children and technology Project. *Computers in Human Behavior, 28*(2), 370–376.

Kaufman, J. C., & Sexton, J. D. (2006). Why doesn't the writing cure help poets? *Review of General Psychology, 10,* 268–282.

Kim, K. H. (2004). *Cultural influence on creativity: The relationship between creativity and Confucianism.* Unpublished Doctoral Dissertation. The University of Georgia, Athens, GA.

Kim, K. H. (2005a). Can only intelligent people be creative? A meta-analysis. *Journal of Secondary Gifted Education, 16,* 57–66.

Kim, K. H. (2005b). Learning from each other: Creativity in East Asian and American education. *Creativity Research Journal, 17,* 337–347.

Kim, K. H. (2006). Can we trust creativity tests? A review of The Torrance Tests of Creative Thinking (TTCT). *Creativity Research Journal, 18,* 3–14.

Kim, K. H. (2008). Underachievement and creativity: Are gifted underachievers highly creative? *Creativity Research Journal, 20,* 234–242.

Kim, K. H. (2009). Cultural influence on creativity: The relationship between Asian culture (Confucianism) and creativity among Korean educators. *Journal of Creative Behavior, 43,* 73–93.

Kim, K. H. (2011a, December). Keynote Speaker. *Successful creativity: Creative climate, creative attitude, and creative thinking.* The Korea Invention Promotion Association & The Korea Ministry of Education, Science & Technology. Seoul, KR, December, 2011.

Kim, K. H. (2011b). The creativity crisis: The decrease in creative thinking scores on the Torrance Tests of Creative Thinking. *Creativity Research Journal, 23,* 285–295.

Kim, K. H., & Hull, M. F. (2012). Creative personality and anticreative environment for high school dropouts. *Creativity Research Journal, 24,* 169–176.

Kohn, A (1993). *Punished by rewards: The trouble with gold stars, incentive plans, a's, raises, and other bribes.* Boston, MA: Houghton Mifflin.

Kohn, A. (2000). *The case against standardized testing.* Portsmouth, NH: Hinemann.

Lewin, T. (2010, July 21). Many states adopt national standards for their schools. *The New York Times.* Retrieved from http://www.nytimes.com/2010/07/21/education/21standards.html.

Lillard, A. S., & Peterson, J. (2011). The immediate impact of different types of television on young children's executive function. *Pediatrics, 128*(4), e1–e6.

Lohman, D. F. (1993). Spatial ability and g. Paper presented at the Spearman Seminar, University of Plymouth. Retrieved from http://www.google.com/url?sa=t&rct=j&q=&esrc=s&source=web&cd=1&ved=0CC4QFjAA&url=http%3A%2F%2Fciteseerx.ist.psu.edu%2Fviewdoc%2Fdownload%3Fdoi%3D10.1.1.111.7385%26rep%3Drep1%26ty

pe%3Dpdf&ei=NmSeUZfxIdOI0QGfuYHgAw&usg=AFQjCNGiNx4I18mq2mFIr
PgiXBfBAx-aJg&bvm=bv.46865395,d.dmQ

McDonough, P. (2009). TV viewing among kids at an eight-year high. Nielsenwire. Retrieved from http://blog.nielsen.com/nielsenwire/media_entertainment/tv-viewing-
among-kids-at-an-eight-year-high/.

Mueller, J.S., Melwani, S., & Goncalo, J.A. (2012). The bias against creativity: Why people
desire but reject creative ideas. *Psychological Science, 23*, 13–17.

National Commission on Excellence in Education. (1983). *A nation at risk: A report to the
nation and secretary of education*. Washington, DC: U.S. Department of Education.

NCLB. 2001. No Child Left Behind Act of 2001, 20 U.S.C. § 6319 (2008).

Paulhus, D.L., Wehr, P., Harms, P.D., & Strasser, D.I. (2002). Use of exemplar surveys
to reveal implicit types of intelligence. *Personality and Social Psychology Bulletin, 28*,
1051–1062.

Rideout, V.J., Foehr, U.G., & Roberts, D.F. (2010). *Generation M2: Media in the lives
of 8–18 year-olds*. Kaiser Family Foundation. Retrieved from http://www.kff.org/
entmedia/upload/8010.pdf.

Rideout, V.J., Vandewater, E.A., & Wartella, E.A. (2003). Zero to six: Electronic media in
the lives of infants, toddlers, and preschoolers. Kaiser Family Foundation. Retrieved
from http://www.kff.org/entmedia/upload/Zero-to-Six-Electronic-Media-in-the-
Lives-of-Infants-Toddlers-and-Preschoolers-PDF.pdf.

Rietzschel, E.F., Nijstad, B.A., & Stroebe, W. (2010). The selection of creative ideas after
individual idea generation: Choosing between creativity and impact. *British Journal
of Psychology, 101*, 47–68.

Rose, L.H., & Lin, H.T. (1984). A meta-analysis of long-term creativity training programs.
Journal of Creative Behavior, 18, 11–22.

Rothenberg, A. (2001). Bipolar illness, creativity, and treatment. *Psychiatric Quarterly, 72*,
131–147.

Runco, M.A., & Richards, R. (Eds.). (1997). *Eminent creativity, everyday creativity, and
health*. Norwood, NJ: Ablex.

Schubert, D.S.P., & Biondi, A.M. (1975). Creativity and madness: Part I-The image of the
creative person as mentally ill. *Journal of Creative Behavior, 9*, 223–227.

Scott, G., Leritz, L., & Mumford, M. (2004). The effectiveness of creativity training: A
quantitative review. *Creativity Research Journal, 16*, 361–388.

Simonton, D.K. (2009). *Genius 101. The Psych 101 Series*. New York: Springer Publishing.

Tomopoulos, S., Dreyer, B.P., Berkule, S., Fierman, A.H., Brockmeyer, C.A., &
Mendelsohn, A.L. (2010). Infant media exposure and toddler development. *Ar-
chives of Pediatrics & Adolescent Medicine, 164*(12), 1105–1111.

Torrance, E.P. (1966). *Torrance Tests of creative thinking*. Benseville, IL: Scholastic Testing
Service.

Torrance, E.P., & Torrance, J.P. (1973). *Is creativity teachable?* Bloomington, IN: Phi Delta
Kappa Educational Foundation.

Treffinger, D.J., Isaksen, S.G., & Dorval, K.B. (2006). *Creative problem solving: An introduction* (4th ed.). Waco, TX: Prufrock.

United States. National Commission on Excellence in Education. (1983). *A nation at risk:
The imperative for educational reform: A report to the nation and the secretary of edu-
cation, United States department of education*. Washington, DC: The Commission:
[Supt. of Docs., U.S.G.P.O. distributor].

Vandewater, E.A., Bickham, D.S., & Lee, J.H. (2006). Time well spent? Relating television
use to children's free-time activities. *Pediatrics, 117*(2), 181–191.

VanTassel-Baska, J., Avery, L.D., Hughes, C.E., & Little, C.A. (2000). An evaluation of
the implementation of curriculum innovation: The impact of William and Mary units
on schools. *Journal for the Education of the Gifted, 23*, 244–272.

Wang, L., Beckett, G.H., & Brown, L. (2006). Controversies of standardized assessment in school accontability reform: A critical synthesis of multidisciplinary research evidence. *Applied Measurement in Education, 19,* 305–328.

Whitson J.A., & Galinsky, A. D. (2008). Lacking control increases illusory pattern perception. *Science, 322*(5898), 115–117.

Section II

THE COMPONENTS OF CREATIVITY

5

INSIDE-THE-BOX: AN EXPERTISE-BASED APPROACH TO CREATIVITY IN EDUCATION

Robert W. Weisberg
Temple University

Michael Hanchett Hanson
Teachers College, Columbia University

Fostering creativity has become a goal of many teachers, educational advocates (Partnership for 21st-Century Skills, 2009), and policy makers. For example, several states are considering using creativity indexes as part of school evaluations (Robelen, 2012). However, that simple intention can go in many different directions.

The term *creativity* is used in many ways: it can refer to a kind of product, different kinds of processes, personality traits, various types of experience, or a long-term cultural judgment. Each of those definitions is linked to various bodies of research and one or more creativity theories; for review, see chapters one and two; see also Runco (2007) and Sawyer (2012). For education, many of these theories can be useful (see chapter two). Many educational techniques for promoting creativity, however, focus on one particular theory concerning how the creative process is carried out: divergent thinking (Guilford, 1950; Plucker, 1999; Torrance, 2002), or thinking "outside-the-box."

This chapter presents a different view of the creative process, based on the idea that creativity is an application of expertise for the purpose of innovation (Gruber & Wallace, 1999; Weisberg, 2006). That is, creativity is based on "inside-the-box" thinking. This expertise-based approach to creativity better matches real-world creative work and the needs of education than does an emphasis on outside-the-box idea generation, associated with divergent thinking.

DIVERGENT THINKING

In his presidential address to the American Psychological Association, Guilford (1950) called on psychology to turn its attention to creativity and proposed the idea of divergent thinking. He saw creativity as a trait that differentiated individuals and measured through tests. The trait could be defined by a series of characteristics, primarily the following: fluency (the ability to produce many different ideas); flexibility (not staying within a limited number of categories when producing ideas); originality (producing ideas other people do not produce—statistically improbable ideas); and elaboration (detailed ideas).

Guilford's (1950) proposals were not based on empirical research. The ideas contained under the umbrella of divergent thinking seemed reasonable to him as the foundation for a theory of creativity. As he noted, the person who produces more ideas will have a greater chance of producing good ones. However, the validity of the divergent-thinking approach to creativity has been questioned; for review, see Weisberg (2006), chapter nine. Do creative thinkers think divergently when they produce creative advances in science, technology, or the arts?

Inside-the-Box Thinking

Case study research examines the skills and processes people use in real-world creative work. That research has shown that people do not rely on divergent thinking. Some people at some points in creative work may try to think of lots of different approaches, but divergent thinking is not necessarily the starting point, or even part of many people's work. Creative people actually think *inside* the idiosyncratic, often complex and interesting boxes they have acquired over their lives. Most observers, being ignorant of the creative thinker's perspective—ways of thinking and knowledge—cannot follow the thought process. They, therefore, conclude that the creative individual worked outside of what was known.

Ways of Thinking

Many educators, psychologists, and philosophers contend that how one thinks and what one thinks are integrally connected (e.g., Baer & Garrett, 2010; Lakoff & Johnson, 1999). As Gruber (1981) observed in his groundbreaking analysis of Darwin's thinking: "information can *only* be incorporated in existing schemes of thought" (p. 108). Ways of thinking and factual knowledge are, thus, key dimensions of the "box" space within which people think.

Furthermore, across case studies of creativity from different domains, Gruber and his colleagues (Gruber & Davis, 1988; Gruber & Wallace, 1999; Wallace & Gruber, 1989) found that *habitual* ways of thinking tend to shape creative people's work over many years. People tend to apply particular principles, preferred paradigms, even groups of metaphors, which they have become adept at using. For example, Keegan (1989) has found that Darwin applied the idea gradualism to his work on coral reefs, earthworms, evolution, and psychology. Hanchett Hanson (2004, 2005) has shown how Bernard Shaw used ironic schemas to analyze situations and produce new ideas across a broad range of social and political topics.

Of course, creative people may add new ways of thinking to their repertoire. Sometimes, they move away from old ways of thinking: changing assumptions or introducing new ideas. In all cases, however, development involves integrating the new with the old in some ways. For example, Darwin abandoned his initial theory of evolution (monad theory) and moved to natural selection, in part, as a result of encountering the principle of superfecundity in Malthus' *Essay on Population* (see text box below). Darwin was not garnering new facts, but integrating a new way of thinking. Even then, the principle of superfecunity was not entirely new. Darwin had encountered the principle before, but had not previously used it in the way he would to develop the theory of natural selection. Indeed, he used the principle of superfecundity very differently than Malthus had. "The conservative Reverend Malthus had seen superfecundity as a threat to the established order, and as an answer he had urged chastity upon the poor. Darwin, in contrast, saw superfecundity as a creative principle, making possible the whole panorama of evolutionary change" (Gruber, 1981, p. 70).

Darwin's theory of natural selection developed over time and included some dead ends (Gruber, 1981). In July 1837 Darwin speculated in his notes that simple new living forms—monads—spontaneously emerged from inanimate matter and then evolved as a result of environmental influences. To keep the number of species more or less constant, Darwin speculated that each monad had a limited life span, like an individual. When the monad died all of the species that had evolved from it would die. He soon revised this theory, giving up the monad life span idea, and then gave up monad theory altogether.

In September 1838 Darwin read Malthus' *Essay on Population*. Four factors came together to produce his insight into natural selection at that point. (1) From his research during the voyage of the *Beagle* (1831–1836) and his search for a cause of species variation, Darwin had become keenly aware of the fact that variation was ubiquitous. (2) Having given up monad theory, he was actively looking for an explanation for new species generation. (3) He had known about natural selection for some time as a way of keeping a species from evolving. For example, in his July 1837 notes he had written about predators keeping prey populations small, leading to in-breeding. He had never considered that natural selection could also *select for* occasional variants until (4) reencountering the idea of superfecundity—producing more offspring than can possibly survive—in Malthus. Far from thinking outside of his box, Darwin integrated the idea of superfecundity with his years of knowledge, experience, and reflection. As a result he saw the full potential of natural selection.

Knowledge

The factual knowledge—data—that creative people use develops in conjunction with ways of thinking, through slow, long-term integration of new information. Again, this development occurs within "the box," not through sudden leaps outside it. Darwin did not need more data when he read Malthus because he had conducted years of research, including the famous voyage of the *Beagle*. Indeed, he had already developed substantial expertise on a number of issues that would inform his new theory, ranging from species taxonomies to coral reef development.

Expertise and Purpose

Thus, creative thinking is one type of expression of expertise. In the course of mastering a domain, one can use expertise in at least two ways, broadly conceived. On the one hand, an individual might try to perfect the techniques that he has been taught, to become as masterful as possible within the conventions of the field. In this case, one is honing expertise to maintain the *status quo*, preserving the traditions of the domain. In contrast, one can also use expertise to go beyond current practice for creative purposes.

A number of different sorts of evidence have been adduced to support the idea of creative thinking as an expression of expertise. First, research has shown that it takes years for an individual to develop the capacity to produce world-class creative work. This finding, known as the *10-Year Rule* (Simon & Chase, 1973; Weisberg, 2006), supports the idea that creative-thinking skills depend on long-term development of expertise. Second, case studies of seminal creative advances in a broad range of domains support the expertise-based view.

The 10-Year Rule in Creative Production

Extensive research has established the 10-year rule for skills ranging from playing chess (Simon & Chase, 1973) and sports to contributing to science and the arts (Ericsson, Krampe, & Tesch-Römer, 1993).

Composition of Classical Music

In a seminal series of studies, Hayes (1989) investigated what he called preparation in the development of creative work across a wide range of domains in the arts. Hayes looked at career development in classical composition, for example, by determining the amount of time required from the time classical composers began musical training until they produced their first masterwork. Hayes defined a masterwork objectively, as a work that had been recorded at least five times when he carried out his analysis. That measure, although simple, reflected the opinions of music professionals (i.e., symphony conductors and record producers) as well as the music-loving public. In addition, the recording-count measure correlates positively with other measures of quality, such as the amount of space given to the analysis of a given piece of music in composers' biographies.

Hayes studied the careers of 76 classical composers. For an overwhelming majority, the first masterwork was not produced until 10 years into the composer's career. Three composers produced masterworks before the 10th year of their career, in years eight and nine. Even Mozart, who began his musical training at an extraordinarily early age (writing music at age six), did not produce his first masterwork until age 21, more than 15 years into his career; see Weisberg (2006), chapter five. See also Simonton (1991), for further analysis of variables affecting preparation time and individual variations.

Composition of Popular Music

The composing career of Lennon and McCartney of the Beatles also illustrates the need for years of preparation (Weisberg, 2006). Lennon and McCartney met on July 6, 1957. The Beatles' first hit record was *Love Me Do*, which came onto the charts in December 1963. That song was followed over the next few years by a string of blockbuster hits, stimulating "Beatlemania," the frenzied fan response that ultimately drove the group to stop touring in 1967. Between the meeting of Lennon and McCartney in 1957 and the issuing of *Love Me Do*, the Beatles had spent years honing their craft; they practiced and worked most of the time. It has been estimated that they performed 1,100 times during the years 1960–1963 alone. That is approximately one performance per day. It should also be empha-sized that the Beatles were spending those hours both by performing others' music (an equivalent of practice) and working on their own music. In other words, they were using their developing expertise for their own clearly creative purpose. So, even assuming no offstage practice at all (which is surely incorrect), the Beatles worked for years to learn their craft. In 1965–1967, approximately 10 years after Lennon and McCartney met the Beatles produced the music, which is considered seminal in the history of rock and roll: the albums *Revolver, Rubber Soul,* and *Sergeant Pepper's Lonely Hearts Club Band.*

Expertise: More than Just Playing Around

People do not develop expertise by simply participating in an activity for a long period of time: playing the piano for 10 years or hitting tennis balls in friendly competition. To become a world-class performer in any domain, including do-mains that demand creative thinking, one must be immersed in that domain over a long period of time, to the exclusion of almost everything else. Ericsson, Krampe, and Tesch-Romer (1993) have proposed that *deliberate practice* is at the heart of achieving world-class levels in any area. Deliberate practice involves a student working with a teacher or coach, who breaks the skill into components. The stu-dent works on the components, first under the teacher's guidance and then alone. Thus, deliberate practice is a highly structured activity, which typically cannot be carried out by a student alone.

Research on the 10-year rule gives a sense of the big picture concerning career development of creative individuals. That research does not, however, examine how people actually use expertise in real-world creative work. To fill in details concerning the creative process, we turn to case study research. Studies across a wide range of domains have demonstrated that creativity can be seen as an expres-sion of expertise. That research has included analysis of Darwin's development of the theory of evolution through natural selection (Gruber, 1981), the discovery of DNA, the invention of the airplane, and Picasso's creation of his painting *Guernica,* among others; for review, see Weisberg (2006). As an example, we will exam-ine Frank Lloyd Wright's creation of *Fallingwater,* his iconic house over a stream (Toker, 2003; Weisberg, 2011).[1]

CASE STUDY: THE DESIGN OF *FALLINGWATER*

Fallingwater is perhaps the most famous private dwelling in the world (e.g., Hoffmann, 1993; Levine, 1996, chapter eight; McCarter, 1997; Toker, 2003; Weisberg, 2011); illustrations of the house can be found in many places on the World Wide Web. In designing this house Wright built on his own expertise, de-veloped over almost 50 years in his career as an architect.

Wright had become well-known early in the 20th century, on the basis of his *Prairie Houses,* so-called because Wright designed them for placement on the flat prairies of the American mid-West (Wright, 1908/2008). However, by the 1930s, his career was in decline. He was essentially ignored by the new generation of modern architects (Levine, 1996, chapter eight). Then he was approached by E. J. Kaufmann, a Pittsburgh businessman and art connoisseur (Gill, 1998), to design a country retreat for the Kaufmann family on Bear Run, a stream running through a wooded area in western Pennsylvania. The creation of *Fallingwater* reinvigorated Wright's career. Soon after the house was built, the house and its creator were on the cover of *Time* magazine, and Wright remained a seminal force in architecture for the rest of his long life.

The most recognizable feature of the *Fallingwater* is its two balconies, constructed of reinforced concrete, soaring over the stream. It seems from photos as if the stream flows through the house, but the stream actually runs under the house, which sits on bolsters that are in the stream. Beams of reinforced concrete are cantilevered over the stream from the bolsters. Those cantilevered beams, with the stream running below, provide support for the living room and its balcony and for the second floor balcony that extends over and beyond the first floor. The central structural feature of the house is a vertical three-story stone core, built around a fireplace, out of which the rooms and balconies extend.

This case study will focus on how Wright designed this extraordinary house. We will use information from the historical record to help us answer questions about Wright's creative thought process. How did he get the idea to place the house essentially over the stream? How did he think of using a cantilevered structure to produce the desired effect? Where did Wright get the idea of constructing a house with two balconies extending out of a central core? Finally, did the design for

Figure 5.1   *Fallingwater*

Source: Courtesy of Robert P. Ruschak, Western Pennsylvania Conservancy.

Fallingwater come all at once or develop incrementally, in small movements from what Wright had done in the past?

The Location of the House: Wright's Established Principles of Design

Kaufmann thought that the house would be set on the south bank of the stream, below and facing the falls, and therefore with a view of them (Weisberg, 2011). However, Wright set the house on the opposite bank, over the falls, which made viewing the falls impossible. In justifying that placement, it has been reported that Wright told Kaufmann: "I want you to live with the waterfall, not just to look at it, but for it to become an integral part of your lives": a recollection of one of Wright's apprentices in McCarter (1997), p. 7. However, there may be a more basic reason why Wright placed the house over the falls: he may have had no choice, given his own well-established principles of design. One of Wright's rules of design was that a house should be oriented to the southeast, so that there would be sunlight in every room for at least part of the day (Hoffmann, 1993, p. 17). Placement of the house facing the falls, as Kaufmann had desired, would have provided the house with a northeastern exposure, making the interior spaces dark much of the time. Wright's placement of the house came directly out of his expertise. The outcome of placing the house on the north bank, making the stream a more intimate part of living in the house, might have been a bonus arising from Wright's rules of house placement. Thus, at this basic step in the design of *Fallingwater*, we do not need to postulate out-of-the-box thinking in order to understand why he placed the house as he did: he simply applied his rules of design to a new situation, in order to solve the problem of where to place the house.

A Structure Cantilevered over a Waterfall: Reusing the Old

Wright visited the site on Bear Run on December 18, 1934. Almost 20 years later, he discussed the development of the idea for the house during that visit. "There in a beautiful forest was a solid, high rock-ledge rising beside a waterfall and the natural thing seemed to be to cantilever the house from that rock-bank over the falling water" (Wright, in an interview televised May 17, 1953, quoted in Toker (2003), p. 137). Let us consider why building a house cantilevered over the stream might have seemed to Wright to be "a natural thing."

In one way, Wright was the perfect architect to build a house near a waterfall: for many years he had been drawn to houses built near or over waterfalls. Wright spent time in Japan beginning in 1905, supervising the construction of his *Imperial Hotel* in Tokyo (Toker, 2003, p. 154). During that time, he developed an intense interest in Japanese art, particularly woodblock prints. Wright brought back from Japan prints of houses near waterfalls. He also brought back many photos and postcards from that trip, and Toker reported that 25 percent of them were of waterfalls.

In addition to his general interest in houses near waterfalls, Wright had specific experience building such a structure. When Wright was designing his compound at *Taliesin*, in Wisconsin, he had a stream dammed to produce a pond and a spillway—an artificial waterfall—(Smith, 1997, p. 64; Toker, 2003, p. 154). In the mid-1920s (i.e., some 10 years before designing *Fallingwater*), Wright had a

power plant built to provide electricity for *Taliesin* through hydroelectric generation. The power plant was a small building cantilevered over that artificial falls.
Thus, a building cantilevered over a waterfall was "natural" to Wright because
he had built a very similar building already. He was working within his expertise
when he designed *Fallingwater*. The location matched well with Wright's expertise, which allowed him to use the past to construct something new, built on what
had come before. Again, his thinking process was basically conservative; he used
his knowledge to deal with a new situation that matched reasonably closely with
something he had done in the past.

A HOUSE WITH TWO BALCONIES
EXTENDING OUT OF A CENTRAL CORE:
A Variation on a Wright Theme

Let us now consider the specific design for *Fallingwater*; did it come to Wright in
a creative leap outside the box, or did it also build on Wright's expertise? As noted
earlier, Wright had acquired fame around the turn of the 20th century, primarily
as a result of the development of his *Prairie Houses*. One striking feature of the
*Prairie House*s was low overhanging roofs, which sometimes were flat, designed
to provide continuity with the flat expanse of the prairie (Wright 1908/2008,
p. 35). Those overhanging roofs, which are cantilevered structures, are very similar
to the roof of *Fallingwater*. One difference between many of the *Prairie Houses*
and *Fallingwater* is that the former have the lower balcony extending farther than
the upper, which is opposite to the situation in *Fallingwater*. However, at least one
Prairie House had the upper balcony extending farther than the lower so, again,
there was precedent in Wright's own work. The Kaufmanns' desire to entertain
large groups of guests in their new house might have played a role in Wright's
extending the upper balcony, a dramatic addition, which also served the practical
purpose of accommodating more people.

Furthermore, *Fallingwater* did not start that way. Toker (2003) has examined
Wright's original drawing for *Fallingwater*, called *plan 166*, and has concluded
that the earliest conception of the house had the lower balcony extending farther.
The upper balcony was brought forward as Wright worked out the details of the
structure.

Still other components of the *Prairie Houses* can also be seen in *Fallingwater*. As
but two of many possible examples, the *Prairie Houses* were built around a stone
core, which contained a fireplace and chimney, which served as the center of the
house. *Fallingwater* had such a core. The stone core of *Fallingwater* also contained
a vertical set of casement windows, extending up through its three stories, and a
similar set of windows can be seen in one of Wright's earlier houses (Hoffmann,
1993, p. 41).

To summarize, one can trace numerous links between *Fallingwater* and Wright's
earlier work. The cantilevered roofs and balconies, terraces, stone walls, and central chimney/fireplace cores, and so forth, were Wright's own "vocabulary" of
elements (Hoffmann, 1995)—his "box." What this discussion means for our understanding of Wright's thinking is that his creativity, at least as exhibited in the
design of *Fallingwater*, was based on the use or re-use of a set of ideas, varied to
meet the contingencies of the specific design problem that he was facing at the

time. The specific way in which those ideas were manifested varied according to the circumstances—the specifics of the site and the needs of the client—but the core of the project was very similar to what he had done before. Again we see the conservative—inside-the-box—nature of Wright's creative thinking.

All at Once or Incremental?

The final question we consider concerning the creation of *Fallingwater* centers on whether Wright's thought process worked in a creative leap or incrementally. We have seen that when Wright drew *plan 166*, he modified it significantly as he worked, developing the third floor and changing the configuration of the balconies. Those phenomena are evidence for the incremental nature of Wright's thinking. It is also notable that in talking about his own thought process, Wright advocated working mentally on a design before committing anything to paper (Weisberg, 2011). If he followed that strategy in creating *Fallingwater*, then the changes seen on *plan 166* are probably an underestimation of the changes that he carried out, many of which might never have seen paper. Thus, Wright's thought may have been even more incremental in nature than the discussion here has indicated.

Wright's Creative Thinking: Conclusions

Based on our analysis of the development of *Fallingwater*, centered on the historical record, we can draw the following conclusions concerning the Wright's creative-thinking process. First, on a general level, we did not need to invoke what one might call extraordinary thought processes to understand Wright's great achievement. Wright carried out an extended process of solving a problem, and he used his expertise as the basis for the incremental development of the solution. In short, Wright was thinking inside the box, based on his expertise.

More specifically, each aspect of the design of the house that we have discussed developed relatively directly out of Wright's application of his knowledge to the situation he was facing. First, the overall placement of the house was directed by Wright's own, previously established design principles: a straightforward example of solving a problem. Second, his decision to build a house cantilevered over a waterfall resulted from the match between Wright's expertise and the site, combined with the necessity of meeting the needs of the client. Third, the specific design of the house—two balconies extending from a central core—was a site-specific modification of a design scheme that Wright had developed years earlier. Finally, the specifics of the design came about in a series of small steps, as Wright accommodated his developing design to the demands of the new project.

YES, BUT . . .

The Talent Question

Is creative success not a question of talent, rather than expertise directed toward creative goals? Every architect is not Frank Lloyd Wright. What about the poor souls who work really hard and never make it?

Even though many people assume that talent must play a crucial role in expert-level work, the research examining the role of talent in high-level performance is far from conclusive. For example, Sloboda (1996) conducted a study of 257 young people in England learning to play classical music. The study looked at participants at five levels of achievement, ranging from those who had dropped out of the program to students at a highly competitive music school. The results showed very little evidence for effects of talent. For example, the study found no evidence of hardworking failures. The amount of practice was by far the differentiating factor among levels of achievement. In addition, there was no evidence that the most accomplished students (i.e., those who were poised on the brink of careers as international musical soloists) acquired their skills more easily, as the notion of talent implies. The high-achieving students needed the same amount of practice to reach a given level of accomplishment as did the other students who reached those levels, including students who did not ultimately reach the highest levels of achievement. The difference was that the high-achieving students carried out that required practice in a shorter period of time; that is, the "talented" students practiced the same amount, but more intensely. *The clear bottom line is that substantial, immersive work is necessary, whatever the contribution of talent may be.*

Cognitive Inflexibility

In spite of all of the evidence previously cited, expertise and creativity are sometimes seen as contradictory ideas. One reason is that research has found that experts can be prone to functional fixedness, inflexibility, and bias. For example, expert bridge players have difficulty accommodating rule changes imposed by researchers (Sternberg & Frensch, 1992). Medical specialists exposed to information about a patient tend to develop diagnostic hypotheses within their specialty, even when evidence indicates that the correct diagnosis should come from a different specialty (Hashem, Chi, & Friedman, 2003). One possible explanation for these findings is that the assumptions of one's field are no longer questioned after a certain point of training and practice. It is sometimes assumed that such findings raise problems for the idea that creativity depends on utilization of one's expertise.

This research, however, has not focused on people whose long-term purpose is creative work. It has found from case study research that just having knowledge was not enough to result in creative accomplishment (Gruber & Davis, 1988; Wallace & Gruber 1989; Gruber & Wallace, 1999). The key was that the creative person organized her thinking process for a creative purpose. Bridge players have utilized their expertise *for* the rules of bridge, not to accommodate new rules, and medical specialists have spent thousands of hours learning to focus on their specialty.

How people organize their thinking is not just in their minds, but also through their practices, circumstances, and associates. For example, Lennon and McCartney brought very different sensibilities and musical styles to their collaboration. Their interactions produced outcomes beyond those which either could have produced alone. Similarly, Wright had a challenging site to push him to adapt a Prairie Style solution in *Fallingwater*. In other words, one aspect of creative work can be finding a variety of ways to extend one's thinking, sometimes including accessing and incorporating others' expertise.

Implications for Education

Every architect is not Frank Lloyd Wright, and only a few of today's students will achieve comparable levels of eminence in their fields. Furthermore, much of the formation of Wright's expertise came after his formal education. In many cases, the 10-year-rule clock starts after, or outside of, formal education. Seldom does the first work in one's field come during K–12 years, and few schools are equipped to—or would want to—provide the kind of immersive work that leads to expertise. (Exceptions include music conservatories, some dance programs, and some athletic programs.) What then is the role of general education in the development of creativity, if there is to be a role at all?

To answer this question, let us start with what is assumed to be the usual role of education. The same issues and, therefore, the same question about the role of education could apply to the development of expertise used for conventional ends. For example, education serves the scholar and the great teacher, who may master and help preserve a domain without producing innovation. We do not question the critical role of education in enabling those career paths. The very idea of education is to lay foundations for such pursuits, introducing students to existing knowledge, methods of research, histories of discovery, and ongoing concerns of the fields in which they may ultimately immerse themselves. In other words, through education, students acquire and learn to use their "boxes." The expertise-based approach is, thus, a particularly fitting way to think about creativity in education.

An Expertise-Based Approach to Creativity in Education

Approach

How would integrating inside-the-box creativity then change traditional education? This is uncharted territory. Comparison of teaching practices and policy benchmarks (e.g., Common Core State Standards Initiative, 2010) to the inside-the-box view of creativity, however, suggests some small but potentially powerful additions to current practices:

1. Explicitly introduce the idea of creativity as an application of expertise, including examples (cases, biographies).
2. Provide settings where students can develop expertise on issues of particular interest to them, and have them practice using their knowledge for both conventional and creative ends.
3. Encourage reflection (metacognition) on when and how students use knowledge to do creative work as opposed to conform to current standards.
4. Emphasize the importance of motivation—finding what students enjoy doing and working hard at those pursuits.

Example

In science units, students can read about, and reflect on, the work of major innovators like Galileo, Edison, Darwin, Einstein, or Crick and Watson. How did these thinkers gain their expertise, and how did they use what they knew to produce major innovations in science? A key point of that exercise would be to expose students to the fact that "great innovations" come about through processes not that different from the processes they can carry out (if different at all). Then, in addition to the general knowledge covered in any unit, teachers can ask the students to "become experts" on specific topics of interest to them. The students can reproduce classic experiments in the field and then, based on their knowledge, generate their own hypotheses, design their own experiments and/or produce their own inventions.

None of the practices just described are, by themselves, unusual. They are common practices and/or established benchmarks in education. Furthermore, this overall approach would work for other subjects and across a wide range of ages. Accounting for different levels of knowledge and the development of metacognitive abilities, these basic curriculum elements can apply to a unit on worms in elementary school or to a history unit in high school or to graduate programs in psychology or music education. What is distinctly different here is organizing these techniques to promote inside-the-box creativity.

A Note on Metacognition

Research on expertise seems to indicate that being aware of one's thinking and the rules of the domain is important early in skill development but then becomes more and more automatic (Feltovich, Prietula, & Ericsson, 2006). With increasing education, writing, playing music, conducting an experiment, or even conducting research should become increasingly automatic as students gain proficiency. Requests for metacognitive reflection may need to be sensitive to this point. As students are learning new processes and encountering new fields of knowledge, asking them to reflect on their thinking can be helpful, including reflection on the reasons for their decisions to use knowledge to creative ends and reflection on their assumptions. As processes become automated, however, students may have more difficulty describing how they are thinking because a characteristic of automation is *not* thinking about the process. Education also has to allow the processing of their skills to become automatic for the development of their expertise.

A Deeper Implication

Of course, another distinction of this approach would be moving away from outside-the-box imperatives. That move should put more value on the students' perspectives. If people are constantly told to *think differently*—outside-the-box—the inevitable implication is that the ways they already think are inadequate. Thus, beyond the real-world relevance of the expertise-based approach to creativity, and beyond its fit with the mission and tools of education, this approach serves students' development more constructively. Their creative work emerges from their lives, including their diverse community and home lives and *all of their education*, as part of who they are, not as a result of a constant demand to be different.

CONCLUSION

The expertise-based view of creativity appears to be more consistent with real-world creative work than are theories that focus primarily on idea generation, like divergent thinking. Research on the period of preparation within a discipline before people make major creative contributions has resulted in "the 10-year rule." In addition, case study research across many domains has shown that creative works tend to be based on previously acquired knowledge and ways of thinking. The results may appear to be "outside-the-box" for onlookers, but the creative person is working inside her idiosyncratic, often complex and interesting "box," acquired over a lifetime of education and work.

The expertise—inside-the-box—view of creativity also fits particularly well with the mission and tools of education. Education is designed to lay foundations for expertise. Through education, students acquire and learn to use their box. Comparison of teaching practices and policy benchmarks in the context of the inside-the-box view of creativity suggests some small but potentially powerful additions to current practices, involving the following: introduction of the inside-the-box idea to students; juxtaposition of conventional and creative uses of knowledge in assignments; development of metacognitive skills important in early applications of expertise; and maintenance of motivation necessary for the long-term, hard work necessary to development of expertise. Finally, the inside-the-box view of creativity challenges students to create from within their rich life experiences as well as all of the resources of their education. Creativity becomes part of who they are, not a constant imperative to be different.

NOTE

1. This case study is based on the firm data of historians' analyses of the development of this seminal creative achievement, rather than solely on Wright's reports concerning how he worked, which can be unreliable (Gill, 1998).

REFERENCES

Baer, J., & Garrett, T. (2010). Teaching for creativity in an era of content standards and accountability. In R. A. Beghetto & J. C. Kaufman (Eds.), *Nurturing creativity in the classroom* (pp. 6–23). New York: Cambridge University Press.

Chase, W. G., & Simon, H. A. (1973). The mind's eye in chess. In W. G. Chase (Ed.), *Visual information processing* (pp. 215–281). New York: Academic Press.

Common Core State Standards Initiative (2010). *Common core standards for English language arts & literacy in history/social studies, science and technical studies.* Council of Chief School State Officers (CCSSO) and National Governors Association (NGA). Retrieved from http://www.corestandards.org/the-standards.

Ericsson, K. A., Krampe, R. T., & Tesch-Römer, C. (1993). The role of deliberate practice in acquisition of expert performance. *Psychological Review, 100,* 363–406.

Feltovich, P. J., Prietula, M. J., & Ericsson, K. A. (2006). Studies of expertise from psychological perspectives. In K. A. Ericsson, N. Charness, P. J. Feltovich, & R. R. Hoffman (Eds.), *The Cambridge handbook of expertise and expert performance* (pp. 41–67). Cambridge, UK: Cambridge University Press.

Gill, B. (1998). *Many masks: A life of Frank Lloyd Wright.* New York: Da Capo Press.

Gruber, H. E. (1981). *Darwin on man: A psychological study of scientific creativity* (2nd ed.), (pp. 97–174). Chicago, IL: University of Chicago Press.

Gruber, H. E., & Davis, S. N. (1988). Inching our way up Mount Olympus: The evolving systems approach to creative thinking. In R. J. Sternberg (Ed.), *The nature of creativity: Contemporary psychological perspectives* (pp. 243–270). Cambridge, UK: Cambridge University Press.

Gruber, H. E., & Wallace, D. B. (1999). The case study method and evolving systems approach for understanding unique creative people at work. In R. J. Sternberg (Ed.), *Handbook of creativity* (pp. 93–115). Cambridge, UK: Cambridge University Press.

Guilford, J. P. (1950). Creativity. *American Psychologist, 5,* 444–454.

Hanchett Hanson, M. (2004). Dialogue with history: Roles of irony in thinking about new kinds of war. *Metaphor and Symbol, 19*(3), 191–212.

Hanchett Hanson, M. (2005). Irony and conflict: Lessons from Shaw's wartime journey. In D. B. Wallace (Ed.), *Education, Art and morality: Creative journeys* (pp. 19–44). Dordrecht, NL: Kluwer Academic Press.

Hashem, A., Chi, M.T.H., & Friedman, C. P. (2003). Medical errors as a result of specialization. *Journal of Biomedical Informatics, 36*, 61–69.

Hayes, J. R. (1989). *The complete problem solver.* (2nd ed.). Hillsdale, NJ: Erlbaum.

Hoffmann, D. (1993). *Frank Lloyd Wright's Fallingwater: The house and its history* (2nd ed.). New York: Dover.

Keegan, R. T. (1989). How Charles Darwin became a psychologist. In D. B. Wallace & H. E. Gruber (Eds.), *Creative people at work.* New York: Oxford University Press.

Lakoff, G., & Johnson, M. (1999). *Philosophy in the flesh.* New York: Basic Books.

Levine, N. (1996). *The architecture of Frank Lloyd Wright.* Princeton, NJ: Princeton University Press.

McCarter, R. (1997). *Fallingwater: Frank Lloyd Wright.* New York: Barnes & Noble.

Partnership for 21st-Century Skills (P21) (2009, December). P21 Framework Definitions. Retrieved from http://www.p21.org/overview/skills-framework.

Plucker, J. A. (1999). Is the proof in the pudding? Reanalyses of Torrance's (1958-present) longitudinal data. *Creativity Research Journal, 12*(2), 103–114.

Robelen, E. W. (2012). States mulling creativity indexes for schools. *Education Week, 31*(19). Retrieved from http://www.edweek.org/ew/articles/2012/02/02/19creativity_ep.h31.html?tkn=TRQF6okSlzg%2FGU44%2BodNo%2BfwVSuZCymOfkfH&intc=es.

Runco, M. A. (2007). *Creativity theories and themes: Research, development and practice.* Burlington, MA: Elsevier Academic Press.

Sawyer, R. K. (2012). *Explaining creativity: The science of human innovation* (2nd ed.). New York: Oxford University Press.

Simon, H. A., & Chase, W. G. (1973). Skill in chess. *American Scientist, 61*, 394–403.

Simonton, D. K. (1991). Emergence and realization of genius: The lives and works of 120 classical composers. *Journal of Personality and Social Psychology, 61*(5), 829–840.

Sloboda, J. (1996). The acquisition of musical performance expertise: Deconstructing the "talent" account of individual differences in musical expressivity. In K. A. Ericsson (Ed.), *The road to excellence: The acquisition of expert performance in the arts and sciences, sports, and games* (pp. 107–126). Mahwah, NJ: Erlbaum.

Smith, K. (1997). *Frank Lloyd Wright's Taliesin and Taliesin West.* New York: Abrams.

Sternberg, R. J., & Frensch, P. A. (1992). On being an expert: A cost-benefit analysis. In R. R. Hoffman (Ed.), *The psychology of expertise: Cognitive research and empirical AI* (pp. 191–203). New York: Springer Verlag.

Toker, F. (2003). *Fallingwater rising: Frank Lloyd Wright, E. J. Kaufmann, and America's most extraordinary house.* New York: Knopf.

Torrance, E. P. (2002). *The manifesto: A guide to developing a creative career.* Westport, CT: Ablex Publishing.

Wallace, D. B., & Gruber, H. E. (1989). *Creative people at work.* New York: Oxford University Press.

Weisberg, R. W. (2006). *Creativity: Understanding innovation in problem solving, science, invention and the arts.* Hoboken, NJ: John Wiley & Sons.

Weisberg, R. W. (2011). Frank Lloyd Wright's Fallingwater: A case study in inside-the-box creativity. *Creativity Research Journal, 23*(4), 296–311.

Wright, F. L. (2008). In the cause of architecture. In B. B. Pfeiffer (Ed.), *The essential Frank Lloyd Wright: Critical writings on architecture* (pp. 34–51). Princeton, NJ: Princeton University Press. Original published 1908.

6

MOTIVATION IS EVERYTHING

Beth A. Hennessey
Wellesley College

Motivation is everything. Motivation marks the boundary between what we are capable of doing and what we actually will do in any given situation. Without the right kind of motivation, we are unlikely to take risks, play with ideas, or accept the possibility of failure. Without the right kind of motivation, creativity is nearly impossible.

A little over 30 years ago, while teaching elementary school, my intuition and experience had already taught me these lessons. My classroom in Denver was composed of a mixed group of kindergarten, first and second graders. Almost without exception, the kindergarteners arrived wide-eyed and excited about anything and everything I put in front of them. No more room to continue a drawing on the front side of the paper? No problem. Just turn over the paper and continue it on the back. No more empty milk cartons in which to plant some seeds? No problem. Almost anything could become a flowerpot in these five-year-olds' eyes. Dictate and illustrate a story about an underwater civilization. What fun! The possibilities for a fanciful city at the bottom of the ocean were infinite. Yet, by the time these same children had reached second grade, far too many of them had become rule-bound and self-conscious. Their excitement about learning and meeting new challenges had been replaced with professed boredom and reluctance to push themselves or try new things.

I worried constantly about my students' plummeting motivation and creativity and wondered what I could do as a teacher to help children hold onto the excitement, interest, and creative spirit they had as five-year-olds entering school. How could I set up my classroom so that it was optimally conducive to motivation and creativity? My familiarity with the research literature now tells me that I was not the only teacher who observed students losing motivation and excitement about learning. Working in a variety of settings and using a wide range of measures, a number

Preparation of this chapter was supported in part by a grant from the MIT International Design Center and the Singapore University of Technology and Design.

of investigators have found children's reported intrinsic motivation in school to decrease steadily over time (Anderman & Maehr, 1994; Harter, 1981; Lepper, Sethi, Dialdin, & Drake, 1997). Also, with this plummeting motivation comes drops in creativity and other qualitative aspects of performance. Even as far back as 1980 when I was teaching in Denver, a small group of social psychologists had already begun to explore this connection between motivation and performance.

GOOD PLAYER AWARDS AND EXPECTED REWARDS

One of the first empirical findings specifically linking *creative* performance and motivation came about almost by accident. In 1973, Lepper, Greene, and Nisbett set out to investigate the effect of expected reward on young children's motivation for drawing. These researchers selected into their study only preschoolers who displayed an especially high level of interest in using magic markers. Children met individually with an investigator and were randomly assigned to either a constraint or no-constraint condition. Children in the expected reward group were told that if they made a drawing, they would be awarded a "Good Player Certificate." Children in the control/no-reward and unexpected reward groups made their drawings without any expectation of reward.

Results revealed that working for an expected "Good Player Award" significantly decreased these preschoolers' interest in and enjoyment of the drawing task. Children who had made drawings for the experimenters in order to receive a Good Player Award spent significantly less time using the markers during subsequent free-time periods than did their no reward or unexpected reward peers. Moreover, this undermining of interest persisted for about a week beyond the initial experimental session.

Because Lepper and colleagues had set out to examine the impact of expected reward on task motivation, they had not originally planned to code or systematically examine the overall quality of the children's pictures. However, a casual examination of the products made in the three experimental conditions showed what these researchers believed was important between group differences. Also, a subsequent systematic assessment of the globally assessed quality of the drawings confirmed this view. Products produced under expected reward conditions were found to be of significantly lower quality than products made by the unexpected reward or control, no reward groups. How was it that this simple, one-time offer of a Good Player Award could serve to undermine the motivation and performance of preschoolers who were passionate about using magic markers? It is precisely this research question that captured my attention and propelled me back to graduate school.

THE MAGIC MAKER STUDY

Researchers and theorists now understand a good deal more about the interplay between motivational orientation and quality of performance. Adopting experimental procedures much like those employed in the "Magic Marker Study," my colleagues and I have carried out numerous investigations in which students of all ages are randomly assigned to constraint or no-constraint (control) conditions and are then asked to produce tangible products and make self-reports of task interest and enjoyment. These investigations, which center on the intersection between motivation and creative behavior, then conclude with an assessment of product creativity and a comparison of motivational orientation and creative performance across groups. Studies like this, many of which have been conducted in real-world classroom environments, have taught us a great deal about the impact of extrinsic constraints. If I were to return to teaching elementary school today, I would have the benefit of knowing about of all sorts of do's and don'ts, principles backed by years of careful experimentation. Our laboratory and classroom-based demonstrations as to how to preserve and promote student motivation and creativity can be translated into practical recommendations for educational reform. The first step in learning from this rich and ever-growing literature is to understand the difference between intrinsic and extrinsic motivation.

Intrinsic motivation is the motivation to approach a task or problem out of sheer interest in the activity itself. An intrinsic motivational orientation carries with it an excitement about the challenges that lay ahead. The solution to a problem or the eventual outcome of a project may not be at all obvious, but somewhere deep down inside the student believes that she has the requisite skills necessary for a successful outcome. Extrinsic motivation, on the other hand, is the motivation to do something for some external goal, some incentive outside of the task itself that is driving task engagement, such as an impending evaluation or the promise of a reward. More than 30 years of exploration into the role played by motivational orientation in the creative process have led my colleagues and me to the Intrinsic Motivation Principle of Creativity; intrinsic motivation is conducive to creativity, whereas extrinsic motivation is usually detrimental (Amabile, 1983, 1996).

EXPECTED REWARD, EXPECTED EVALUATION, COMPETITION, TIME LIMITS, AND SURVEILLANCE

This list sounds very much like the recipe for how to set up the typical American classroom. Unfortunately, however, each of these ingredients has consistently been demonstrated to be a powerful killer of intrinsic motivation (Hennessey, 2003). In fact, this list of extrinsic constraints has been shown to undermine both the intrinsic motivation and the creative behavior of students at all grade levels. Hundreds of empirical investigations have underscored the fact that intrinsic motivation is an especially delicate and fleeting state. This ingredient so essential to creative performance is easily destroyed, and educators wishing to preserve and promote their students' motivation must work diligently to do so. Student intrinsic task motivation cannot be taken for granted.

In the classroom, intrinsic motivation is almost always preferable to an extrinsic motivational orientation. Generally speaking, extrinsic motivation will consistently lead to better performance only on tasks requiring rote recitation, precise performance under strong time pressure, and the completion of familiar, repetitive procedures. An intrinsically motivated state, characterized by deeply focused attention, enhanced cognitive functioning, and increased and persistent activity (Alexander & Murphy, 1994; Maehr & Meyer, 1997), leads to deeper, more long-lasting learning and better problem-solving on open-ended tasks (McGraw, 1978; McGraw & McCullers, 1979).

Empirical data supporting this proposition come from a variety of sources. As early as 1913, Dewey identified the link between student interest or curiosity and effort expended in the classroom; and, in 1967, Simon empirically demonstrated that learners driven by intrinsic motivation and curiosity try harder and exert more consistent effort to reach their learning goals.

Guthrie, Wigfield, Metsala, and Cox (1999) reported that intrinsically motivated young readers read more and showed significantly higher levels of comprehension and recall than did students who were not excited by or engaged in the reading process. In fact, there have been a variety of investigations showing that intrinsic interest leads to more elaborate and deeper processing of texts.

In 2000, McDaniel, Waddill, Finstad, and Bourg found that students asked to read uninteresting narratives focused on individual text elements, such as extracting proposition-specific content, whereas readers of interesting texts tended to engage in organizational processing of information. In fact, a large number of related investigations have demonstrated that when students approach new concepts with high levels of curiosity and interest, information is better learned and remembered (Flink, Boggiano, & Main, 1992; Gottfried, 1990; Harter & Jackson, 1992; Hidi, 1990; Lepper & Cordova, 1992; Tobias, 1994).

Importantly, intrinsic motivation promotes far more than memory and persistence. Students' motivational orientation also helps to determine the kinds of activities they will choose to pursue in the first place. When given a choice of open-ended tasks requiring a creative solution, extrinsically motivated students tend to opt for the easiest possible problems (Condry & Chambers, 1978; Pittman, Emery, & Boggiano, 1982). Intrinsically motivated learners, on the other hand, are more likely to take risks and explore solutions to questions or activities that represent for them an appropriate level of difficulty and challenge. How is it that intrinsic interest promotes exploration and risk-taking so necessary for creative performance? Some theorists have proposed that one of the most important functions of task motivation is the control of attention. Studies of a phenomenon termed optimal experience or "flow," for example, point to a link between creative behavior and a highly pleasurable state in which persons of all ages become so immersed in an activity or problem that they lose all sense of time and place (Csikszentmihalyi, 1993, 1997).

THE MAZE METAPHOR

However, when an extrinsic constraint is imposed on a student's behavior, a portion of the cognition, concentration, and energy that should be devoted to an activity or problem requiring a creative solution is instead directed toward an impending reward, deadline, or evaluation. Amabile (1996) offers a maze metaphor to illustrate this phenomenon. She points out that an open-ended creativity-type task is very much like a maze. There is one starting point but a variety of exit points and many different paths to those exits. Most importantly, some of those exits, those solutions, are much more elegant or creative than others. In situations where a reward has been promised or an impending evaluation looms large, the goal is to play it safe and get in and out of the maze as quickly as possible.

However, if a creative idea or problem solution is to be generated, it is essential that the student become immersed in the maze itself. In fact, if creative breakthroughs are to happen, students, teachers, and persons of all backgrounds and ages must be willing to experiment with alternative pathways and risk hitting dead ends. At the core of many conceptualizations of the intrinsically motivated state, this willingness to play in the maze is the issue of control. Most contemporary theoretical models developed to explain the undermining effects of extrinsic constraints rest on the assumption that, in the Western world at least, each of us is driven by an innate need to preserve a sense of autonomy and self-determination.

We strive at all times to feel an internal locus of control and act as origins of our own behavior (Amabile 1996; Deci, 1992: Deci & Ryan, 1985; Hennessey 2003). This formulation has been successfully applied to classrooms at all levels and has also helped to explain a small body of seemingly contradictory findings offered by a group of investigators trained in the behaviorist tradition.

These researchers present the strongly contrasting view that creativity can be *easily increased* by reward and other extrinsic incentives and that the detrimental effects of extrinsic constraints occur only under limited conditions that can be easily avoided. At the core of the disagreement are important differences in the definitions of creativity driving investigations, whether the experimental activities employed are formulaic or truly creativity-type tasks and the instructions given to study participants. Such controversy is healthy for any field and has generated a number of new avenues of study including investigations into so-called immunization effects and a sort of motivational synergy that combines elements of intrinsic and extrinsic orientations (Amabile, 1996; Hennessey, 2003).

After many years of sharing the difficult message with teachers that they were killing students' motivation and creativity day in and day out, my challenge as a researcher became how to help students to maintain their intrinsic task motivation even in the face of powerful extrinsic constraints like competition and expected reward. In a series of three studies, my colleagues and I decided to look at an extrinsic constraint as a kind of germ or virus and wondered whether it might be possible to inoculate children against its usually negative effects. Our goal was twofold: to strengthen intrinsic motivation; and to provide antibodies (techniques) for fighting the negative effects of extrinsic motivation. While it may not be practical, realistic or even possible to remove all vestiges of the five killers of intrinsic motivation and creativity from the classroom environment, students can be helped to focus on the intrinsically interesting, fun, and playful aspects of their schoolwork. They can be coached in ways to make even the most routine assignment more exciting, and they can be taught strategies that will help them to distance themselves from socially imposed extrinsic constraints, such as rewards. This potential for teachers to immunize students against some of the negative effects of expected reward or other extrinsic constraints has, in fact, been demonstrated empirically (Hennessey, Amabile, & Martinage, 1989; Hennessey & Zbikowski, 1993).

FIVE WAYS TO PROMOTE CREATIVITY

At the core of these successful interventions are five concrete steps that teachers seeking to preserve students' intrinsic motivation and promote creativity must take: (1) Teachers must work diligently to create an interpersonal atmosphere that allows students to feel in control of their learning process; (2) Toward this end, they must step back and critically review the incentive systems that are currently in place; (3) In situations where extrinsic incentives cannot be removed, students must be helped to distance themselves from those constraints as much as possible; (4) They must be encouraged not to worry so much about what the students around them are producing or what their classmates are thinking about their own work. Instead, they must be helped to remember that what is really important is that they enjoy what they are doing and always try their best; (5) and finally, students must be helped to become more proficient at recognizing their own strengths and weaknesses.

In short, teachers striving to preserve and promote young learners' intrinsic motivation for the mastery of new material, the completion of open-ended assignments, and engagement in projects requiring creativity must strive to capitalize on students' own, existing interests. Seldom, if ever, do adults take the time to help children to reflect about the subject areas, activities, and challenges they most enjoy. However, even kindergarteners and first graders can understand the concept of intrinsic motivation, and children at all grade levels can be helped to identify the kinds of lessons, movies, books, or projects that get them most excited. Conversations with teachers and other school staff can help children to more concretely identify their passions. Students can be encouraged to think about and articulate the exhilaration they feel when learning about particular topics or engaging in the activities they love, and they can also be helped to explore the ways these passions might best be pursued both in and out of school. Teachers, too, can share their own interests and model for their students the ways in which they exercise creativity in their own lives.

To sum up, a complex array of factors contributes to an intrinsically motivated orientation and the likelihood of creative performance. When presented with an open-ended activity or problem, the intrinsically motivated student feels curious and stimulated. Task engagement is perceived to be free of strong external control; as progress is made on the problem, there emerge feelings of competence, mastery, and self-efficacy. Importantly, each of these hallmarks of intrinsic motivation focuses on an internal phenomenological state: Intrinsic motivation is assumed to be the result of a primarily individualized process. Yet, creativity must also be seen as a social phenomenon. Even the most gifted and talented of students cannot go it alone. They need classroom and overall school environments that promote an intrinsic motivational orientation and that are reasonably free of extrinsic constraints. They also need the license to experiment with ideas and make mistakes and the time and materials to do so. Yet, even if all of these conditions are met, they will not suffice. Intrinsic motivation is only one of several essential ingredients for creative performance.

In order for a creative solution to be found or a creative idea or product to be generated, a student must approach a problem with the appropriate *domain skills* (background knowledge and expertise in a given discipline or area, such as a mastery of the periodic table), *creativity skills* (willingness to take risks, experiment, play with idea), and *task motivation* (intrinsic not extrinsic). Under ideal circumstances, the coming together of these three factors forms what Amabile (1997) terms the "creative intersection." See figure 6.1.

Generally speaking, educators are fairly successful in giving background knowledge and requisite skill sets to their students. In essence, the delivery of information and basic skills training is seen as the primary charge of the schools. Even creativity skills such as brainstorming, suspending judgment or "piggy-backing" off of someone else's ideas are often formally taught and/or informally modeled. From the perspective of a teacher, librarian, or school administrator hoping to promote their students' creativity, it is the motivational piece of this componential model that can prove to be the most problematic. If the classroom environment, the overall atmosphere of a school or the district-wide science fair, is not conducive to intrinsic motivation, then all the domain knowledge and creativity skills in the world will not make up for this deficit.

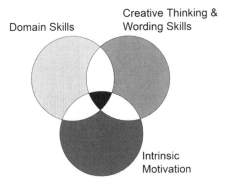

Figure 6.1 The Creativity Intersection

At issue is the fact that students are likely to demonstrate high levels of intelligence or musical talent or technical skill across a wide variety of situations. These ability areas are best conceived of as relatively stable *traits*. Yet, creative behavior is never a given, never constant. None of us are optimally creative 100 percent of the time. Creative performance depends, in large part, on motivational orientation, which is highly variable and very much a situation-dependent *state*.

WHAT ARE TEACHERS TO DO?

Clearly, intrinsic motivation is crucial both for students' retention of new or difficult material and for the creativity of their performance. However, this essential ingredient is very much situation-specific and easily undermined. The immunization studies described earlier (Hennessey, Amabile, & Martinage, 1989; Hennessey & Zbikowski, 1993) reveal one avenue, one set of important steps that teachers can take to preserve and even build on student intrinsic motivation. Research conducted by investigators like Cordova and Lepper (1996) suggests another related course of action with the recommendation that teachers construct classroom situations that allow for multiple opportunities for students to exercise self-determination coupled with the contextualization and personalization of lessons. Studies show that individualized or small-group instruction incorporating elements of choice of what to learn and how to learn is one of the key tools teachers can use to maintain and grow student intrinsic motivation. Importantly, however, there is nothing magic about "learning by doing" activities like those advocated by Dewey and popularized during the open classroom movement of the 1970s. Hands-on activities will not guarantee intrinsic interest or creative behavior. Experiential learning in and of itself is just learning. Also, group activity is not always conducive to creativity. Working in teams can often lead to a convergence of thought rather than creative breakthroughs (Treffinger & Isaksen, 1992; Treffinger, Isaksen, & Dorval, 2006).

Yes, teachers today have the benefit of an increasingly nuanced understanding of the importance of motivation. Empirical research tells us that many of the practices educators take for granted can be especially damaging to student intrinsic motivation and creative performance. If only U.S. schools could be purged of competition, coercive reward systems, controlling evaluation methods, and the like. But old habits die hard. The reality is that, in this age of accountability and NCLB regulations, the current U.S. educational climate is fraught with more extrinsic constraints than at any other time in our nation's history. Teachers now face all sorts of new sources of scrutiny as they "teach to the test" and worry that their salaries, and maybe even their ability to keep their jobs, may be dictated by their students' scores. Children attend pep rallies and chant slogans reminding them to "do their best" on upcoming high-stakes examinations. Entire schools branded by labels like "failing" or "underperforming" push on against incredible odds to boost student performance. Competition, expected evaluation, rewards, time limits, and surveillance have now been legislated. Extrinsic motivation reigns supreme and the intrinsic motivation and creativity of students (and their teachers) are in peril.

Having spent my entire career exploring the question of how best to set up classroom environments so that they are optimally conducive to student intrinsic motivation and creativity, it is easy to understand the excitement that I felt when I first learned that my home state of Massachusetts had passed a bill mandating that schools provide frequent, high-quality opportunities for students to engage in creative work. Upon closer examination, however, I worry that this effort being spearheaded by well-meaning politicians, business leaders, and educators may do more harm than good. To be fair, the details are still being worked out. However, it appears that Massachusetts, as well as Oklahoma, California, and a handful of other states, is moving toward the implementation of a so-called creativity index (Robelen, 2012) designed to rate public schools on how well they teach, encourage, and foster creativity in students. One of the primary tools, if not *the* primary measurement device, underlying this initiative is a tally of the number of opportunities, including science fairs, debate clubs, theater productions, and after-school enrichment programs, each school provides for students to engage in creative activities. In the words of the originator of the Massachusetts bill, Dan Hunter, "The Creative Challenge Index will also provide incentive for teachers to use their creativity and to be recognized for their innovative talents. Teachers are necessarily creative" (Hunter, 2008, p. 23). Or are they?

WHAT ARE LEGISLATORS TO DO?

Above all else, politicians and their educational advisors working to construct the Creative Challenge Index and other measures of a school's success in promoting student creative behavior must first understand that student *and teacher* creativity does not come easily. Creativity must not be trivialized. Creative behavior is the result of a confluence of domain skills, creativity skills, and task motivation. Given the pressures of NCLB regulations and testing, it is already the rare teacher who can find the time, much less the motivation, to build opportunities for student creativity into the school day. The last thing teachers need is a creativity index that amounts to nothing more than another punitive checklist against which their own performance and the performance of their students will be judged. Also, even if teachers were given the resources, the license, and the time to organize science fairs, theater productions, and other open-ended activities, there is no guarantee that students' creativity would be increased.

Motivation is everything. Lawmakers must turn their attention to classroom climate and the motivational orientation of both students and teachers. Rather than enforcing a simplistic tally of creative opportunities, state standards must focus on the far more difficult question of whether schools are doing everything they can to slowly but surely create a community of curious, enthusiastic, and empowered young learners and innovators. Legislators will find that that there are no easy measurement tools to be had here. Unlike academic achievement that can, at least to some extent, be reliably and validly assessed with the use of standardized tests, motivational orientation must be seen as an ever-changing variable. Any measurement tools that are developed will need to depend upon qualitative as well as quantitative data, and even the best tools will yield only snapshots in time rather than robust classroom or school-wide scores. Children's self-reports of motivational orientation will need to be combined with teachers' ratings of their students' motivation as well as inventories of classroom or overall school climate (Fraser, 1990; Moos & Trickett, 1987).

Of course, it will also be important to measure the creativity of children's work. Recognizing that creativity, like motivation, is situation-specific and highly variable, policy makers would do well to focus on the consensual assessment of actual products rather than scores earned on paper-and-pencil tests such as the Torrance Tests of Creative Thinking or TTCT (Torrance, 1990). The best indicator of student motivational orientation will be the quality, novelty, originality, and usefulness of the tangible products they produce—artwork, essays, newspapers, presentations, community service projects, plays, and concerts. The assessment of product creativity will take time and effort, but it is possible and can be done "in house" without the need for additional resources or specialized materials. Creativity may be difficult to define, but it is something that we recognize when we see it. In fact, virtually all of the studies outlined earlier, empirical investigations of the impact of environmental constraints on student motivation and creativity, used classroom teachers' assessments as their main creative outcome measure. Following the guidelines outlined by Amabile and colleagues for the Consensual Assessment Technique (CAT) (Amabile, 1982; Hennessey & Amabile, 1999; Hennessey, Amabile, & Mueller, 2011), and guided only by their own subjective definitions of creativity, teachers consistently show high levels of inter-rater agreement when they are asked to independently assess the creativity of student products relative to one another rather than against some abstract norm. At present, there is even an innovative online experiment spearheaded by the Council of Chief State School Officers (CCSSO) allowing teachers to collect, review, and publish student work demonstrating continuums of student performance on college and career-ready skills; go to http://www.edsteps.org/CCSSO/Home.aspx.

THERE ARE NO QUICK FIXES

Creativity is never easy. In this age of accountability and high-stakes testing, teachers must be given the support they need to find the intrinsic motivation, the sheer energy and enthusiasm, to provide opportunities for their students to engage in open-ended thinking and exercise their creativity skills. Students must be placed in classroom environments that have been carefully constructed so as to allow for their intrinsic motivation to surface and flourish. Also, if teachers are truly committed to optimizing the conditions for creativity in schools, policy makers and educational experts must find the intrinsic motivation and courage to move beyond a simplistic "quick fix" mentality of checklists and rating scales toward a far more complex and difficult reworking of our nation's educational system. Motivation is everything!

REFERENCES

Alexander, P.A., & Murphy, P.K. (1994). *The research base for APA's learner-centered principles.* Presented at the annual meeting of the American Educational Research Association, New Orleans, LA.

Amabile, T.M. (1982). Social psychology of creativity: A consensual assessment technique. *Journal of Personality and Social Psychology, 43,* 997–1013.

Amabile, T.M. (1983). *The social psychology of creativity.* New York: Springer-Verlag.

Amabile, T.M. (1996). *Creativity in context.* Boulder, CO: Westview.

Amabile, T.M. (1997). Motivating creativity in organizations: On doing what you love and loving what you do. *California Management Review, 40,* 39–58.

Anderman, E.M., & Maehr, M.L. (1994). Motivation and schooling in the middle grades. *Review of Educational Research, 64,* 287–309.

Condry, J., & Chambers, J. (1978). Intrinsic motivation and the process of learning. In M.R. Lepper & D. Greene (Eds.), *The hidden costs of reward* (pp. 61–84). Hillsdale, NJ: Lawrence Earlbaum.

Cordova, D.L., & Lepper, M.R. (1996). Intrinsic motivation and the process of learning: Beneficial effects of contextualization, personalization and choice. *Journal of Educational Psychology, 88,* 715–730.

Csikszentmihalyi, M. (1993). *Flow.* New York: Harper Collins.

Csikszentmihalyi, M. (1997). *Creativity: Flow and the psychology of discovery and invention.* New York: HarperCollins.

Deci, E.L. (1992). The relation of interest to the motivation of behavior: A self-determination theory perspective. In K.A. Renninger, S. Hidi, & A. Krapp (Eds.), *The role of interest in learning and development* (pp. 43–70). Hillsdale, NJ: Lawrence Erlbaum.

Deci, E.L., & Ryan, R.M. (1985). *Intrinsic motivation and self-determination in human behavior.* New York: Plenum.

Dewey, J. (1913). *Interest and effort in education.* Boston, MA: Houghton Mifflin.

Flink, C., Boggiano, A.K., & Main, D.S. (1992). Children's achievement-related behaviors: The role of extrinsic and intrinsic motivational orientations. In A.K. Boggiano & T.S. Pittman (Eds.), *Achievement and motivation: A social-developmental perspective* (pp. 189–214). New York: Cambridge University Press.

Fraser, B.J. (1990). *Individualized classroom environment questionnaire.* Melbourne: Australian Council for Educational Research.

Gottfried, A.E. (1990). Academic intrinsic motivation in young elementary children. *Journal of Educational Psychology, 82,* 525–538.

Guthrie, J.T., Wigfield, A., Metsala, J.L., & Cox, K.E. (1999). Motivational and cognitive predictors of text comprehension and reading amount. *Scientific Studies of Reading, 3,* 231–256.

Harter, S. (1981). A new self-report scale of intrinsic versus extrinsic orientation in the classroom: Motivational and informational components. *Developmental Psychology, 17,* 300–312.

Harter, S., & Jackson, B.K. (1992). Trait vs. nontrait conceptualizations of intrinsic/extrinsic motivational orientation. *Motivation and Emotion, 16,* 209–230.

Hennessey, B.A. (2003). The social psychology of creativity. *Scandinavian Journal of Educational Research, 47,* 253–71.

Hennessey, B.A., & Amabile, T.M. (1999). Consensual assessment. In M. Runco & S. Pritzker (Eds.), *Encyclopedia of creativity* (pp. 347–359). New York: Academic Press.

Hennessey, B.A., Amabile, T.M., & Martinage, M. (1989). Immunizing children against the negative effects of reward. *Contemporary Educational Psychology, 14,* 212–227.

Hennessey, B.A., Amabile, T.M., & Mueller J.S. (2011). Consensual assessment. In M.A. Runco & S.R. Pritzker (Eds.), *Encyclopedia of creativity* (2nd ed., Vol. 1) (pp. 253–260). San Diego, CA: Academic Press.

Hennessey, B.A., & Zbikowski, S.M. (1993). Immunizing children against the negative effects of reward: A further examination of intrinsic motivation training techniques. *Creativity Research Journal, 6,* 297–307.

Hidi, S. (1990). Interest and its contribution as a mental resource for learning. *Review of Educational Research, 60,* 549–571.

Hunter, D. (2008). A proposal to nurture American creativity: The Creative Challenge Index. *MASCD Perspectives,* Fall, 22–24. Retrieved from http://www.mascd.org.

Lepper, M.R., & Cordova, D.I. (1992). A desire to be taught: Instructional consequences of intrinsic motivation. *Motivation and Emotion, 16,* 187–208.

Lepper, M.R., Greene, D., & Nisbett, R.E. (1973). Undermining children's intrinsic interest with extrinsic rewards: A test of the overjustification hypothesis. *Journal of Personality and Social Psychology, 28,* 129–137.

Lepper, M.R., Sethi, S., Dialdin, D., & Drake, M. (1997). Intrinsic and extrinsic motivation: A developmental perspective. In S.S. Luthar, J. Burack, D. Cicchetti, & J.R. Weisz (Eds.), *Developmental psychopathology: Perspectives on adjustment, risk, and disorder* (pp. 23–50). New York: Cambridge University Press.

Maehr, M.L., & Meyer, H.A. (1997). Understanding motivation and schooling: Where we've been, where we are, and where we need to go. *Educational Psychology Review, 9,* 371–409.

McDaniel, M.A., Waddill, P.J., Finstad, K., & Bourg, T. (2000). The effects of text-based interest on attention and recall. *Journal of Educational Psychology, 92,* 492–502.

McGraw, K.O. (1978). The detrimental effects of reward on performance: A literature review and a prediction model. In M. Lepper & D. Greene (Eds.), *The hidden costs of reward* (pp. 33–60). Hillsdale, NJ: Erlbaum.

McGraw, K.O., & McCullers, J. (1979). Evidence of a detrimental effect of extrinsic incentives on breaking a mental set. *Journal of Experimental Social Psychology, 15,* 285–294.

Moos, R.H., & Trickett, E.J. (1987). *Classroom environment scale manual* (2nd ed.). Palo Alto, CA: Consulting Psychologists Press.

Pittman, T.S., Emery, J., & Boggiano, A.K. (1982). Intrinsic and extrinsic motivational orientations: Reward-induced changes in preference for complexity. *Journal of Personality and Social Psychology, 42,* 789–797.

Robelen, E.W. (2012). Coming to schools: Creativity indexes. *Education Week, 31,* 1, 12–13.

Simon, H.A. (1967). Motivational and emotional controls of cognition. *Psychological Review, 74,* 29–39.

Tobias, S. (1994). Interest, prior knowledge and learning. *Review of Educational Research, 64,* 37–54.

Torrance, E.P. (1990). *The Torrance Tests of creative thinking norms-technical manual figural (streamlined) forms A & B.* Bensenville, IL: Scholastic Testing Service.

Treffinger, D.J., & Isaksen, S.G. (1992). *Creative problem solving: An introduction.* Sarasota, FL: Center for Creative Learning.

Treffinger, D.J., Isaksen, S.G., & Dorval, K.B. (2006). *Creative problem solving: An introduction* (4th ed.). Waco, TX: Prufrock.

7

THE CREATIVE TAPESTRY: COLLABORATIVE PARTNERSHIPS

Gail Bush
National Louis University, Emerita

Exploring collaborative partnerships of the "Big-Cs" is fascinating due to the magnitude of their creativity (Gardner, 2008, p. 80). What about the decidedly pedestrian rest of us? What is it about collaborative partnerships that feel so natural, so generative, so true to our creative spirits however pedestrian they might be on the grand scale of life? Is it always a match made in creativity heaven or do collaborative partnerships rely on the temperament and dispositions of the partners just as all human interactions do? Also, the most important question relative to the topic of this book: what is the role of collaboration within the context of creativity?

Collaborative partnerships abound in every aspect of the arts and sciences. They seem to be a natural element within the habitat of creativity. Even those brilliantly profound discoveries and inventions that have only one name associated with them are the result of the efforts of others working sometimes in collaboration but always building upon knowledge laid bare by others in their community. Albert Einstein is known predominantly as a singular creative genius. Development psychologist Howard Gardner (1993) identifies Einstein as "confident in his beliefs, but increasingly alone." Gardner reports that Einstein's friends felt that he was in his own world, out of step, and out of touch (p. 125). However, there was his classmate and friend Marcel Grossman standing by him, without whom the mathematics required for his discoveries would have been problematic; long discussions with Michelangelo (Michele) Besso from the patent office led to new insights; Mileva Marić, the first Mrs. Einstein, was a constant sounding board; and as creativity and collaboration scholar Vera John-Steiner writes, the Danish physicist Niels Bohr and Einstein shared both a friendship and profound differences in thought about quantum mechanics development. Their fundamental stumbling block was over what John-Steiner calls conceptual complementarity, the complementary relations between ideas. Einstein, not willing to accept Bohr's understanding of the concept, proposed his own. While Bohr disagreed with Einstein's counterargument, he was nonetheless grateful for the motivation it gave him to think deeper about the concept (John-Steiner, 2000, pp. 52–53, 55). Gardner (1993) also reports that Einstein did indeed value the opportunity to discuss new ideas and "thanked Besso explicitly for a conversation that led to the special theory of relativity" (p. 103).

THE CREATIVE TRAJECTORY

Four C Model of Creativity by Ronald A. Beghetto and James C. Kaufman (2009) suggests a trajectory of creativity that may help readers understand the importance of developing children's creativity by providing a variety of supports. "Big-C" creators are eminent and monumental legendary geniuses. Who has not heard of Charles Darwin or Albert Einstein? However, their eminence began somewhere and was developmental in nature. Three additional Cs—"mini-c," "little-c," and "Pro-c," inform our understandings about the development of creativity. Mini-c creativity, which is likely the genesis of creativity, results in the "novel and personally meaningful interpretation of experiences, actions, and events" (p. 3) when teachers, parents, and mentors encourage curiosity, exploration, and the habits of mind to continually engage children in more creative insights, processes, and products. Mini-c creativity represents students' first efforts to address the universality (or near universality) of creative potential. The little-c level may be reached "after repeated attempts and encouragement" (p. 6) as well as years of practice and acquisition of expertise as a highly accomplished chef, artist, or musician. At the Pro-C level, the creator has attained a higher level of creative expertise albeit not at the eminence level, but nevertheless changing their professional domain by introducing new ideas and associations or ways of doing.

Note: See Kaufman and Beghetto (2009) for a complete description of the Four C Model of Creativity.

Throughout this book the reader will find definitions of creativity that focus on particular facets of understanding of the concept. To distinguish collaboration within the context of creativity it might be explained simply that one necessary condition of creativity is that it is deemed creative by the community and that collaborative partner represents the beholder. The relationship itself provides a microcosm for each partner, access to a safe haven in which to think broadly, deeply, and without limits. The social nature of collaboration is integral to creativity throughout, both during the creative process and consequentially as the product is accepted or rejected by the community. If the creative process is parsed into steps—brainstorming precedes action, and subsequently the collaboration moves forward. The threads that are woven together making each collaborative tapestry durable are a shared language representing the vision, trust and respect, multiple perspectives, and the social context within which it thrives.

The creative tapestry is unique, has depth, is textured, and tells a story. Many creative collaborative partners have particular necessary elements that they have researched. Arts educator and scholar Eliot Eisner (1964) found that creative individuals place a sense of humor as a top element. Funny thing about humor, it is much more satisfying to share than to laugh alone. Physicist Richard Feynman, no stranger to the humorous side of life, felt that desire was the driving force behind a successful collaboration. Creativity and collaboration scholar Vera John-Steiner (2000) identifies a shared vision, multiple perspectives, competency in skills and training, and a fascination with the partner's contributions as commonalities among collaborative duos. The tattered tapestry has tangled threads that do not withstand the elements, the dispositions, or the environment. As with any relationship, there are no guarantees of a successful outcome. Also, there are some well-known creative duos to be discussed later in this chapter who seem to thrive on the angst and anguish and thereby produce highly creative products borne of the emotional friction and others who were could-have-beens.

TEJIENDO PALABRAS/WEAVING WORDS: LANGUAGE AS A WAY OF BELONGING (SORIA, 2011)

Cultural anthropologists have come to view language as a way of belonging to the community. The area of study called ethnosemantics, also known as ethnolinguistics, grew to popularity within the field in the middle of the 20th century (Harris, 1968). Cultures are defined through concepts as structured through their languages. Even the minor unit of a subculture will communicate as its own culture—even one as small as a collaborative duo. Anthropologist Edward T. Hall studied intercultural communication not only through language but also through social distances that permeate cultures. As subcultures follow the same patterns, the communication developed by a collaborative partnership includes more than just language but also physical space; the collaboration defines the environment within which the partnership dwells. Hall (1976) believed that we have a drive to collaborate as we evolve through both our biology and our creations. This drive is one of the basic principles of living. Other scholars take similar approaches to arrive at the conclusion that collaboration is a function of the human condition, that we need each other for a full menu of survival rationales.

This drive is realized through speech as we pursue practical activities in our lives and schooling. It is the particular speech used that connects us to the culture. Shared language allows us to belong to each other. Cultural communities and professions have shared language; the arts and music each have their own languages; as do age groups especially adolescents. Collaborative partners develop speech patterns and their own language to move their communication forward. It seems to be a symbiotic development—the phenomenon of the collaboration causes the language to develop, and the language then serves to move the participants toward their shared goal. Russian philosopher and contemporary of Lev Vygotsky, Mikhail Bakhtin (1986), identifies the following "social speech types—social dialects, characteristic group behavior, professional jargon, generic languages, languages of generations and age groups, tendentious languages, languages of the authorities of various circles and of passing fashions, languages that serve the specific sociopolitical purposes of the day" (p. 262). Bakhtin believed that we appropriate the language of others with whom we communicate. Wertsch

(1990) suggests that Bakhtin's specific attention to these forms of discourse high-light the socioculturally situated communicative phenomena (p. 119).

This focus on dialogue as a natural condition of humankind has a rich his-tory. The popular instructional method of Socratic seminar is based on shared in-quiry as established by the eponymous Greek philosopher. Plato scholar Herman Sinaiko (1998) explores the commonality between a most unlikely pairing in his essay "Socrates and Freud: Talk and Truth." Sinaiko contends that both scholars were after the truth, and that talk was the only vehicle that would allow them to achieve that elusive goal. According to Sinaiko (1998), "Socrates seems to have argued that the key to understanding the nature of things lies in the world as it appears to the one particular soul that is most important to each of us—our own" (p. 8). Gaining self-knowledge, as in knowing thyself, was his singular focus. It sounds counterintuitive. In order for Socrates to strive toward his goal, he needed to be surrounded by his colleagues. As Sinaiko (1998) writes,

> his enterprise is communal . . . the plurality of voices, the clash of opinions, the attempt to persuade others of what you think you really know, the rig-orous and unstinting scrutiny of every opinion, the common search for fal-lacies, weaknesses, ambiguities, self-deceptions, unfounded certainties—all these and more are essential to that search for self-knowledge. (p. 11)

The controversial father of psychoanalysis, Sigmund Freud, shared with Socrates an enduring belief in the importance of talk. For Freud, the talking cure discourse established between the psychoanalyst and the patient, was a pathway through the conscious mind into the unconscious mind. His theory comes screeching into our own minds when we inadvertently give voice to a Freudian slip. Talk is the only ve-hicle to take us on this journey to the truth, to self-knowledge, to the unconscious mind. While Sinaiko finds this pairing curious, the similarities in the motivation for discourse as the primary tool to self-discovery are undeniable.

IT HANGS FROM HEAVEN TO EARTH: TRUST AND RESPECT (SIMIC, 1999)

Vera John-Steiner (2000) reports in *Creative Collaboration* that while shared vi-sion and multiple perspectives are necessary elements for collaborative success, fas-cination and respect for the partner's contribution is also required. It is the trust factor that takes time to develop over multiple interactions. Taking risks takes trust a step further. While it is of critical importance when striving to achieve creative outcomes to feel that one has wings, taking risks in a collaborative relationship depends upon a rock-solid foundation of trust with a partner.

Trust and respect also feed into the sense of mutuality, as coined by John-Steiner (2000), and based on Vygotsky's sociocultural perspective that "creative activities are social, that thinking is not confined to the individual brain/mind, and that con-struction of knowledge is embedded in the cultural and historical milieu in which it arises" (p. 5). Vygotsky's focus then is on interdependence of the development processes and the role of language as a tool in that construction. It is the shared risk-taking within the collaborative dynamic that adds value to the creative process. Perhaps it helps us to be a little bit more open-minded, intellectually curious, and tolerant of ambiguity if we are not alone. There is a built-in safety net, someone who understands the broader context, to share in the dissonance and reward, which promotes a stronger appeal to venture together into new challenges and opportunities. However, the dimensions of the creative individual as described by Mihaly Csikszentmihalyi seem counter to the basis of a productive partnership. Both oversensitivity and stubbornness seem like logical character traits for the highly creative and unlikely as positive affects for collaboration. Yet, balancing these difficult personality traits is the appreciation for and almost craving of the novel, the new, the unique and abhorrence for the mundane, the usual, and the ordinary. One of the ironies of the creative temperament is that it is both oversensitive and craves novelty. Again, within our realm of the little-Cs, mutual respect diffuses the oversensitivity while having a different perspective presented affords novelty, a new way of seeing (Martindale, 1999, p. 144–145). There is a delicate balance found between skepticism and appreciation for new ideas and the stimulation that novelty generates.

Sharing distinct perspectives with each other, ideas one would not have conjured alone, is acutely satisfying to our creative selves. How do we reconcile this with our oversensitivity and perhaps frail egos? Csikszentmihalyi (1996) describes numerous paradoxical traits that dwell within the complex composition of creative individuals such as intelligence and naiveté, physical energy and quietude, wisdom and childishness, and opposite ends of the spectrum between extroversion and introversion. Perhaps the fact that these conflicts naturally reside within the creative individuals favors collaboration. The dialectics present in a collaborative partnership becomes just another in the list of antithetical traits of complex personalities, and in this scenario the traits are spread over two personalities. If indeed our creative selves engender such complexities, the comfort of an equally complex partner with whom one might grow to trust and respect is a rare value that cannot be denied.

MANY COLORED THREADS: MULTIPLE PERSPECTIVES (GOETHE, 1885, 2009)

While some might enter collaborative partnerships with trepidation and a healthy skepticism, most often we acclimate to the process, share a language, and grow to appreciate the different perspective offered. Developing that sensibility that accompanies the safe place within the collaborative environment offers a feeling of satisfaction when we share a sense of progress and productivity. It is likely that partners integrate some of that diverse approach and grow in a manner that would be impossible working singularly in isolation surrounded by our one perspective afforded to us as members of the human race. The basis for this affinity toward having a partner in crime runs deep within our humanity.

Psychologist Jean Piaget, when asked about creativity and how he got his ideas, claimed to have three methods. First, he suggests that one read nothing in one's own field. Second, he recommends reading in related fields, and lastly, he suggests having a theoretical whipping boy to use as a motive. When asked about his recommendation of reading in related fields, Piaget responded

It goes without saying that you should read nothing in your own field. If you approach a topic by reading everything that's been written on it, it's much harder to find new things . . . Related fields? Because I think any exploration of knowledge must by nature be interdisciplinary. It's impossible to dissociate real steps forward of the intelligence from logicians' and mathematicians' axiomatization or formalization of them, and so forth. It's impossible to isolate the individual from the social environment, and so forth. (Bringuier, 1977, pp. 126–128)

Piaget's perspective speaks to two essentials within this discussion of the value of collaboration within the context of creativity. When he speaks of not reading within the field but only outside the field to generate new ideas, he is suggesting that it is not productive. We must know our fields of study; we must be masters of our domain if our works are to enhance the field by offering something to be considered creative. If not, our outcomes would not be deemed to be novel, to extend beyond what is accepted as the norm within a domain. Therefore, Piaget does not feel that reading within one's domain will benefit creativity unless there are significant differences of opinion that might be explored. However, reading outside, in related fields, will reap fresh ideas, new ways of seeing, and new constructs through understanding the language of the related field. It is our role to synthesize what we read, to identify new patterns, make connections, and develop novel approaches. Piaget demonstrates this approach using the study of intelligence as an example where one would read biology, mathematics, logic, sociology, and other fields of study. Piaget, speaking about reading research, suggested that partnerships that elicited more creativity would be those that are populated by partners from different but related fields. Each partner has a lens that sees through the construct of her field, the language of the field, the historical and cultural context of the field. The most creative collaborative partners will embody the research in their own fields, and the multiple perspectives brought to the partnership will ignite more creative sparks.

The second essential that might be gleaned from Piaget's interview is the concept of the unity of knowledge, popularized by E.O. Wilson (1998) in *Consilience: The Unity of Knowledge*. As Wilson writes, consilience is not a new idea, but it certainly conflicts with our propensity toward the construction of knowledge through disciplines. There are artificialities, which are promulgated for the neat and tidy delivery of curriculum content and seem to have gone haywire in the postmodern era. Within reason it is understandable that there must be a method to divide and conquer the world of knowledge. However, the study within microspecialties has overshadowed fundamental understandings within macrodomains and made for faulty foundations of knowledge. Ultimately it is the coming together afterward, that Wilson claims philosophers and scientists alike seem to abhor (p. 12–13). Understanding that the big questions of our day require an ability to see patterns across disciplines and make sociocultural historical connections aligns our thinking toward the concept of consilience. Believing in the unity of knowledge, we can see the natural benefits of a shared vision, appreciating multiple perspectives, and the respect and acceptance of a partner's contributions to a collaborative relationship. Psychologist Jean Piaget was interviewed by Bringuier long before biologist E.O. Wilson wrote *Consilience: The Unity of Knowledge*, but taking him at his word, one can only imagine his delight upon reading this book which would be considered outside his field.

COLORS INTERMINGLE. THEIR TEXTURES SOCIALIZE: SOCIAL APPLICATIONS (NORCROSS, 2011)

Language and its role as a developmental tool were discussed earlier in this chapter. John Dewey (1910) explicates language not as intellectual in and of itself or even of having high pursuits of conveying knowledge. Dewey sees language as having two much more basic functions closely related to a consideration of the affective aspect of collaboration: the first "motive for language is to influence (through the expression of desire, emotion, and thought) the activity of others; its secondary use is to enter into more intimate sociable relations with them" (p. 179). Dewey's view draws a distinction from the intellectual use of language; rather, it presupposes an ulterior motive for sociability beyond the common popular concept. Vygotsky (1978) contends that it is the convergence of speech and practical activity that lead to intellectual development (p. 24). While Vygotsky is focusing on the development within children, Csikszentmihalyi (1990, 1996) believes that as we develop intellectually and in all other ways throughout life, we continue to seek incrementally more challenges. These new challenges are generative and feed into our creative appetites. The phenomenon of collaboration then creates both the opportunity as described by Dewey and Vygotsky for language to have a practical application and the environment to feed the creative soul as artists' colonies, writers' workshops, and all varieties of "birds of a feather" communities attest.

TO WEAVE A NEW FORM OF THOUGHT: COLLABORATIVE CHARMS (VICUÑA, 1996)

The value of collaboration within the context of creativity has an undeniable track record of evidence from the arts to sciences and everything in between. Csikszentmihalyi believes that the creative self is complex and is its own paradox. We know that diverse perspectives deepen collaboration and are instrumental in the understanding of the unity of knowledge. A few well-renowned pairs have been mentioned in large part due to the enormous undertaking of John-Steiner. As one would suspect, each pairing is unique within their domain, their historical and cultural context, and the individual characteristics of each partner. John-Steiner applies a particular meaning of complementarity as productive interdependence to the manner in which different sorts of persons collaborate together. This application would be fitting for most of the effective partnerships under study. For an exploration of underrepresented areas of concentration, here are just a few more to add a measure of grist for our mill.

Physicist Richard Feynman had a strong sense of desire, a well-developed sense of humor, profound intellect, and as a theoretician, a distinct inability to communicate. He was vibrant, dedicated, and thought at a rapid pace. He was decidedly an original. Freeman Dyson was a mathematician who followed Feynman's work and became enthralled by the mind and the man. As the translator of Feynman's ideas, Dyson, used his mathematical prowess and thereby provided a key role in the development of quantum electrodynamics. Feynman's preference was to be a problem finder without the pesky detail of problem-solving. It would only slow him down. Dyson employed mathematics to solve these problems as Feynman would have already moved on to another topic. It is John-Steiner's contention that complementarity between partners with differences in temperament and working styles leads to "the broadening of a collaborative partner's intellectual and artistic possibilities" (2000, p. 46).

The well-known pairing of artists Frida Kahlo and Diego Rivera exemplify John-Steiner's element of the gift of confidence, "belief in a partner's capabilities is crucial in collaborative work" (2000, pp. 126–127). The tumultuous couple had an unshakable conviction in the talent of their partner. Their fascination with each other's artistic expression fed their creative souls. Kahlo was often working through pain and insecurities. It was Rivera who encouraged Kahlo to show and sell her paintings. In turn, Kahlo's critique of Rivera's work was of immense importance to him. Their relationship around their work was built on trust, dwelled in respect, and grew to be of critical necessity to them both. John-Steiner uses Kahlo and Rivera as a basis for the expansion of Vygotsky's zone of proximal development (ZPD) (1978) to include the emotional sphere. ZPD is most often considered to be "the distance between the child's actual developmental level as determined by independent problem solving and the level of potential development as determined through problem solving under adult guidance or in collaboration with more capable peers" (p. 86). Vygotsky was concerned with the unity of learning processes and internal developmental processes as social processes well within the cognitive realm. John-Steiner extrapolates ZPD from child development to adult human development, moves to the affective domain, and discusses the emotional environment that is created by the nature of the collaborative partnership. It seems reasonable to assume that the proximal zone created by collaborative partners has a balance of development. In some partnerships the balance may remain stable as it did in Kahlo and Rivera; in others on more equal emotional, social, or intellectual footing, the balance might shift throughout the collaborative process.

THE INTERLACING OF WARP AND WEFT: COLLABORATIVE STRUGGLES (VICUÑA, 1996)

Earlier in this chapter Albert Einstein was introduced as a collaborative thinker. It was his long-standing debate with Danish physicist Niels Bohr that illuminated collaborative pairings who agree to disagree. As John-Steiner (2000) reports, Bohr used the term complementarity "for the apparent contradiction between two mutually exclusive properties" (p. 44). While Howard Gardner (1993) claims that the scientists' discussion continued for over 30 years, Bohr was not swayed toward objective reality; and Einstein was not moved to support complementarity (p. 125). It is difficult to imagine, however, that the debate that Bohr so keenly appreciated did not impact the development of either of their insights. John-Steiner (2000) reports that Bohr

> loved to be contradicted in order to get deeper into the subject, but he progressed best when the person with whom he thrashed out the problem had the same attitude as himself, not only in approaching the problem but also in needing to penetrate its depth to the uttermost. (p. 45)

Lest we be misled to thinking that all collaborative partnerships are smooth sailing, climb upon the *H.M.S. Pinafore* for a ride. The famously incompatible duo of Gilbert and Sullivan produced the most popular operettas of Victorian England. W.S. Gilbert was the librettist who wrote the plots and the lyrics; Arthur Sullivan was the classically trained composer who first composed hymns and then operas. Together they are credited with leading to the development of musical theater. From all reports, Gilbert was humorous, gregarious, and confrontational; he appreciated satire, farce, and conjecture. Sullivan sought realism in his work, abhorred conflict, and felt that Gilbert's perspective was demeaning to his wealthy friends and patrons. Theirs was a highly productive yet topsy-turvy collaboration that ended in a legal battle and never to be reconciled (Ainger, 2002; Dillard, 1991). From the arts to the sciences, controversy follows collaborative partnerships. Harry Truman's contention that it is amazing how much we could get done if we did not care who received the credit comes to mind.

It would be an unfathomable feat to document all the never were, the almost, the could have been, and the if only. However, it remains a remarkable oddity that the immensely popular duo of Crick and Watson still goes unchecked by so many schooled in creativity studies. Less well known is "the third man of the double helix" Maurice Wilkins, and perhaps the most curious and definitely unresolved part of this storied collaboration is the role of Rosalind Franklin (Nova, 2007; Sayre, 1975; Stephenson, 2003; Watson, 1980; Wilkins, 2005). It seems safe to claim from the most reliable sources that Franklin and Wilkins had a difficult relationship; Franklin had a decidedly deductive scientific inquiry style, and Wilkins chose to attach himself to the competitive nature of the Crick and Watson partnership. That Wilkins surreptitiously shared information gleaned by Franklin with Crick and Watson is uncontested. Wilkins showed Crick and Watson the famous x-ray crystallization Photo 51 developed by Franklin without her permission (Stephenson, 2003, p. 14). He also shared unpublished internal reports. In an unusual twist of reasoning, it is reported, sometimes as "strokes of luck" (Gardner, 1993, p. 33) and also "if one considers various components of the ultimate model of DNA, all of them were available to only Watson and Crick" (Weisberg, 1993, p. 248).

While the underpinnings of the discovery of the double helix have many interpretations, there are two factors that are outstanding within this discussion of the value of collaboration within the context of creativity. First, it does seem safe to surmise that it was the capacity of Crick and Watson to take a leap of imagination given (however allegedly ill-gotten) the information. This is where their two different knowledge bases came into focus and, with trust and respect for each other's mastery of their domains they were both willing to take that intuitive leap together. Second, and sadly, it was not in Franklin's character to collaborate. It was not how she was raised; it was not what she had experienced in her previous work, and it did not come naturally to her. One might say that it was neither in her nature nor her nurture, simply not in her DNA.

As much of this tale of tangled threads of collaboration has a happy ending for our popular duo, it is for history to decide how the story of this legacy will unfold. Our lesson is in the study of collaboration as a complex relationship that mirrors what Csikszentmihalyi (1996) calls "The Creative Personality" (p. 51). The dimensions of complexity that he identifies could just as easily be describing collaborative partnerships as they weave their creative products: long hours of concentration along with significant rest; smarts and childishness; responsibility and irresponsibility; imagination and reality; extroversion and introversion; humble and proud; diminished gender stereotyping; rebellious, independent, and traditionalist within the domain; passionate and objective; and oversensitivity and great enjoyment (Csikszentmihalyi, 1996, pp. 55–73). Consider that our creative selves balance these traits within our own personality. Then imagine a partner who magnifies and illuminates this capacity to create within an environment replete with a shared communication and vision, trust and respect, multiple perspectives, mastery of domain knowledge, and a drive to collaborate.

THE WORLD IS A TAPESTRY WE WEAVE WHILE WALKING BACKWARD (COCKBURN, 1988)

The lessons learned from collaborative partnerships are cumulative. They tend to be organic and generative; they build our creative capital for our next grand adventure. The author's own collaborative history includes many partners along the way, but only three who stand out as significant.

As a practitioner in a suburban high school, my partner was a former swim coach. This was a collaboration that had the most practical applications for our immediate work. We were profoundly productive, coming from vastly different backgrounds to the same field. We developed deep trust and respect, understanding that we did not need to know what the partner knew, but trusting that our shared vision would serve as our compass. When working on a project and an idea would come to both of us simultaneously we immediately deemed it a "pure thought" and ran with it. We always followed it, did not question it—it sprang so naturally as a product of our mutuality, and we gave it the power we felt it deserved. We received national recognition for our efforts and went on to impact educators around the country through our presentations and writing.

My next noteworthy collaboration was in a college of education. As a professor with a coterminus appointment to create a graduate program and a teaching center, I partnered with a professor whose background again was in direct opposition to my own. We also had deep sociocultural differences. Together we quickly learned each other's ways of working and found common ground that felt visceral. We forged a collaborative partnership that produced creative academic programming, grant opportunities for book ownership for children, and literary events that created a community for children's literature educators that did not exist.

Also, most recently, my most deeply rewarding collaborative relationship is with my writing partner. Together we have conducted empirical research and in our documentation and presentation activities have succeeded in moving our field forward. Our collaborative partnership was perhaps the most coherent and yet vulnerable of all because writing is a very personal form of expression. Many of the characteristics identified by Csikszentmihalyi surfaced within our own creative selves, as did the elements studied by John-Steiner in collaborative duos. In each of these remarkable experiences, it was not just the creative products that mark the partnerships. It is also the magic of those collaborative spaces within which we dwelled that fed our creative spirits.

In *A Sense of the Mysterious: Science and the Human Spirit*, physicist and writer Alan Lightman (2005) pens,

> I hold no illusions about my own achievements in science, but I've had my moments, and I know what it feels like to unravel a mystery no one has understood before, sitting alone at my desk with only pencil and paper and wondering how it happened. That magic cannot be replaced. (p. 176)

Lightman eloquently describes my feeling about the value of collaborative partnerships, especially within the context of creativity. There is nothing quite like the pure thought experience shared by two or more partners in the throes of creativity. It speaks directly to the inner creative self, cutting through the layers of the mundane, the usual, the ordinary, the expected. As complex as it is, as daring as it might seem, it is simply a human experience not to be overlooked, not to be understated, not to be missed.

REFERENCES

Ainger, M. (2002). *Gilbert and Sullivan: A dual biography.* Oxford, UK: Oxford University Press.

Bakhtin, M. (1986). The problem of speech genres (V. McGee, Trans.). In C. Emerson & M. Holquist (Eds.), *Speech genres and other late essays* (pp. 60–102). Austin, TX: Univ. of Texas Press.

Bringuier, J. C. (1977). *Conversations with Jean Piaget.* Chicago, IL: University of Chicago Press.

Cockburn, A. (1988). The world is a tapestry we weave. In *Alistair Cockburn: Poems.* Retrieved from http://alistair.cockburn.us/Poems.

Csikszentmihalyi, M. (1990). *Flow: The psychology of optimal experience.* New York: HarperCollins.

Csikszentmihalyi, M. (1996). *Creativity: Flow and the psychology of discovery and invention.* New York: HarperCollins.

Dewey, J. (1910). *How we think.* New York: Heath.

Dillard, P. H. (1991). *How quaint the ways of paradox!* Metuchen, NJ: Scarecrow Press.

Eisner, E. W. (1964). *Think with me about creativity.* Dansville, NY: Owen Publishing.

Gardner, H. (1993). *Creating minds: An anatomy of creativity seen through the lives of Freud, Einstein, Picasso, Stravinsky, Eliot, Graham, and Gandhi.* New York: Basic Books.

Gardner, H. (2008). *Five minds for the future.* Boston, MA: Harvard Business Press.

Goethe, J. W. (1885/2009). *Many colored threads from the writings of Goethe.* Charleston, SC: Bibliobazaar.

Hall, E. T. (1976). *Beyond culture.* New York: Doubleday.

Harris, M. (1968). *The rise of anthropological theory: A history of theories of culture.* New York: Thomas Y. Crowell.

John-Steiner, V. (2000). *Creative collaboration.* New York: University of Oxford Press.

Kaufman, J. C., & Beghetto, R. A. (2009). Beyond big and little: The Four C Model of Creativity. *Review of General Psychology, 13*(1), 1–12.

Lightman, A. (2005). *A sense of the mysterious: Science and the human spirit.* New York: Random House.

Martindale, C. (1999). Biological bases of creativity. In R.J. Sternberg (Ed.), *Handbook of creativity.* Cambridge, UK: Cambridge University Press, 137–152.

Norcross, C.M.R. (2011). Navajo weaver. *Arabesques: Cultures and dialogue.* Retrieved from www.arabesques- editions.com/journal/cristina_norcross/03115616.html.

Nova. (2007) *DNA—Secret of photo 51.* (DVD). United States: PBS.

Sayre, A. (1975). *Rosalind Franklin and DNA.* New York: W.W. Norton.

Simic, C. (1999). Tapestry. *Charles Simic: Selected early poems.* New York: George Braziller.

Sinaiko, H. L. (1998). Reclaiming the canon: Essays on philosophy, poetry, and history. New Haven, CT: Yale University Press.

Soria, M. (2011). Libro, tejiendo palabras/Weaving words. Retrieved from http://23sandy .com/works/products-page/poetic-pen/libro-tejiendo.

Stephenson, A. (Spring 2003). Collaboration and competition: Rosalind Franklin's story. *The natural selection,* 14–15.

Vicuña, C. (1996). The origin of weaving. In *The world of poetry.* Retrieved from http:// www.worldofpoetry.org/cv_p1b.htm.

Vygotsky, L. S. (1978). *Mind in society: The development of higher psychological processes.* Cambridge, MA: Harvard University Press.

Watson, J. D. (1980) *The double helix: A personal account of the discovery of the structure of DNA.* New York: Touchstone Publishing.

Weisberg, R.W. (1993). *Creativity: Beyond the myth of genius.* New York, NY: Freeman.

Wertsch, J. (1990). The voice of rationality. In *Vygotsky and education: Instructional implications and applications of sociohistorical psychology,* edited by L.C. Moll. Cambridge, UK: Cambridge University Press, 111–126.

Wilkins, M. (2005). *The third man of the double helix: The autobiography of Maurice Wilkins.* Cambridge, UK: Oxford University Press.

Wilson, E. O. (1998). *Consilience: The unity of knowledge.* New York: Alfred A. Knopf.

8

ENCOURAGING CREATIVE ACHIEVEMENT: HOW TO DEVELOP THE HABITS OF MIND NECESSARY FOR CREATIVE PRODUCTION

Lori J. Flint
East Carolina University

My first tenure-track position in higher education involved (among other duties) teaching a required graduate-level educational psychology course for practicing educators. Hailing from approximately 10 to 15 different rural, suburban, and urban school districts, these teachers were there to earn master's degrees. They came expecting to be taught, and, because they were teachers, I expected them to also be eager learners.

With over a decade of school volunteerism, several years of teaching experience, and a newly minted PhD in gifted and creative education, I was determined to teach well, using all the tools at my disposal. To me, teaching well meant teaching the way I wanted my students to teach, not just lecturing or telling them how to teach. I read dozens of articles and books on the topic and created a course that was learner-centered, involved social learning, and was constructivistic in nature. I created interesting, open-ended, creative assignments for my students and expected students to reciprocate with engagement.

What I frequently got instead was confusion, frustration, and sometimes, downright animosity. Why, I wondered, are these students behaving this way when I am asking them to do authentic, meaningful work? Knowing that teachers should never blame students for a lack of success, I sought to improve my practice by studying adult-learning theory, observing students, and speaking with colleagues. I began to understand the several factors undermining my efforts at teaching in these ways. This newfound knowledge led me to create a recipe for eliciting the sorts of responses I had hoped for all along.

FACTORS THAT INHIBIT CREATIVITY

The Demise of "Yes, of Course I Can?"

As you read earlier in this book, on top of everything else we must teach, we now also have mandates for creativity coming from business, industry, state governments, and even federal agencies. Creative teaching and creative learning are wonderful, desirable, and beneficial to both students and teachers; however, not everyone comes equally equipped to engage in creative production.

Ask a young child to create a song, picture, or object, with little direction, and the odds are that the challenge will be enthusiastically embraced. Make the same request of the same child in late elementary school or beyond, and one is likely to be met with a "how do you want me to do it?" or "I don't get it." Ask an adult learner to do creative open-ended assignments, and there is likely to be confusion, or even hostility. Why? What happens between the early years and adulthood to make most people uncomfortable doing creative work? According to author Robert Fulghum, in his book *Uh-Oh* (2010):

> When asked why the limitations, college students answer that they do not have talent, are not majoring in the subject, or have not done any of these things since about third grade, or worse, that they are embarrassed for others to see them sing or dance or act.

How do people become like this? Are these innate characteristics, or do we mold students into performance machines? Why are students, especially adult students, so bothered by such an assignment?

In my estimation, based upon working through literally thousands of open-ended, inquiry-based projects with students, the issue is convergence. That is, most of these students have been taught according to principles of pedagogy as both children and adults and have been taught to seek *the* one correct answer; thus, they are unsure as to how to proceed when given little direction and asked to create something unique.

Performance-Focused Culture

What happened was school, with all its demanding peer pressure, standardized tests, and insistence on competitive performance goals (See Pintrich box on following page). Because of this, young children often spend their full days of kindergarten sitting at desks completing worksheet after worksheet, or being drilled in reading, instead of learning through play. From reading thousands of teacher education fourth year interns' end-of-course papers, I know that recess, the dress up and pretend centers, and any free time to explore have gone the way of the dinosaur in many classrooms. Replacing them are neat rows of desks where movement, talking, and questioning are discouraged, and punitive rules are strictly enforced. In many districts indicators of growth have been replaced with letter grades that provide no information but do make students feel bad when they don't achieve to the level of their peers or to the expectations of their teachers or parents. (For more information about how the current performance-focused culture developed in U.S. schools, see chapter four.)

In an era when many students have been conditioned to come to school with primarily performance goals, that is, getting good grades or passing the test, it can be challenging to creatively engage students of any age. Somehow, passing tests has become the goal of education, rather than a result of effective teaching and learning (Watkins, 2010), and we try to force achievement by pressuring students and imposing performance goals on them.

Pintrich, 2000, examined individuals' motivation to achieve, also called goal theory. From studying the work of numerous educational psychologists, he has discerned three distinct types of achievement motivation:

- **Mastery (or Learning) Goals:** Focus on learning new skills and knowledge, transforming oneself into a better person, and achieving self-defined success. Students with these goals generally choose more interesting, more challenging work and then work hard to understand and succeed at it.
- **Performance (or Ego) Goals:** Focus on outperforming others, being perceived as competent without putting in much work, on winning and avoiding failure. Students with these goals choose easier, more defined work that allows them to be seen as successful by others, or, if they fail, to have good excuses for why they failed.
- **Social Goals:** Focus on relationships, social status, and other social rewards for achieving. Students with this attribution work because they want particular people to like and accept them.

Compulsory Education and Traditional Pedagogy

Most of us understand that some students remain in school only because attendance is compulsory. Though each state sets its own rules about who must attend school and for how long, the typical required attendance range is from six years to 16 years. What some may not know, however, is that in order to satisfy a state's requirements for being "highly qualified" under the federal Elementary & Secondary Education Act, Public Law PL 107-110, otherwise known as the No Child Left Behind Act of 2002 (NCLB, 2002), many *teachers* are now required to earn particular degrees within a predetermined time frame in order to maintain their teaching credentials. Thus, a new type of compulsory education exists: for the educators who, just like their younger counterparts, often do not want to be there. Having taught all day, some are resentful about having to spend time away from their families or spend thousands of dollars on an education they neither care about nor desire.

While we can and do require children to attend school and behave the way we want them to, trying to enforce such regulation with adults who are resistant about being in a required class in a required degree program is something altogether different. This is because most adult learners and many of today's savvy younger students operate according to the rules of *andragogy* rather than pedagogy. Pedagogy is the generally accepted definition of the science of teaching and learning, but actually, it is the teacher-centered, traditional, stand-and-deliver approach favored for dealing with children. In this approach, the teacher or school librarian stands at the center of everything instruction-related: curriculum, decisions about how teaching will occur, and whether something has been learned, while the student is submissive to the teacher and her whims. Using a pedagogical approach with adults is contraindicated because, by definition, adults are supposed to be self-determined beings who make their own decisions everywhere in life except, perhaps, in school.

Andragogy (Knowles, 1968), on the other hand, is learner-centered and inquiry-based. Andragogy supposes a certain level of independence in the learner and expects learners to use prior knowledge to help determine the following: what extra information they want to attain; how they attain it; and how to apply new knowledge and information. Originally intended as a paradigm for how adults learn, it has morphed into a true alternative to the pedagogical approach, as a learner-centered way of educating students of all ages. In the andragogical classroom, the teacher's responsibilities include the following: creating a psychologically safe environment for learners; expecting learners to have choices in the planning process; helping learners to decide their own particular learning needs; fostering the creation of their own learning goals; enacting those objectives; and evaluating their own learning (Galbraith, 1998).

MOVING FROM PEDAGOGY TO ANDRAGOGY

Students of all ages acculturated into a performance or ego orientation become accustomed to being told what to do and how to do it. Rather than thinking independently and creatively, they tend to strive for the one "right answer," needing constant reassurance that they are doing their work the "right way," often developing anxiety when presented with open-ended work. Such students also have a low tolerance of ambiguity (or for the unknown) and thus experience a great deal of cognitive dissonance when confronted with the unknown. Moving students from an intolerant and pedagogical stance to an andragogical one takes effort on the part of a teacher/facilitator, but after working on this with thousands of students of all ages, I can confidently attest that it can be accomplished through a systematic approach that includes the following: training thinking; developing a tolerance of ambiguity; providing incubation time; establishing an environment of psychological safety; and building trusting, respectful relationships.

Training Thinking

Dewey, in his work *How we Think* (1933, pp. 30–32), discusses the need for learners to adopt three attitudes that encourage thinking: a) open-mindedness, b) whole-heartedness, and c) responsibility. By training thought or employing metacognition (thinking about our thinking) in these three ways, we become ready to open our minds to new experiences rather than merely passing judgment on the unfamiliar or that we perceive to be too challenging. He also discusses the need for open-mindedness, because, in the words of an unknown author, "The human mind is like a parachute. It functions best when open."

Costa and Kallick (2001) are known for their sixteen *Habits of Mind*, defined as "having a disposition toward behaving intelligently when confronted with problems, the answers to which are not immediately known" (p. 1). Put another way, they are ideals that thinking human beings should employ when approaching problems to which there are no known or easy answers. Contextualizing a problem or situation by sorting through these and then selecting one or more as lenses through which to view or begin to solve the problem helps train the mind and also reduce anxiety. The resulting experience of success leads to further development of one's habits of mind, creating a positive cycle of appropriate risk-taking and problem-solving success.

SIXTEEN HABITS OF MIND OF COSTA AND KALLICK

- Persisting
- Developing emotional competence
- Listening with understanding and empathy
- Thinking flexibly
- Thinking about thinking (metacognition)
- Striving for accuracy and precision
- Questioning and posing problems
- Applying prior knowledge to new situations
- Thinking and communicating with clarity and precision
- Using the senses to gather data
- Taking responsible risks
- Creating, imagining, and innovating
- Responding with wonderment and awe
- Finding humor
- Thinking interdependently
- Learning continuously.

Source: Adapted from Costa and Kallick (2001).

Developing a Tolerance of Ambiguity

Many students experience a "freak-out" moment, otherwise known as cognitive dissonance, when given an open-ended, complex, and undefined task. This is because many of them have an intolerance of ambiguity. There are many definitions of this much-studied, though still little understood concept. One is Ehrman's triarchic concept, described in Grace (1998, p. 23) as

the ability to take in new information . . . to hold contradictory or incomplete information without either rejecting one of the contradictory elements or coming to premature closure on an incomplete schema . . . [and] to adapt one's existing cognitive, affective, and social schemata in light of new material.

Ehrman and Oxford (1990) expanded the definition to describe a set of personality characteristics, specifically including the willingness to take appropriate academic risks. Ely (1989) defines tolerance of ambiguity as how well one accepts confusing situations or tasks, especially those with no clear lines of demarcation, that is, no clear beginning or end or direction.

According to Frenkel-Brunswik, tolerance of ambiguity (AT), "generalizes to the entire emotional and cognitive functioning of the individual, characterizing cognitive style, belief and attitude systems, interpersonal and social functioning, and problem solving behavior" (Furnham & Ribchester, 1995, p. 180).

Studies linking AT and personality type have shown that many of the people least tolerant of ambiguity are the very ones who tend to become educators, thus perpetuating that cycle of conformity referred to elsewhere in this book. If we want to break that cycle, we must create creativity-friendly environments where ambiguity and openness are embraced and students are encouraged to explore and learn without risk of reprisal or criticism (Selby, Shaw, and Houtz, 2005); we should train these characteristics *into* our students and not out of them as we currently do:

> "sensitivity to problems . . . aesthetic sensibilities . . . curiosity . . . sense of humor . . . playfulness . . . fantasy . . . thinking . . . risk-taking . . . tolerance for ambiguity . . . tenacity . . . openness to experience . . . adaptability . . . intuition . . . willingness to grow . . . openness to feelings . . . unwillingness to accept authoritarian assertions without criticism . . . examination . . . integration of dichotomies."
> (p. 303)

Reading all these definitions helps us understand that tolerance of ambiguity is a characteristic we need to help our students develop, but it is a concept with which most teachers and teacher educators remain unfamiliar.

The evidence is clear: if we want teachers who are creative and user friendly, who teach with passion, who are open-minded and possess all of these other characteristics, we must school them in these ways as children, reinforce their learning as young adults and help create masters when teaching educators in advanced degree programs. As for those who come to us with the old ways of thinking, fear, anxiety, and intolerance of ambiguity, already entrenched in their personalities, we need to do some deconstruction before we can reconstruct.

But, how do you get students to tolerate ambiguity and open inquiry? What should an educator know to facilitate an effective learning experience for all participants? He should be prepared for an onslaught of questions regarding open-ended assignments because many students are not at all comfortable with open-endedness, especially when no examples are provided, and when it comes to uncertainty about their grades.

Providing Incubation Time

In researching resources for this book, I came across a TED Talk by Jason Fried (2010, in resources appendix—videos—*Why Work Doesn't Happen at Work*), who writes about collaboration and creativity. In this talk, he says, "people need long stretches of uninterrupted time" if they are to accomplish great creative work. Instead, he says, we spend too much time at work starting and stopping and wind up getting nothing done. This resonated with me because I definitely find this to be the case: I go to work to attend meetings and teach classes, but I do my real thinking work in my home office, or on the back porch. I cherish my work-at-home days because I know, "There is no greater enemy of effective thinking than divided interest" (Dewey, 1933, p. 31), and at home I can lock myself away from distractions.

School days are much the same: interruptions interspersed with jagged little bits of instructional time. Students are constantly busy, doing what they are told to do in multiple domains. Because little to no time in today's typical school day is devoted to thinking about or creating original integrated, multidisciplinary work, something will have to change in the way we do school. Interestingly, John Dewey

(1933) said much the same thing 80 years ago: that we need to reduce the quantity of disconnected facts we teach and increase the time to think about them while also preventing it all from becoming disconnected bits jumbled to the point of nonsense. Instead, he says, we need to teach students that, "To carry something through to completion is the real meaning of thoroughness, and power to carry a thing through to its end or conclusion is dependent upon the existence of the attitude of intellectual responsibility" (p. 33). This learner-centered approach is the message of the newly adopted Common Core: teach concepts and skills, not facts; provide opportunities for meaningful, interdisciplinary, thoughtful work; and do so in the time it really takes, not the usual 50-minute lessons to which we've become accustomed.

What does that look like in a real classroom? In one school in which I worked, fourth and fifth-grade teachers met to discuss how to effectively teach 19th-century European immigration to the United States. First, we identified what we wanted the students to learn, then we went off and read and learned more ourselves, came back and discussed what we'd learned, had the aha moment of deciding to stage a simulation of what it was like to come into the United States through Ellis Island, and finally, enacted that. Afterward, we debriefed the extremely successful experience we had staged for over 100 students and discussed what we needed to change next time. In essence, we followed what Wallas (1926) described as a four-step process of creation: preparation, incubation, illumination, and revision. Torrance (1993) says, "in fact, one can detect the 'Wallas process' as the basis for almost all the systematic, disciplined methods in existence throughout the world today" (p. 233). He later refined the idea into a practical three-stage instructional model "that provides opportunities for incorporating creative thinking abilities and skills into any discipline at any level from preschool through professional and graduate education and the elderly" (p. 233). He calls this method his *incubation model of teaching* (Torrance, 1979).

Heightening Expectations and Motivation

In stage one, the educator, whether school librarian or teacher, presents a problem, a dilemma, or an assignment, which sparks a desire or need to know in the student. The presentation of the open-ended assignment typically leads either to excitement on the part of students who are more open and tolerant of ambiguity, or cognitive dissonance on the part of others.

Deepening Expectations or Digging Deeper

What happens next is the period of answering a lot of questions, allowing students to discuss their ideas with each other, and thus constructing their own understanding of what is being asked for and how each might accomplish that task. This process is crucial to obtaining high-quality products from students, and it takes time. When I do a project like this with students, I have learned to allow approximately eight to 10 weeks from start to finish; that is the *incubation time*. During this period, we share ideas, discuss, brainstorm, and so on, but we do not examine examples. Some students find the lack of examples intimidating or anxiety-provoking; yet, this can be quite freeing for others. Most students' attitudes lie somewhere in between.

Going Beyond or Keeping It Going

The idea here is that once students experience that initial excitement about learning and create something personally meaningful for themselves, they find ways to internalize what they've learned and incorporate that information or those skills into their being. In other words, they have actually learned, learning being a permanent change in behavior caused by experience.

Providing time for deep thinking is crucial to the success of creative production. This gives students time to engage in authentic inquiry-based learning, to incubate ideas, toss them around, and really get into the project, develop the question they want to answer, or choose a topic. Most students become quite wrapped up in a project once they take ownership of it and will find themselves vacillating between one idea and another, learning while investigating, and then discarding one after another.

To create something new and wonderful takes time, thus the incubation process. Brains have a remarkable ability for automaticity, and therefore teach students to use this to their advantage. Instead of stressing about a project, have them read and re-read the instructions until they are firmly in their heads as they go about daily business. Teach them to surf the Internet, find lots of good material to develop their ideas, and then create a sort of mental soup comprised of all those bits and pieces. Let it simmer, visit the pot occasionally to stir, add new ingredients, or adjust the flavor. And remember, "a first rate soup is more creative than a second-rate painting" (Maslow, 1968).

CREATIVE PRODUCT

Though teachers today are occasionally still specialists in one narrow field or subject area, more often we are called upon to be education generalists. With reduced funding and increased inclusion, we frequently must serve a wide variety of learners and abilities within one classroom.

Given that, it behooves us to examine our understanding of learners and how we consider them as individuals, as categories of learners, and as part of the overall group of students we teach. Demonstrate your understanding of the interrelationship of various learners to one another and the greater educational system in a graphic metaphor. That is, create a graphic representation of such.

No examples will be supplied *

Note: Some students in this class could find this assignment challenging to exceptionally challenging. It might prove anxiety-provoking for some; yet, it might also be quite freeing for others. Most students will find their attitudes lie somewhere in between. The assignment will be discussed and rediscussed, reason-checked, hashed out, ideas examined and approved, and as a result, progress will be made by all. In order to complete this assignment several intrapersonal factors are required:

Tolerance of ambiguity
Incubation process

Metacognition

Open-mindedness

Trust.

This assignment will conclude with a gallery-type presentation of all projects on the same evening. Students will celebrate their efforts and evaluate one another's products. In addition, the professor will conference individually with each student.

Students will not be assessed according to their creative ability, but based upon the following criteria:

- Does your product graphically and clearly represent your understanding of the topic?
- Does your product appear neat, show attention to detail, appear to be the product, which a graduate student is capable?
- Does your product adequately convey the complexity of this issue/topic?

The information in this box represents an open-ended assignment used with master's level educators in an advanced educational psychology course. The resulting products have been illustrative of deep metaphorical thinking.

Rationale for this will be discussed in class.

Inviting Learning and the Walk of Faith

Bringing students of any age around to new ways of thinking requires that teachers and school librarians have patience, a low need for control, a sense of humor, and the ability to quickly establish a mutually trusting relationship within an environment of psychological safety. Students have not always encountered such environments in the past, so may come to us with fear, mistrust, or apathy from prior educational encounters, and it is our job to invite them to learn in new ways.

Tomlinson (2002, p. 7) discusses invitational learning as

needs that teachers can address to make learning irresistible: affirmation, contribution, purpose, power, and challenge. Sometimes, teachers find that the learning environment is key to meeting student needs. Sometimes the mode of instruction is key. Generally, environment and instruction work in tandem to invite, inspire, and sustain student learning. Together, they make the content important.

Here is a little more information about invitational learning according to Tomlinson.

- Students need to know that they are important in your classroom or library. They need to feel like they are in a place of physical and psychological safety: the only place in which meaningful academic and creative risks can occur.

Students need to feel that their needs, interests, and ideas are heard. This is *attribution.*

- Students want to know that their presence makes a difference, that they are an integral part of your team. They bring with them ideas and capabilities, or *contributions* that can help everyone succeed.

- Students need to understand what they do in your environment, why they do it, and that the work is meaningful and authentic. There must be a *purpose* to the work, and that the student is reflected in it.

Two other key components to invitational learning and successful creativity are *power* and *challenge.* Too many students today go to school powerless over their learning; they are permitted no choices, or given work that is low-level, rote, and repetitive. Yet, when a challenge is presented in an invitational environment, students "accomplish things here that I didn't believe were possible" (Tomlinson, 2002, p. 9).

When educators meet these needs in a kind, caring, and consistent fashion, students begin to trust and engage in whatever you challenge them to do. One obstacle we often encounter along the way, however, is time. Sometimes, we do not keep our students for long (one semester, or even less), which makes it difficult to build the rapport essential to a creative environment. Experience has taught me that when students are afraid of failure, especially on open-ended ambiguous assignments, I need to engage in this discourse:

"It is *my* job as your facilitator to provide the scaffolding needed for you to be successful. This means guiding your inquiry, sparking ideas, putting you in touch with people, ideas, and resources that can assist you in your quest. The assignment will be discussed and re-discussed, reason-checked, hashed-out, ideas and project plans examined and tweaked or approved, and as a result, progress will be made by all. Sometimes I will quell your anxiety, and other times I may even incite it a bit. That is part of the art of teaching—knowing when to push and when to back off a bit. Here's where I invite you to learn and ask you to walk that walk of faith—trust that as your teacher I am here to help you succeed, not to play gotcha with you. I will incorporate principles of andragogy vs. just those of pedagogy to help get you where you need to be. What is material is that I assume the responsibility for creating and maintaining an environment where appropriate academic and intellectual risk-taking are both encouraged and valued.

It is *your* responsibility to become comfortable with and develop a tolerance for ambiguity, that feeling of not knowing where you are going before you start. How could you? As a learner, you need to feel a bit disequilibrated, or unbalanced, to provide that impetus for learning and kick start the process, just as your students do or will do."

Saying these words, or something like them with students in every course I teach, has truly changed the ways in which students respond to ambiguous assignments. They quickly learn to trust, and that the other students and I will help them get where they need to go. They know we will defer judgment, not judge or shoot down their ideas, and thus begin to enjoy the process of learning so much more then they had. I have seen incredible growth in some of the most reticent or disengaged students, including risk-taking in how they choose to deliver their work: visual arts, stone carving, quilting, food, moviemaking, singing original songs, and more.

STRIVING FOR SELF-ACTUALIZATION

In 1943, Abraham Maslow proposed a positive theory of motivation that we have come to know as his hierarchy of needs. In this theory, we understand that human beings have lower order, or deficit, needs that include physiological needs, safety needs, and belongingness needs. Only once these are satisfied can people begin to address their growth needs, first esteem and then move toward the pinnacle of the hierarchy: self-actualization. Even if all other needs are met, Maslow says

> we may still often (if not always) expect that a new discontent and restlessness will soon develop, unless the individual is doing what he is fitted for. A musician must make music, an artist must paint, a poet must write, if he is to be ultimately happy. What a man *can* be, he *must* be. (p. 98)

In 1968 Maslow redefined self-actualization, not as a fixed state where we arrive at that pinnacle, but as episodic, something we move toward and away from throughout our lives.

By bringing creative teaching and learning into our classrooms, teaching our students to think deeply, giving them the time in which to do it, developing their tolerance for ambiguity, and inviting learning we create safe zones in which episodes of self-actualization can occur. These successes breed future success, maybe not this week, or this month, or even this year, but they do breed eventual success. When we develop these habits of mind and disposition, we all benefit, not just our students.

REFERENCES

Costa, A., & Kalick, B. (2001). Describing habits of mind. Adapted from Costa & Kallick (2000), *Habits of mind: A developmental series.* Alexandria, VA: Association for Supervision and Curriculum Development. Retrieved from http://www.ccsnh.edu/docu ments/CCSNH%20MLC%20HABITS%20OF%20MIND%20 COSTA-KALLICK%20DESCRIPTION%201-8-10.pdf.

Dewey, J. (1933). *How we think.* Boston, MA: Houghton Mifflin.

Ehrman, M., & Oxford, R. (1990). Adult language learning styles and strategies in an intensive training setting. *The Modern Language Journal, 74,* 311–327.

Ely, C. (1989). Tolerance of ambiguity and use of second language learning strategies. *Foreign Language Annals, 22* (5), 437–445.

Fried, J. (2010). *Why work doesn't happen at work* [video file]. Retrieved from http://www .ted.com/talks/jason_fried_why_work_doesn_t_happen_at_work.html.

Fulghum, R. (2010). *Uh-Oh* (p. 229). Random House, Inc. Kindle Edition.

Furnham, A., & Ribchester, T. (1995). Tolerance of ambiguity: A review of the concept. *Current Psychology, 14*(3), 179.

Galbraith, M. (1998). *Adult learning methods.* Malabar, FL: Krieger Publishing Company.

Grace, C. (1998). Personality type, tolerance of ambiguity, and vocabulary retention in CALL. *Calico Journal, 15*(13), 19–45.

Knowles, M.S. (1968). Androgogy, not pedagogy! *Adult Leadership, 16,* 350–352, 386.

Maslow, A. (1943). A theory of human motivation. *Psychological Review, 50*(4), *370–96.* Retrieved from http://psychclassics.yorku.ca/Maslow/motivation.htm.

Maslow, A. (1968). *Toward a psychology of being.* New York: D. Van Nostrand.

No Child Left Behind (NCLB) Act of 2001, Pub. L. No. 107-110, § 115, Stat. 1425 (2002).

Pintrich, P. (2000). An achievement goal theory perspective on issues in motivation terminology, theory, and research. *Contemporary Educational Psychology, 25,* 92–104. Retrieved from http://www.unco.edu/cebs/psychology/kevinpugh/motivation_project/resources/pintrich0 0.pdf.

Selby, E., Shaw, E., & Houtz, J. (2005). The creative personality. *Gifted Child Quarterly, 49* (4), 300–314.

Tomlinson, C. (2002). Invitations to learn: Do students care about learning? *Educational Leadership, 60*(1), 6–10.

Torrance, E. P. (1979). An instructional model for enhancing incubation. *Journal of Creative Behavior, 13,* 23–25.

Torrance, E. P. (1993). Understanding Creativity: Where to Start? *Psychological Inquiry, 4*(3), 232–234.

Wallas, G. (1926). *The art of thought.* London, UK: Watts.

Watkins, C. (2010). *Learning, performance and improvement.* Research Matters (34). International Network for School Improvement, London Centre for Leadership in Learning, Institute of Education, University of London, London.

9

ACTING ON CURIOSITY: WHAT'S CHANGED, WHAT HASN'T, AND WHAT EDUCATORS CAN DO

Marilyn P. Arnone
Syracuse University

Ruth V. Small
Syracuse University

The important thing is not to stop questioning.

—Albert Einstein

The Standards for the 21st-Century Learner (AASL, 2007) support curiosity as a critical disposition for learning. Curiosity can be the spark that ignites creativity, the topic of previous chapters in this book, and thus it is an important consideration for establishing a learning environment that fosters creativity. Curiosity has always been and always will be critical to intellectual development, problem-solving, and creativity. Some things never change. Yet, something about curiosity has changed. It is how our students *act* on curiosity. Emerging technologies continue to provide new contexts for acting on one's curiosity (Arnone, Small, Chauncey, & McKenna, 2011). The purpose of this chapter is to explore what has and what has not changed and the implications of these changes for educators.

The following brief background on the study of curiosity over the past five or more decades presents the reader with a number of definitions of curiosity and explanations of how curiosity works. While these definitions capture the spirit of curiosity, they do little to help educators operationalize a plan to stimulate students' curiosity for learning in an age of ubiquitous technologies or to consider the potential effects of not having information and digital literacy skills on curiosity. They also provide little insight on how curiosity may lead to deepening levels of interest or to engagement.

This chapter also provides two scenarios that illustrate how differently a middle school–aged child might act on curiosity today, as opposed to several decades ago, with implications for educators. It concludes with recommendations for librarians, teachers, and other educators on ways to foster and support students' curiosity in today's information and technology-rich world.

BACKGROUND ON CURIOSITY

Curiosity motivates scholarship. A curious student will want to explore and learn. Curiosity is motivation, which is intrinsic, as opposed to motivation, which comes as a result of external incentives, such as rewards or threats of test taking. To instill curiosity in a child is to encourage her/his disposition to learn. (Arnone, 1992, p.3)

Curiosity has been explored from a multiplicity of perspectives over the years. Some of the earliest explanations for curiosity held that, like other behaviors, it was presumed to be instinctive (McDougall in 1926 cited in Pintrich and Schunk, 2002). Such views, however, fail to adequately address any connection between curiosity and learning. Drive theories emphasize one's tendency to act on curiosity in order to return to a homeostatic or stable condition, a view also rejected by later theorists.

Much of our present understanding of curiosity has been influenced by the seminal work of Daniel Berlyne, often called the "Father of Curiosity." Berlyne associated curiosity with exploratory behavior and made a distinction between *diversive* and *specific exploration*. Diversive exploration occurs when a person seeks new experiences, possibly due to boredom or changelessness, while specific exploration is a result of uncertainty or conceptual conflict. He related specific exploration to *epistemic* curiosity or what he termed "the brand of arousal that motivates the quest for knowledge and is relieved when knowledge is procured" (Berlyne, 1960, p. 274). Later theorists referred to specific versus diversive curiosity, acknowledging the multifaceted nature of the construct.

EXAMPLE OF DIVERSIVE VERSUS SPECIFIC CURIOSITY

You may be able to identify students who come into the library looking for a change. They may scan the library seeking an experience whether it be playing a computer game or surfing the stacks. This would be *diversive* curiosity. On the other hand, the student who asks you a question about a topic is exhibiting *specific* curiosity.

While earlier theories posited that an optimal state of curiosity was homeostasis and that activity occurred when there was a displacement from the optimum (Walker, 1981), Berlyne believed that humans strive to maintain an intermediate amount of what he called *arousal potential*.

What Is Arousal Potential?

Stimuli that have the power to affect arousal include uncertainty, complexity, incongruity, conflict, surprise, and suddenness of change. Depending on the collative variability of the stimuli (i.e., how easy or difficult it is for a person to collate or compare stimuli with what the person is already familiar), arousal level may be increased and curiosity induced. Stimuli, which deviate to the extremes are considered aversive because a person will strive to keep the incoming stimuli near an optimal level, which is somewhere in between the extremes. Berlyne attests to a moderate amount of uncertainty as being pleasurable, however. This dimension of curiosity is important for planners of instruction, as it provides clues for strategies that may be effective in triggering curiosity such as posing an intriguing question, presenting a statement that contradicts what students already know, or presenting a situation in which students themselves discover ambiguity or things that do not make sense, leading to inquiry. The example that follows illustrates the latter strategy used in a lesson on evaluating web-based resources.

EXAMPLE OF INCONSISTENT INFORMATION

The school librarian at an elementary school is collaborating with a classroom teacher who is presenting a unit on mammals. The team decides to take an opportunity to teach the importance of evaluation skills in conducting research. They direct the students to an intentionally bogus website about the largest mammals on earth where numerous factual errors are encountered. While at first accepting of the site, students gradually notice errors and inconsistencies. The information they find contradicts what they know to be true, and it just doesn't make sense. The collaborative team acknowledges their discovery, and students are primed for a lesson on evaluation criteria.

Note: A search on "bogus websites" will generate numerous sites on a variety of topics.

What about Individual Differences?

Individuals differ in their preference and tolerance for curiosity arousal. This can vary widely from individual to individual and from occasion to occasion. When a student encounters a situation in which he is uncertain about the answer to a question, for example, a state of emotional tension and physiological and neurological arousal can be observed. "The state of tension is what Berlyne called curiosity and the resultant behavior—exploration" (Day, 1982, p. 19). Day and Berlyne (1971) both agree that individuals differ in tolerance and preference for arousal potential, stating "When confronted by a specific amount of arousal potential, some people will react with positive affect, interest, and exploration. Others may become overly tense and inefficient, and try to reject, avoid, or withdraw from the source of stimulation" (p. 304).

This has implications for educators, as there is no "one-size-fits-all" when designing situations to stimulate students' curiosity. For example, while the boy in the readers' advisory example presented below began to tune out when too many books were shown to him, another child may have preferred even more titles to remain in his Zone of Curiosity about the topic. As school librarians, we need to be looking for individual differences in curiosity to be mindful of the appropriate amount of stimulation to use in raising state curiosity or "curiosity in the moment." We will discuss more about the distinction between curiosity as a state and as a relatively stable trait later in this section.

EXAMPLE OF READERS' ADVISORY

Imagine you are conducting a readers' advisory interview with a middle school boy who is curious about wartime inventions. You have asked all the right readers' advisory questions and have found one book by Charles Gibson that shows how various technologies like guns, iron battleships, submarines, and other war inventions evolved. Those are just the types of inventions he is curious about, he enthusiastically tells you. He is in the *Zone of Curiosity*. Feeling good about your success, you find numerous other books on the topics. However, you soon notice a look on his face that signals he is tuning out. He may now be beyond the right amount of arousal for his individual needs. You take his cue. Pulling back on most of the books you found, you suggest that he take home the one or two books that initially piqued his curiosity. He smiles and leaves eagerly to dig for answers to his curiosity questions.

Berlyne conducted several studies related to an individual's intolerance for ambiguity and simplicity–complexity. One study showed that those who were intolerant of ambiguity also demonstrated a preference for familiarity, symmetry, and such things as black-and-white solutions. Another study found a positive correlation between tolerance of ambiguity and self-confidence. When seeking needed information through exploratory and epistemic behavior, a person must deal with ambiguity, but as Berlyne (1960) notes "this means that the conflict must be faced and borne for a while" (p. 216).

A number of researchers followed up on Berlyne's work. Day (1982), for example, proposed a curvilinear relationship between level of arousal and performance. At one end of the curve, too little stimulation would cause the individual to sink into boredom, lose interest, and possibly withdraw from a situation. At the opposite end, too much stimulation may cause an individual to become anxious and again withdraw or become ineffective. The central area of the curve is what

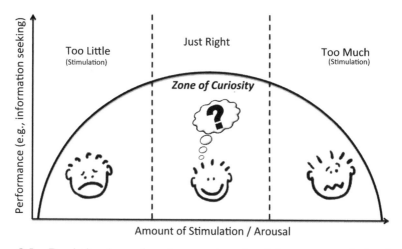

Figure 9.1   Persisting in exploration requires the right amount of stimulation.

Source: It helps to illustrate this relationship and was developed by the authors based on Day's research and explanation of the Zone of Curiosity (1982).

Day (1982) called the *Zone of Curiosity* where the individual experiences optimal arousal and can approach and explore her environment until the conceptual concept triggered by curiosity-evoking stimuli can be resolved.

Pre-service school librarians are taught to ask students a number of questions in order to hone in on their interests, needs (e.g., reading for an assignment or for pleasure), and developmental levels and guide them to appropriate books and electronic resources. It is also important to recognize body language and nonverbal cues (Peck, 2010). Both questioning and observation can be essential to discovering the right amount of stimulation to keep your student in the Zone of Curiosity.

Maw and Maw (1964, 1965, 1966) built upon Berlyne's work and operationally defined curiosity. Their definition, which is of particular relevance to educators, includes both specific and diverse aspects of curiosity. Curiosity is demonstrated by an elementary school child in the following cases:

1. reacts positively to new, strange, and incongruous elements through exploration and manipulation
2. exhibits a need or desire to know more about herself or the environment
3. scans her environment seeking for new experiences
4. persists in examining and exploring to know more about the environment (Maw & Maw, 1964, p. 31).

The third case relates to diverse curiosity whereas the others relate to specific curiosity. As educators we are more concerned with specific curiosity. You will be able to see how students under the first, second, and fourth definition of Maw and Maw are evident in the example that follows in which the librarian uses students' curiosity as a learning motivator.

EXAMPLE OF CURIOSITY TO MOTIVATE LEARNING

When the fifth-grade class arrived for a lesson on the concept of intellectual property, they found a small box on each table in the library. All of them were red, except for one lone yellow box. All of the boxes were closed and had no markings on them except for a small black question mark on the lid. The librarian asked the students not to open any of the boxes as they sat down at the tables. Students' eyes were fixed on those boxes; many wanted so badly to open them and find out what was in them. One boy raised his hand and asked when they would be able to open the boxes. The librarian told him only he could pick up his box and shake it but could not open it. The boy shook the box, and it made a clinking sound. One girl said, "Oh, it's keys!" Another girl said, "I think there are spoons in there." A boy said, "No, it sounds more like money." The librarian then told the class they would be using a web resource that would reveal the secret of the boxes. The students eagerly began exploring the website.

CURIOSITY AS TRAIT OR STATE

Curiosity can be looked at both as a personality feature that is relatively stable (*trait curiosity*) and as a state condition that is dynamic (*state curiosity*) that can be induced by interaction between an individual and the environment (Day, 1982;

Naylor, 1981). Loewenstein (1994) refers to state curiosity in terms of curiosity in a particular situation and trait curiosity as one's capacity to experience curiosity.

Ainley (1987) views curiosity as an approach to novelty and also argues that it is not a unitary construct. She investigated a two-factor structure of curiosity: breadth of interest curiosity style and depth of interest curiosity style. The former consists of "an orientation towards seeking varied and changing experiences" (p. 55) that seems to resemble diversive curiosity. The latter represents an orientation toward "exploring and investigating new objects, events and ideas" (p. 55) in order to better understand them. Depth of interest as a curiosity style is analogous to specific curiosity. The relationship between curiosity and interest is further explored in the next section.

What Are Some Other Perspectives on Curiosity?

Beswick and Tallmadge (1971) offer a cognitive process theory of curiosity. In this view, curiosity is a "process of creating, maintaining and resolving conceptual conflicts" (Beswick, 2000, p. 3) that results when an individual receives an incoming signal or stimulus that does not fit the cognitive map of his world as he has experienced it. Information-seeking happens in order for the individual to create a "best fit" with what he knew before.

The approach of Beswick and Tallmadge (1971) acknowledges that an understanding of the arousal mechanisms (such as those put forth by Berlyne and others) can also provide explanations for observed behavior: "The cognitive and physiological approaches are not necessarily exclusive of each other; nor were they exclusive in Berlyne's basically physiological approach where cognitive processes played an important part in what he called epistemic curiosity" (p. 3). Similarly, the study by Alberti and Witryol (1994) with third and fifth-grade children proposed that curiosity enhanced cognitive development through exploration.

An information-processing perspective is evident in Loewenstein's (1994) interpretation of curiosity. He sees curiosity as a "form of cognitively induced deprivation that arises from the perception of a gap in knowledge or understanding" (p. 1), viewing curiosity itself as aversive while the process of satisfying that curiosity as pleasurable. Kashdan, Rose, and Fincham (2004) view curiosity as a "positive emotional-motivational system associated with the recognition, pursuit, and self-regulation of novel and challenging opportunities" (p. 291).

Arnone et al. (2011) argued that curiosity is so intertwined with the constructs of interest and engagement that a new research agenda is needed in which the three constructs are studied in relation to each other. The definition of Arnone et al. addresses curiosity *episodically* as opposed to as a personality trait although they recognize the importance of trait curiosity. It is the situational triggering of curiosity that educators can influence most. According to their definition, curiosity is a desire for new information or experience that triggers a reaction (exploration, use of information, or new media skills) and resolution (either curiosity is satisfied or the individual withdraws from the curiosity-provoking situation). When curiosity is satisfied (e.g., the individual finds the answer to a curiosity-provoking question), then there is the potential for curiosity to lead to deepening levels of interest such as those proposed by Renninger (2000) and sustained learning engagement. Figure 9.2 graphically represents this definition.

Figure 9.2 illustrates how curiosity, when resolved (or *satisfied*), can lead to interest and engagement in a learning topic. When curiosity has not been satisfied,

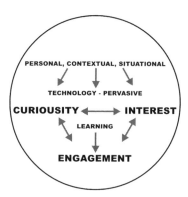

Figure 9.2   How curiosity leads to interest and sustained learning engagement.

Source: From "Curiosity, interest and engagement in technology-pervasive learning environments: A new research agenda," by M. P. Arnone et al., 2011, Educational Technology Research and Development, 59, p. 189. Reprinted with permission from authors.

withdrawal from the learning situation is likely to occur. This may happen due to frustration, anxiety, or boredom (see figure 9.1).

Early childhood educator, Lisa Jacobson has many opportunities to observe children's curiosity being triggered, leading to interest and sustained engagement, as depicted in figure 9.2.

> Sometimes I will give brown paper lunch bags to children and take them on a nature walk just outside the building. They look, gather things like pine cones, twigs, parts of plants or flowers, and explore the area around them. They get very excited when they find their treasures and are eager to share them with their peers and me. We then bring their *finds* back into the classroom and empty their brown bags on the science table. As they start examining all of the treasures, the children begin talking about what they have found. I may begin a discussion by asking questions about their discoveries that often leads to other things they saw outside but didn't bring in like a butterfly, worm, or bug. To help build on their interest, we often will incorporate picture books, magnifiers and other tools that will help to support their growing curiosity. (personal communication, June 12, 2012)

In the absence of any stimulus provided by the educator, children's natural propensity for exploration often results in curiosity, and often the camaraderie of collaborative exploration further fuels individual curiosity. Jacobson sees this regularly on the playground but recognizes children's individual differences in how they respond to curiosity arousing situations.

> Another time, I saw a child pick up a stick and start digging in the dirt. He found a worm and this excited other children to start digging to find worms as well. Most kids were intrigued and explored how their worms looked and felt. One little girl, who was enjoying digging in the dirt, had no desire to touch the worm that she found. Though looking at it from a distance

intrigued her, she chose not to touch it or handle it at all. I respected her wishes but still encouraged her to participate by asking her questions to build her interest more. I picked the worm up and placed it in my own hand so she could look at more it closely. Eventually, she gained enough courage to touch it with one finger. (personal communication, June 12, 2012)

Touching the worm with just one finger was the next step in this child's exploration. Despite the curiosity trigger (discovering the worm), had Lisa not intervened, the child may have withdrawn from further exploration. Instead, there was real potential for more exploration to occur. In fact, while satisfactory resolution of a curiosity episode initiates new learning as the child makes sense of things, Arnone et al. (2011) argue that ". . . it is curiosity's power to both trigger and be triggered through the development and deepening of interest and consequently, the forms of engagement that result in deep learning and effective participation, collaboration, and affinity" (p. 6).

Is Curiosity Related in Some Way to Competence?

The scholarship on competence of White (1959) and Deci (1975) suggested that there was a connection between curiosity and need for competence. Focusing specifically on information literacy competence, a recent study found a significant relationship between curiosity and perceived competence in information skills among more than 1,000 eighth-grade students (Arnone & Reynolds, 2009). It seems intuitive that a child would likely remain in a Zone of Curiosity longer if he has the necessary information skills for finding appropriate information to satisfy the intriguing questions at hand. Without such skills, it is likely that a child could become frustrated or anxious by withdrawing from exploration before curiosity is resolved. Building on figure 9.1, it seems that in order to persist in information seeking to resolve curiosity, there must be both the right amount of stimulation *and* the right skills to do the job.

What Has and Hasn't Changed about Acting on Curiosity

Before we move on to what has and hasn't changed, and considering the situational definition of curiosity presented by Arnone et al., let's travel back in time to a hypothetical situation decades ago when a middle school child encountered a curiosity-arousing event. As you read scenario 1, think about the options a curious child like James had for exploration and its impact on learning.

SCENARIO 1

It is 1972 and James is an eighth-grade student at Rocky Road Middle School in Newbury, Ohio. One afternoon after school, James switches on his family's TV and happens upon a program about a volcano that is erupting in Hawaii. The story ignites James's curiosity and prompts several questions such as: Why do volcanoes erupt? What happens to the people who live near erupting volcanoes? Are kids still able to go to school? How long does it take to get every-thing back to normal? How does this event affect the environment? He asks his mother, who says that she doesn't know the answers but that he should ask his teacher when he gets to school the next day. The following morning at school, James asks his science teacher some of his questions about volcanoes.

His teacher tells him that they'll talk about volcanoes in several weeks, but that he can go to the school library and see what resources it has on vol-canoes. There, James finds a print encyclopedia; he takes the correct volume and reads the section on volcanoes. He finds an explanation of why volcanoes erupt but nothing that would answer his other questions. The librarian shows him a filmstrip on volcanoes and a 1970 *National Geographic* magazine that contains an article showing a color photo of an erupting volcano. Although the vivid oranges and reds of the molten lava in the article and filmstrip look even more intriguing than the scenes he saw on the TV program, there was not much information that would provide the answers to his questions. Giv-ing up, James goes out to play ball after school. He mentions his interest in volcanoes to his friends while he is playing ball. They don't seem too inter-ested, as none of them had seen the TV program on the volcano eruption in Hawaii. They continue their game.

Now let's fast-forward to a similar occurrence set in current times. As you read about Julie in scenario 2, think about how her approach differed from that of James and what new issues face her as she explores and learns.

SCENARIO 2

Let us fast forward to 2013, and Julie is an eighth-grade student at Rocky Road Middle School in Newbury, Ohio. One afternoon after school, Julie re-ceives a tweet from her cousin who lives in Washington State. The tweet states, "Volcano erupting nearby. We are all safe." The story ignites Julia's curiosity and prompts several questions such as: Why do volcanoes erupt? What kinds of things could happen to the people who live near erupting volcanoes? Do schools close when this happens? How long does it take to get everything back to normal? How does this event affect the environment? Julie's interest in the environment also leads her to wonder about what happens inside the volcano just before it erupts and whether there might be a way to use active volcanoes as an energy source.

She sends a text message to some of her friends, sending them the link to an online news story on the volcano eruption and asking if they know any of the answers to her questions. Her friends use social bookmarking to share websites and web resources. Julie's friends are her collaborators and so is a global social network of enthusiasts who have an interest in volcanoes. A twitter hashtag about the event allows instant sharing of information. Jacob shares an interesting website, and Julie types http://kids.nationalgeographic

.com into her laptop's browser. She finds a page on the site where kids her age write blog posts about their travels; one actually saw a volcano erupt in Costa Rica.

Julie leaves this site and googles the term "volcano." Within seconds, she receives 92,400,000 hits, including a web-based question-and-answer service in which experts on volcanoes answer questions online, picture galleries from museums, her local library's collection on volcano-related materials, fact sheets on volcanoes around the world, theory papers (e.g., volcanoes on other planets), video clips, songs about volcanoes, live webcams of actual volcanoes, and much more. She is immediately overwhelmed but decides to select a fact sheet first. Julie finds this boring; therefore she selects an interesting video clip from the National Geographic site, which she downloads onto her PDA, then moves on to a site that has animations of erupting volcanoes. After watching one, she notices another link for tornado animations, clicks on that and is soon connected to more sites about tornadoes.

She continues to explore about tornadoes, doesn't resolve all of her questions on volcanoes, and runs out of time to work on her assigned homework project. At school the next day, her friend Sarah tells Julie about a cool 3-D interactive animation that seemingly takes one inside a volcano as it prepares to erupt. Sarah has loaded it on her handheld device, and she beams the file to Julie. The images get Julie thinking about an invention that harvests molten lava that could be used as a heat source. She starts to collect images, sounds, and text for a voice-over, animated presentation she is creating just for fun, using easy but nonetheless high-tech tools.

What Hasn't Changed

Several things have not changed since the scenario depicted in 1972. Kids are still as curious as ever. They become riveted in specific curiosity as something new or unfamiliar crosses their path like a butterfly emerging from its cocoon. They are full of wonder. An event in nature can trigger a barrage of questions aimed at filling an information gap and a desire to *know*. There remain individual differences in tolerance for uncertainty (not knowing), and the amount of stimulation that can be handled in a curiosity-provoking situation has probably not changed either.

The need to feel competent and master one's environment is likely the same now as well. Also, individuals still need skills that will allow them to successfully find the answers to their curiosity questions.

What Has Changed

Technology has radically changed since James' time and so has the pace at which new and disruptive technologies are emerging. The information cycle itself has changed primarily as a result of technology; news that once took a day to get into the newspaper is spread globally in a matter of seconds through social media. The expectations of consumers to be able to access information whenever needed are higher. The proliferation of misinformation and disinformation has increased as a result of the sheer volume of accessible data. That volume of data also makes it easy to become overwhelmed by too much information. How individuals and groups socialize and exchange ideas continues to evolve. As a result, the context for Julie *acting* on her curiosity is very different than it was for James.

As can be seen in figure 9.3, the authors argue that the study of curiosity should be investigated in light of today's technology-pervasive learning environments and that when studying behaviors within these media environments, the moderating factors of person (e.g., developmental levels, beliefs, etc.) and context (formal, informal, home, school, museum) and situation factors (social influences, specific technology, time, etc.) also must be considered.

Finally, the types of skills and tools that today's curious students must master have also changed. The AASL Standards can help librarians identify the skills required for today's learners that will allow them to be curious (and discerning) explorers and creative problem solvers.

What Educators Can Do to Foster Curiosity for Learning

With the creation of the AASL Standards for the 21st-Century Learner (2007), the burgeoning importance of the Common Core State Standards, and the explosion of information and instructional technologies for teaching and learning, it is no longer optional for educators to ignore the motivational aspects of education. While the focus of learning assessment is currently on knowledge acquisition, educators must not underestimate the role of curiosity and interest in student learning.

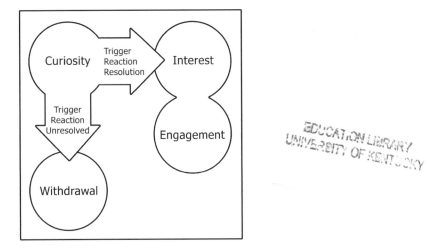

Figure 9.3 Model of curiosity, interest, and engagement (CIE) in new media technology-pervasive learning environments.

Source: From "Curiosity, interest and engagement in technology-pervasive learning environments: A new research agenda," by M. P. Arnone et al., 2011, Educational Technology Research and Development, 59, p. 189. Reprinted with permission from authors.

Arnone and Small (1995) suggested that curiosity can be aroused and sustained in ways that also promote attention, relevance, confidence, and satisfaction in learning what Keller (1987) contends are essential components of motivating instructional design comprised in his ARCS Model of Motivational Design. The ARCS Model is based on a synthesis of motivation theories, such as expectancy-value theory, social learning theory, and was created to stimulate students' intrinsic motivation to learn.

The ARCS Model specifies four broad motivation goals for promoting students' intrinsic motivation and cognitive engagement. They include (1) gaining and sustaining **A**ttention; (2) demonstrating the **R**elevance of the learning experience; (3) building students' **C**onfidence in their ability to be competent in the learning task; and (4) promoting learning **S**atisfaction (Keller, 1987, 1999).

As educators, we need to ensure that all students are prepared to resolve their curiosity questions through the use of inquiry skills that require higher-level thinking. We must create learning environments that encourage exploration and discovery and allow learners to construct meaning and build on prior learning. In the section that follows, we provide suggestions for strategies that promote curiosity in each of Keller's four major components of motivating instruction.

Attention

- Create an atmosphere where learners feel comfortable about raising questions.
- Use technology (e.g., YouTube video, Twitter post) to trigger interest in a topic.
- Recognize students' individual differences in tolerance for stimulation and curiosity arousal during the learning situation.
- Help learners become aware of their incoming information gaps when learning a particular topic.
- Demonstrate the range of technologies that can be used to access and share information on a topic of interest.
- Minimize distractions that may have the potential to eliminate curiosity once aroused.
- Provoke a cognitive conflict using complexity, incongruity, contradiction, and ambiguity.

Relevance

- Model curious behaviors to increase learners' perceptions of the importance of curiosity.
- Use online simulations to demonstrate the importance of a concept or principle.
- Allow students to become engaged and curious about topics or interests in which they already have some knowledge.
- Show students how to search the Internet successfully for information on a topic of interest so they can persist in their curiosity exploration.
- Demonstrate how social media allow students to share ideas and collaborate for learning.
- Create online learning collaboratories where students help scaffold each other. (Be careful to manage potential distraction from such collaborations.)

- Make statements that help learners see the potential value in persisting in a curiosity-arousing situation until the necessary information has been found.
- Allow students to experiment with appropriate new technology applications as alternative strategies for exploring curiosity-stimulating situations.

Confidence

- Align the learning challenge with learners' skills and abilities and at the appropriate level of complexity.
- Provide informative feedback that will help learners see a realistic picture of their information gaps and reinforce their curiosity and interest. Provide *progress* feedback rather than *performance* feedback.
- Develop online tutorials to allow students to practice their information skills in school and/or at home.
- Teach students to use social bookmarking for saving sites that piqued their curiosity.
- Teach them about databases and network technologies to build competence. Perceived competence will allow them to persist longer in their explorations.
- Help them develop personal learning networks to organize their resources, social connections, and so on. This provides support that enhances confidence.
- Help learners have positive expectations for success based on having clear learning goals.
- Have students create a mind map to outline their curiosity questions and identify possible sources of information.
- Encourage active exploration and give learners opportunities to explore curiosity-arousing situations in their own ways.
- Pair students with similar interests but different levels of ability
- Support information-seeking activities with guidance and modeling.
- Allow sufficient time for learners to persist in their explorations or information seeking.

Satisfaction

- Emphasize the intrinsic enjoyment that learners feel as a result of reducing the uncertainty connected with curiosity.
- Be enthusiastic about the learners' accomplishments as they relate to curiosity.
- Allow students to communicate the results of their curiosity-driven projects through podcasting, screencasting, blogs, gaming, and other creative ways.
- Give learners an opportunity to reflect on their curiosity-arousing episodes and their resolution.
- Recognize accomplishment by posting exemplary work on the library or school website.
- Acknowledge any special challenges that students may have encountered in the process of resolving information uncertainty.

- Provide the learner with additional enrichment materials (e.g., books, blogs, websites, etc.) about related areas of interest.

- Inform learners about ways in which they might continue to explore their topic of curiosity.

- If one learner has resolved her uncertainty, allow her to provide guidance and informative feedback to others who are not yet there.

CONCLUSION

It is significant that NASA's first robotic rover to reach, explore, and collect data on Mars was named "Curiosity." Countless books and movies have piqued our curiosity about the red planet and stimulated questions like "Is there life on Mars?" "If there is life, is it friendly life?" "Will earthlings ever set foot on Mars?" Our minds present creative images of what Martian life might be like.

Curiosity is a powerful catalyst for human creativity, discovery, and learning. As educators, it is imperative that we use innovative ways to stimulate and support our students' curiosity, encourage them to explore areas of interest, and become engaged in learning activities whenever and wherever their curiosity takes them.

ACKNOWLEDGMENTS

We wish to acknowledge Dr. Carol Sansone, Professor of Psychology at the University of Utah, for her input on both of the scenarios presented in this chapter.

REFERENCES

Ainley, M. (1987). The factor structure of curiosity measures: Breadth and depth of interest curiosity styles. *Australian Journal of Psychology, 39*(1), 53–59.

Alberti, E.T., & Witryol, S.L. (1994). The relationship between curiosity and cognitive ability in third and fifth grade children. *Journal of Genetic Psychology, 155*, 129–145.

American Association of School Librarians. (2007). *AASL's standards for the 21st-century learner in action.* Chicago, IL: American Library Association.

Arnone, M.P. (1992). *Curiosity as an influencing variable in achievement in an interactive learner control environment.* Doctoral dissertation. Syracuse University, Syracuse, NY.

Arnone, M.P., & Reynolds, R. (2009). Empirical support for the integration of dispositions in action and multiple literacies into AASL's Standards for the 21st-century learner. *School Library Research,* American Library Association. Retrieved from http://www.ala.org/aasl/aaslpubsandjournals/slmrb/slmrcontents/volume12/arnone_reynolds.

Arnone, M.P., & Small, R.V. (1995). Arousing and sustaining curiosity: Lessons from the ARCS Model. *Proceedings of the 1995 Annual Conference of the Association for Educational Communications and Technology,* Anaheim, CA, February 8–12.

Arnone, M.P., Small, R.V., Chauncey, S.A., & McKenna, H.P. (2011). Curiosity, interest, and engagement in technology-pervasive learning environments: A new research agenda. *Educational Technology Research & Development, 59*, 181–198.

Berlyne, D.E. (1954). A theory of human curiosity. *British Journal of Psychology, 45*(3), 180–191.

Berlyne, D.E. (1960). *Conflict, arousal and curiosity.* New York: McGraw-Hill.

Beswick, D.G. (2000). *An introduction to the study of curiosity.* University of Melbourne. Retrieved from http://www.beswick.info/psychres/curiosityintro.htm

Beswick, D. G., & Tallmadge, G. K. (1971). Reexamination of two learning style studies in the light of the cognitive process theory of curiosity. *Journal of Educational Psychology, 62*(6), 456–462.

Day, H. I. (1968). Role of specific curiosity in school achievement. *Journal of Educational Psychology, 59*(1), 37–43.

Day, H. I. (1982). Curiosity and the interested explorer. *NSPI Journal,* May, 19–22.

Day, H. I., & Berlyne, D. E. (1971). Intrinsic motivation. In G. S. Lesser (Ed.), *Psychology and educational practice* (pp. 294–335). Glenview, IL: Scott, Foresman, and Company.

Deci, E. L. (1975). *Intrinsic motivation.* New York: Plenum.

Kashdan, T. B. (2009). *Curious? Discover the missing ingredient to a fulfilling life.* New York: William Morrow.

Kashdan, T. D., Rose, P., & Fincham, F. D. (2004). Curiosity and exploration: Facilitating positive subjective experiences and personal growth opportunities. *Journal of Personality Assessment, 82,* 291–305.

Keller, J. M. (1987). The systematic process of motivational design. *Performance and Instruction, 26*(9–10), 1–8.

Keller, J. M. (1999). Motivation in cyberlearning environments. *International Journal of Educational Technology, 1*(1), 7–30.

Litman, J. A., & Jimerson, T. L. (2004). The measurement of curiosity as a feeling of deprivation [abstract]. *Journal of Personality Assessment, 82*(2), 147–157.

Loewenstein, G. (1994). The psychology of curiosity: A review and reinterpretation. *Psychological Bulletin, 116*(1), 75–98.

Maw W., & Maw, E. (1964). *An Exploratory Study into the Measurement of Curiosity in Elementary School Children.* Cooperative Research Project No 801. Newark, DE: University of Delaware.

Maw W., & Maw, E. (1965). Differences in preference for investigatory activities by school children who differ in curiosity level. *Psychology in the Schools, 2,* 263–266.

Maw W., & Maw, E. (1966). Children's curiosity and parental attitudes. *Journal of Marriage and the Family, 28,* 343–345.

McDougall, W. (1926). An introduction to social psychology (Rev. ed.). Boston: John W. Luce.

Naylor, F. D. (1981). A state-trait curiosity inventory. *Australian Psychologist, 16,* 172–183.

Peck, P. (2010). *Readers' advisory for children and 'tweens.* Santa Barbara, CA: Libraries Unlimited, an imprint of ABC-CLIO.

Pintrich, P. R., & Schunk, D. H. (2002). *Motivation in education: Theory, research, and applications* (2nd Ed.). Columbus, OH: Merrill-Prentice Hall.

Renninger, K. A. (2000). Individual interest and its implications for understanding intrinsic motivation. In C. Sansone and J. M. Harackiewicz (Eds.), *Intrinsic motivation: Controversies and new directions,* 373–404. San Diego, CA: Academic Press.

Walker, E. L. (1981). The quest for the inverted U. In H. Day (Ed.), *Advances in intrinsic motivation and aesthetics.* New York: Plenum Press.

White, R. W. (1959). Motivation reconsidered: The concept of competence. *Psychological Review, 66,* 297–333.

Section III

CREATIVITY IN THE CLASSROOM AND THE SCHOOL LIBRARY OF CURIOUS DELIGHT

The heading of section three draws heavily from Alane Jordan Starko's book *Creativity in the Classroom: Schools of Curious Delight*. D. H. Lawrence (1930) penned *curious delight* in his essay "Making Pictures."

10

---·=◆=·---

CREATIVITY IN THE CLASSROOM: TEACHERS AND LIBRARIANS TOGETHER

Alane Jordan Starko
Eastern Michigan University

Recently, I had a wonderful opportunity to visit schools in China and speak to Chinese educators. Everywhere I went, teachers and administrators asked me the same questions: How can we help our students to be more flexible thinkers? How can we help them be better at creative and imaginative thinking? I was struck by the contrast between these conversations and the ones I most often hear in schools in the United States. In recent years (and for logical reasons), conversations in U.S. schools have focused largely on improving standardized test scores. In China, where test scores—at least for the schools I was visiting—are already high, they recognized those scores as an insufficient goal. They were interested in learning more about the kind of education that has fueled the traditional strengths of the United States in innovation and creativity.

Of course, conversations about the need for creativity are not unique to China. Dr. Kyung-Hee Kim's research (see chapter four) was the subject of *Newsweek's* widely publicized "Creativity Crisis" feature (Bronson & Merryman, 2010), sparking watercooler conversations about creativity across the United States. Yet, there is still a level of ambivalence regarding the role of both critical and creative thinking in American education. On one hand, conversations about a "Creativity Crisis" imply the need to infuse more creative thinking into students' experiences—as long as it does not depress test scores. At the other extreme, the 2012 Republican Platform from the state of Texas stated, "We oppose the teaching of Higher Order Thinking Skills . . . , critical thinking skills and similar programs . . . which . . . have the purpose of challenging the student's fixed beliefs and undermining parental authority" (p.12). Teaching students to think flexibly and creatively will, by its very nature, encourage them to look at the world in new ways. For those who view any challenge to "fixed beliefs" as problematic, creative thinking is likely to be problematic as well.

This means teachers in the United States—and around the world—face the challenge of multiple goals and priorities. Teachers must make sure students learn the required content and learn it in such a way that they are successful on mandated tests. Teachers also must ensure students actually understand the content in sufficient depth that they can apply it outside a testing situation—because if students cannot do that, what is the point? Simultaneously, teachers must help students develop the kinds of thinking that will help them be successful with the content we cannot teach, because it has not yet been developed.

It is a truism that today's students will live in a world not conceived. If, as a young person, I had been given a chance to see the world I live in today, it would have seemed like science fiction. When I went to school, we cooked dinner in a non-microwave oven, dialed our phone from the kitchen wall, spoke to the bank teller when we needed cash, and saw pictures of a room-sized computer in *Life Magazine*. Today, I happily teach courses online, write a creativity blog (creativiteach.me), grumble when the ATM is down, and feel incomplete without my smart phone. None of those things would be possible had I not learned to think flexibly, explore new ideas, and learn independently. Those skills, particularly flexibility, grow even more essential as the world changes at a faster and faster pace. And so, what do schools do?

I propose that schools address these seemingly contradictory goals simultaneously. This is possible if we make *learning for understanding* the center of our efforts. The Active Learning Practices for Schools (ALPs) website (2012), based on Harvard's Teaching for Understanding project, makes distinctions among three important goals in education: knowledge, skills, and understanding. Knowledge and skills represent content "on tap," information, or performances that students can bring forward at will. These are important in any school situation. In contrast, understanding is described at http://learnweb.harvard.edu/alps/tfu/info1b.cfm as "the ability to think and act flexibly with what one knows (para. five)," that is, the ability to put knowledge and skills into action. If we are to teach in ways that help students learn for understanding, by definition, we need to help them use content flexibly. By doing so, we develop understanding, support creativity, and (assuming good assessments) are likely to enhance test scores as well. Such a deal! Thus, we are left with one (albeit complex) challenge. How do we develop classrooms that support both creativity and understanding?

TEACHING FOR CREATIVITY: THREE KEYS

Imagine a classroom in which creativity is welcomed. Maybe you picture an art room or a music studio. You may picture a wildly colorful room, busy students, and an enthusiastic—and perhaps eccentric—teacher. Our stereotypes of teaching for creativity sometimes lean toward Robin Williams' costumed character leaping across desks in the movie *Dead Poets Society* (or perhaps something out of Hogwarts). However, neither my talents nor my agility make it likely that I will be levitating feathers, dressing up, or clambering across the furniture in most of my classes. Does that mean my ability to create a classroom full of creativity is limited? No.

As I have thought about this dilemma, it has become clear that I want to do two different things. I want to teach creatively—*creative teaching*—and I also want to teach in a manner that supports student creativity—*teaching for creativity*—but, they are different. In creative teaching, the teacher is creative. Creative teachers use their creativity to design innovative lessons, create stimulating classroom environments, and engage their students in interesting projects. However, creative teaching does not necessarily guarantee that the *students* will have a chance to be creative. If the teacher presents a highly engaging lecture while dressed as Henry VIII, but the students are required only to comprehend and repeat the facts about Henry, it may be creative teaching, but it was not teaching for creativity.

As I have considered the things teachers can do to create a classroom in which creativity can flourish, I have found they cluster in my mind into three categories, or keys. Key No. 1 is to develop a creativity-friendly classroom environment. Key No. 2 is to teach the skills and attitudes of creativity. Key No. 3 is to teach the creative methods of the disciplines. I will describe each one briefly and then elaborate on how they may be implemented in classrooms and supported by libraries.

- Key No. 1: *Developing a creativity-friendly classroom* entails creating a classroom atmosphere in which both the physical environment and the classroom's emotional climate are supportive of creativity. It is a classroom in which the routines, procedures, and classroom culture encourage flexible thinking. It is a place in which it is not only safe to ask questions, find problems, and seek to solve them, but where those behaviors are also enthusiastically welcomed.
- Key No. 2: *Teaching the skills and attitudes of creativity* entails explicitly teaching students about creativity. Does this not make perfect sense? How can we expect students to think more creatively if they do not understand creativity as a goal? Teaching the skills and attitudes of creativity includes teaching about the lives of creative individuals, the nature of the creative process, and strategies that can be used to generate creative ideas.
- Key No. 3: *Teaching the creative methods of the disciplines* requires teaching students how individuals are creative in the disciplines they study. In science, for example, this type of teaching requires learning the processes of scientific investigation, in addition to the concepts and generalizations resulting from such investigations in the past. This is more complex than teaching the five steps of the scientific method although that is a place to start. Real science rarely progresses in such neat and predictable steps. Learning how creative scientists operate entails learning the kinds of questions scientists ask and the investigative methods they use. It examines the obstacles that can impede progress, the circuitous paths that can lead to success, and the skills necessary to conduct investigations. Parallel kinds of knowledge can be examined for any field in which creativity emerges. Helping students find and solve problems in the disciplines is a key way to integrate creativity into core content.

Each of these keys is important in itself, but when combined they provide multiple opportunities for students to exercise their creativity, as well as an atmosphere in which those efforts are nurtured. Simultaneously, they provide the opportunity to learn content for understanding—a wonderful two-for-one package.

KEY NO. 1: DEVELOPING A CREATIVITY-FRIENDLY CLASSROOM

Everyone who creates creates somewhere. When I explore my artistic creativity in mosaic, I work in a mosaic studio. I write in my office. I create recipes in my kitchen.

Each of those spaces provides resources and support for the types of creativity I try to exercise there. The creativity literature is full of stories (some true, some apocryphal) about creative individuals who had to work in a particular place, using specific tools. Environment matters. In schools, our classrooms impact students' creativity on both a physical and emotional level. When considering a classroom supportive of creativity, we must ask ourselves what kind of physical environment will be most conducive to students' learning and creativity, and what kind of emotional climate will be most supportive of students' learning and creativity?

There are several bodies of research relevant to these questions, but we will consider just one: the research regarding intrinsic motivation. Amabile (1989, 1996, 2001) developed a three-part model of creativity that focused attention on intrinsic motivation as an essential element of the creative process. The three parts of her model included domain-relevant knowledge and skills (the knowledge base in which the creativity is based), creativity-relevant processes, and task motivation. Generally, intrinsic (task) motivation, as opposed to extrinsic (performance) motivation, is associated with increased creative performance. That is, in most circumstances, individuals who are approaching a creative task based on their interest and desire to address the task, as opposed to seeking an external reward, are more likely to produce a creative outcome.

Intrinsic motivation is an essential element for many aspects of education. Chappuis, Stiggins, Chappuis, and Arter (2012) wisely pointed out:

> The decisions that contribute the most to student learning success are made, not by adults . . . , *but by students themselves. Students* decide whether the learning is worth the effort required to attain it . . . *Students* decide whether to keep learning or to quit working. [italics original] (p. 8)

Helping students to be motivated by the tasks at hand is essential, not just for creativity, but for learning as well.

No activity, in and of itself, is intrinsically motivating. It can only be so to a particular person, at a particular time, but there are characteristics more commonly associated with intrinsically motivating activities. The first and most obvious characteristic is interest. Individuals are more likely to be motivated by ideas and activities that have captured their interest. Who wants to spend time doing something they perceive as boring or without value? A second aspect is competence. As individuals perceive themselves to be improving and gaining competence, they are more motivated to continue. Think about a time you gained a new skill. As you realized you were improving, you were much more likely to want to continue. I am finding that true of my novice efforts at mosaic making. I have never worked in the visual arts before and approached the idea with considerable hesitation. However, as I have gained skill and seen my efforts improve, I find myself wanting to take additional classes and even branch into related arts. This is tied to a third hallmark of intrinsic motivation: the importance of choice. We are much more likely to want to engage in an activity of our own choosing than one that is mandated.

Unfortunately, some of the variables that are associated with diminished intrinsic motivation will sound very familiar to anyone who works in schools. In her early work, Amabile called these "creativity killers," which are evaluation, surveillance, reward, competition, and lack of choice. I envision school personnel shaking their heads as they recognize the abundance of these creativity killers in schools.

Fortunately, as Amabile's work continued, she modified her position to make the relationship between intrinsic motivation and creativity a bit more nuanced, "Intrinsic motivation is conducive to creativity; controlling extrinsic motivation is detrimental to creativity, but informational or enabling extrinsic motivation can be conducive particularly if initial levels of intrinsic motivation are high" (1996, p. 119). That is, intrinsic motivation is supportive of creativity. Some types of extrinsic motivation are harmful to creativity, but some are not. Of course, our task is to determine which is which and how best to use them in classrooms.

Supporting Intrinsic Motivation in Classrooms

Exploring all the ways that we can support intrinsic motivation in classrooms is far beyond the capacity of one short chapter, but here are a few points to consider.

- Think about when and how students can choose within the required curriculum. Can you devise a project in which the same content could be expressed in several ways and let students select one? Can students choose from among books in a given genre? Can you assign a task that can be completed several different ways and have students explain their choice—without having one correct method? The options for choice are myriad. Just be aware that when students have choices, all the choices must include the equivalent opportunities for learning and demonstrating knowledge of content.

- The type and timing of feedback is an essential component of intrinsic motivation. This is part of what Stiggins (2005) calls "assessment *for* learning," which also can be considered "assessment *for* creativity." Remember that a sense of growing competence increases intrinsic motivation. If students get clear informational feedback in time to adjust and improve their performance, you have supported the kind of motivation that will make creativity possible—regardless of whether the specific assignment at hand requires creative thinking. In the same way, helping students thoughtfully assess their own progress will also enhance their sense of progress and control over their learning processes.

- Study, and be thoughtful about, the use of rewards. Providing extrinsic rewards (stickers, pizza parties) for creative activities can actually decrease students' creative efforts. It is almost as if they think, "If I'm not getting a prize, why bother?" Rewards that come as a happy surprise rather than an expected payoff are much less problematic.

- It is becoming increasingly clear that creative endeavors are often team efforts. Students must have opportunities to work both on individual creative challenges that are matched to their skills and interests and also on group assignments that require genuine contributions from all participants. Planning such assignments demands considerable teacher creativity in order to avoid the dreaded, "Now I have to do all the work or it will not get done" phenomenon. *Teaching* students both how to work independently, and how to work in a group (as opposed to simply ordering them to do so) is an essential part of this process.

- A classroom that supports creativity is a place that welcomes questions—not just the type of questions that clarify content, but the kind that reflects genuine curiosity and wonder about the world. Teaching students to ask such questions,

Figure 10.1 **"If I'm not getting a prize, why bother?"**

Source: Used with permission of author, Christopher T. Jones.

and then treating them with respect, is an essential aspect of a creative classroom culture.

- A creativity-friendly classroom gives students experiences with inquiry-based instruction, in which students raise questions, solve problems, analyze data, and draw conclusions. Such processes provide the scaffolding and experiences that can lead to genuine creative inquiry.

- Amabile (1996) has demonstrated that students can be "inoculated" against the negative impact of extrinsic rewards through example. Listening to a peer express delight in learning for its own sake is contagious. Talk to students about your own joy in learning and help them share it.

Finally, a creativity-friendly classroom considers the physical space, and how it affects students' creative endeavors. This includes not only basics such as adequate space for materials and procedures for readily changing furniture from individual to group-work configurations, but also the kinds of sensory stimuli included in the room. As in many educational dilemmas, this is a place where balance is essential. There are students for whom an overly stimulating environment can be distracting and detract from learning. On the other hand, creative ideas require input, and that includes new and interesting experiences provided regularly. Consider how autumn leaves, an interesting shell, a new type of music, a book of photographs, or an antique kitchen item may change the atmosphere. Walking into a classroom should spark curiosity and stimulate questions.

Supporting Intrinsic Motivation in School Libraries

How can librarians support key No. 1? Developing a classroom atmosphere that supports creativity requires a broad range of teaching skills. Teachers need information on inquiry learning, formative assessment, appropriate feedback, differentiation, developing high-quality projects, and a host of other topics. With increasingly limited professional development budgets in most schools, many of these skills will need to be developed through print, media, and online resources. School libraries need not be just for students. The development of a strong professional collection will greatly enhance teachers' options for learning and growth. Working with teachers to identify their needs and interests can help assure the collection will be well used. Of course, the library itself should be an interesting and visually inviting place. Consider what kind of space might not only encourage students to read, but also encourage them to question, ponder, and wonder.

KEY NO. 2: TEACHING THE SKILLS AND ATTITUDES OF CREATIVITY

It stands to reason that if we want students to exercise creativity, they need to know that creativity is a goal, and know what that goal looks like. Expecting students to be creative without explaining what that means, how it might operate in school, and why it is important, is not so different from expecting students to factor equations without any instruction. Why would we think they would be able to do that? Also, why would they think it was important? Helping students understand that creative thinking is both important and welcomed is particularly important with older students who may have spent more years learning that every question has one right answer (often "B") and their task is to identify it.

Many strategies are designed to assist individuals in generating original ideas. A number of these strategies originated in business, where new ideas are essential for maintaining a competitive edge. Most of these are based on divergent thinking, assuming that by producing many varied ideas, individuals are more likely to come up with more good ones. There is evidence that such strategies can be effective in assisting both children and adults in producing novel appropriate ideas; however, exactly why or under what circumstances they work is not always clear. It could be that some strategies mimic or stimulate the cognitive processes that underlie creativity; or, perhaps these strategies help to develop the attitudes or habits of mind that facilitate creativity: independence in judgment, willingness to explore multiple options, and persistence beyond the first idea. In any case, familiarity with strategies designed to enhance creative thinking provides individuals a set of tools to use as they explore their creative behaviors. Instead of sitting and waiting for the Muse to strike, students can use deliberate strategies to channel their thoughts in new directions.

Teaching the basic creative-thinking skills like brainstorming or SCAMPER would fit under this key (Starko, 2010). So would the teaching about inventors and inventions or analyzing biographies of creative individuals to find out how they generated ideas or dealt with discouragement. Explicit teaching of the importance of curiosity, strategies of problem-finding, or discussions about the importance of dealing with failure also would fit into this category.

Having tools, however, is not always sufficient. The practice of creative thinking does not automatically result in the transfer of such skills to other circumstances. It is imperative students be taught how to use them, when to use them, and under what circumstances they might be useful. Using creative-thinking tools in diverse circumstances can enhance the possibility that they will be seen, not as diversions, but as valuable approaches to life's dilemmas. One way to simultaneously teach the importance of transfer and maximize learning for understanding is to use creative-thinking strategies to process core content. For example, brainstorming is a strategy for generating ideas, useful in solving problems. There is little point in "brainstorming" things that are, for instance, the color red. That does not solve a problem. However, you could use brainstorming to generate alternative choices for a story character, or options a historical figure might have used to solve his dilemma in a different way. Such activities require thoughtful consideration of the content at hand as well as flexible thinking, with opportunities to develop both understanding and creativity.

How can librarians help? Be alert for books supportive of creative thinking. These might include any of the following.

- Books in which the characters solve problems in inventive ways can provide role models for creativity. Fictional characters such as *The Paper Bag Princess* (Munsch, 2002) and *Bud not Buddy* (Curtis, 1999), or even *The Great Brain* (Fitzgerald, 2004) and *Harriet the Spy* ((Fitzhugh, 2001) can inspire students' own inventiveness.

- Books in which young people find their creative voice can encourage students to find their own. For example, *Ish* (Reynolds, 2004) can be an example for students from six to 96. Books such as *Perfect Square* (Hall, 2011) could help students recognize that happiness can come amidst challenge and transformation, essential for young people who may feel a bit different in their creativity.

- Books that provide alternate points of view, for example, *The True Story of the Three Little Pigs* (Scieszka, 1996)—or even *Cinderella Skeleton* (San Souci, 2000), are good examples of flexible thinking. Students can also benefit from books that present multiple perspectives on historical events, from *George vs. George* (Schanzer, 2004) to *Everybody's Revolution* (Fleming, 2006) or for older students, Greenhaven Press's *Opposing Viewpoints in American History* series.

- Books about inventors and inventions, particularly inventions by young people, can inspire budding inventors. Be sure that the school library's collection is diverse and includes books and information about inventors who vary by race, gender, and culture so that students begin to understand the breadth and depth of human creativity.

- Biographies of creative people can provide examples both of creative thinking and of the challenges of the creative process. These can range from picture books like *Balloons over Broadway* (Sweet, 2011) to longer biographies. Autobiographical descriptions of the creative process, for example, *Honoring Our Ancestors* (Rohmer, 1999), can be particularly helpful. Again, approach the biographies with some caution. Avoid stories in which historical figures appear to have lived charmed and perfect lives. Understanding how creative people struggled with challenges is an essential lesson.

- Books that can be used to spur students' creativity can come in a myriad of forms. *If You're Hoppy* (Sayre, 2011) can be used to inspire students to create new song lyrics. *Little Paper Planes* (Jones, 2012) can be used to spark new paper planes or works of art. *Names for Snow* (Beach, 2003) can inspire metaphor; *The Aunts Go Marching* (Manning, 2003) can spur exploration with homophones whereas *12 Ways to Get 11* (Merriam, 1996) examines even computation in flexible ways. Books that present new creative forms with which students can experiment: reversible poetry from *Mirror Mirror* (Singer, 2010); delightful concrete poems can also be helpful from *Technically, It's Not My Fault* (Grandits, 2004).

You'll notice that most of my example books are picture books. Picture books are not just for young children. Their short length and high interest make them useful for teaching to all ages, from preschool to graduate school. Of course, the general principles and categories already listed are appropriate for books at all levels, websites, and other media. One of the greatest services librarians can provide teachers is to help them find such resources. Any time you find a book or web resource that helps the reader look at the world just a little differently, teachers who are trying to facilitate creativity would love you to share these resources with them.

KEY NO. 3: TEACH THE CREATIVE METHODOLOGIES OF THE DISCIPLINES

Creative individuals are creative in something. That is, Georgia O'Keefe was a creative artist. Scott Joplin was a creative musician. Steve Jobs was a creative inventor. Creativity does not exist in a vacuum, but in a discipline (or disciplines). The disciplines we teach in schools have grown as a result of the creative efforts of individuals working within them. One way we can help students both envision creativity, and develop their own, is to teach them how creativity operates in the disciplines we teach.

This means we must teach at least two key things. First, students must gain enough understanding of the major concepts, generalizations, and big ideas of the discipline to be able to question and explore knowledgeably. Second, they must learn the techniques and methodologies (as well as habits of mind) of creative individuals in the field. Whatever the content area, students must learn the kinds of problems that are explored in that area, how they are addressed, and how information is shared. Students of science must learn not just facts and rules, but how science works. Young writers must learn the kinds of questions and problems writers face, and how they address them. Of course, the level and sophistication of techniques used will vary enormously with grade level, but the general principle remains; if students are to work creatively in content areas, they must learn both the content and the methods of the subjects they study.

Perhaps the easiest way to envision this distinction is in history. Students learning history must learn the facts about what occurred, as well as generalizations that help them understand why the facts matter. However, they should also learn what historians do—for example, the difference between observations and inferences when they approach artifacts. Asking historical questions can begin in elementary grades with inquiries as simple as "How is being in first grade today similar or different from being in first grade when our parents were in school?" Such questions can be answered through eyewitness testimony (parent interviews) and perhaps even primary documents (family photographs, old report cards). Of course, older students can address more complex questions using a wider range of historical sources. There is a wealth of primary documents online, available for student inquiry in ways undreamed of just a few years ago. Understanding that new historical knowledge is generated in similar ways—and that it grows and changes, as sources are uncovered—is key to students' understanding of creativity in that field.

How can librarians help? There are two types of resources that are valuable when students are learning the creative methods of the disciplines. First, students need access to primary sources with which to learn and practice creative processes.

Depending on the field, this can mean online historical documents or print reproductions of primary artifacts. It may mean books demonstrating the writing processes of prominent authors. For example, I once had a reproduction of the original manuscript of Dickens' *A Christmas Carol*. Seeing the edits and changes in that document was a powerful demonstration of the importance of editing! In the sciences, students may need access to simulations, where the actual primary materials would be too expensive or dangerous. While there are many useful primary resources online, the sheer volume can be daunting. Helping teachers locate and use appropriate primary sources can be a huge service.

How-To Is Not Inquiry

The second type of resources is "how to" books/resources that teach students how to investigate and ask questions in various disciplines. These could include books about the scientific method, authors' advice on writing, or descriptions of strategies for analyzing artifacts. Again, be cautious. Beware of books that purport to teach students how to explore, but then proceed to tell them exactly how every experiment is supposed to turn out, or provide explicit directions for each poem or drawing. If an author tells me to put one plant in a sunny window and one in a cupboard, and then tells me the one in the cupboard will grow yellow and spindly, why should I carry out the experiment? I already know what will happen. This is not inquiry. This is not science. "Copy my drawings exactly" is not art.

In fact, a steady diet of such books can warp students' understanding of the discipline. I once was in a children's bookstore looking for books that would teach students to ask scientific questions and conduct investigations, but without providing the answer on the next page. The clerk asked if he could help me, and I explained my quest. I said I wanted the students to be able to work like real scientists, without having the answers in advance. The clerk looked puzzled. "But scientists know the answers," he said. Now, I looked puzzled. He continued. "Even in my college physics class (clearly his standard for advanced science!), we always knew the answers. Scientists just do the experiments to prove it." Needless to say, I stopped hoping for assistance. This young man's experiences in science classes had left him with an impression of inquiry that was more akin to following the directions on boxed macaroni and cheese than genuine science. Please, please help students find books that are based on science rather than macaroni.

Taken together, the three keys for creativity in the classroom can help students learn in ways that will support both in-depth learning and creative thinking. They also make teaching and learning more fun! Taking creative roads with students can never be boring because we never know exactly where they will lead. May you enjoy all your rambles!

REFERENCES

ALPs. (2012). Teaching for understanding introduction. Retrieved from http://learnweb .harvard.edu/ALPS/tfu/info.cfm.

Amabile, T. M. (1989). *Growing up creative*. New York: Crown.

Amabile, T. M. (1996). *Creativity in context: Update to the social psychology of creativity*. Boulder, CO: Westview.

Amabile, T. M. (2001). Beyond talent: John Irving and the passionate craft of creativity. *American Psychologist, 56*(4), 333–336.

Beach, J. K. (2003). *Names for snow.* New York: Hyperion Books for Children.

Bronson, P., & Merryman, A. (July 10, 2010). The creativity crisis. *Newsweek Magazine.* Retrieved from http://www.thedailybeast.com/newsweek/2010/07/10/the-creativity-crisis.html.

Chappuis, J., Stiggins, R., Chappuis, S., & Arter, J. (2012). *Classroom assessment for student learning: Doing it right using it well.* 2nd ed. New York: Pearson.

Curtis, C. P. (1999). *Bud not buddy.* New York: Yearling.

Fitzgerald, J. (2004). *The great brain.* New York: Puffin.

Fitzhugh, L. (2001). *Harriet the spy.* New York: Delcourt.

Fleming, T. (2006). *Everybody's revolution.* New York: Scholastic.

Grandits, J. (2004). *Technically, it's not my fault.* New York: Clarion Books.

Hall, M. (2011). *Perfect square.* New York: Greenwillow Books.

Jones, K. L. (2012). *Little paper planes.* San Francisco, CA: Chronicle Books.

Manning, M. J. (2003). *The aunts go marching.* Honesdale, PA: Boyds Mills Press.

Merriam, E. (1996). *12 ways to get 11.* New York: Aladdin Paperbacks.

Munsch, R. (2002). *The paper bag princess.* Buffalo, NY: Annick Press.

Platform and Rules Committee Republican Party of Texas. (2012). *2012 State Republican Party platform.* Retrieved from http://www.texasgop.org/about-the-party.

Reynolds, P. (2004). *Ish.* Somerville, MA: Candlewick Press.

Rohmer, H. (Ed.). (1999). *Our ancestors.* San Francisco, CA: Children's Book Press.

San Souci, R. D. (2000). *Cinderella skeleton.* New York: Voyager Books.

Sayre, A. P. (2011). *If you're hoppy.* New York: HarperCollins.

Schanzer, R. (2004). *George vs. George.* Washington, DC: National Geographic.

Scieszka, J. (1996). *The true story of the three little pigs.* New York: Puffin.

Singer, M. (2010). *Mirror mirror: A book of reversible poetry.* New York: Dutton Children's Books.

Starko, A. J. (2010). *Creativity in the classroom: Schools of curious delight.* New York: Routledge.

Stiggins, R. (2005). From formative assessment to assessment for learning: A path to success in standards-based schools. *Phi Delta Kappan, 87,* 4, 324–328.

Sweet, M. (2011). *Balloons over Broadway.* New York: Houghton Mifflin.

11

THE APPLICATION OF COMMON CORE STATE STANDARDS TO FOSTER CREATIVITY AND CURIOSITY

Carolyn Coil
Pieces of Learning

The Common Core State Standards (also known as the Common Core Standards or CCSS) result from an initiative begun by the states and coordinated by the National Governors Association Center for Best Practices (NGA Center) and the Council of Chief State School Officers (CCSSO). As of this writing, the CCSS are K–12 standards in English Language Arts (ELA) and mathematics. Literacy in history/social studies, science, and technical subjects are specifically addressed in the 6–12 Common Core State Standards. However, because the K–12 ELA standards focus heavily on informational texts, we could say that science and social studies are covered when students use informational texts in these subject areas throughout all grade levels in the CCSS.

These standards provide educators with wide latitude in both content and in ways to teach. The Common Core State Standards do not focus on specific content mastery. Instead, they rely on major concepts, ideas, and skills that direct students to use the content to examine questions, look at multiple issues, and find a variety of ways to solve problems. The CCSS were developed with the goal of defining the knowledge and skills students should have within their K–12 educational careers so that they will graduate from high school capable of succeeding in entry-level, credit-bearing academic college courses, and/or workforce-training programs (National Governors Association Center for Best Practices, Council of Chief State School Officers, 2010).

COMMON CORE STATE STANDARDS AND CREATIVE THINKING AND QUESTIONING

Because the CCSS are both general and conceptual in nature with broader curriculum application and a problem-solving focus, they can potentially lay the groundwork and provide the framework for higher-level thinking including creativity and curiosity in ways that lower-level test prep curricula never can. The CCSS should not lead to a regimented, scripted curriculum focusing on students passing standardized tests. Instead, they have the potential to provide opportunities for developing creativity through the integration of new ideas, technology, the arts, and higher-level questioning.

A better way to teach creative thinking is by using ill-structured problems representative of real-life situations in which there is no obvious answer. Ill-structured problems should be authentic and relevant to students (Howard, McGee, Shin, & Shia, 2001) and allow for numerous creative alternative solutions instead of one correct answer (Meacham & Emont, 1989). The CCSS provide many opportunities for students to use creative thinking as they discuss and find evidence-based solutions to ill-structured problems.

Common Core English Language Arts College and Career readiness (CCR) Anchor Standards at www.corestandards.org are K–12 standards that define what students should know and be able to do by the end of each grade level; these become more complex as students advance in grade levels. The Anchor Standards in Reading, Writing, and Speaking and Listening that I have used in the example lessons/units in this chapter are delineated in the text that follows.

Do not think that you are limited to these specific standards if you want to encourage creativity and curiosity! While certain CCSS were chosen for each lesson/ unit, nearly every unit of work that teachers develop could use a number of different Common Core ELA Anchor Standards. In the examples written for this chapter, I have made use of two for writing and two for reading that seem particularly appropriate in developing creativity through higher-level thinking and problem-solving:

Writing—Text Types and Purposes

Write narratives to develop real or imagined experiences or events using effective technique, well-chosen details, and well-structured event sequences.

Writing—Research to Build and Present Knowledge

Draw evidence from literary or informational texts to support analysis, reflection, and research.

Reading—Key Ideas and Details

Read closely to determine what the text says explicitly and make logical inferences from it; cite specific textual evidence when writing or speaking to support conclusions drawn from the text.

Reading—Integration of Knowledge and Ideas

Analyze how two or more texts address similar themes or topics in order to build knowledge or to compare the approaches the authors take.

Common Core State Standards and the Arts

A second way to foster creativity and curiosity using the CCSS is by integrating the arts into instruction in nearly all subject areas and disciplines. Arts integration can be defined as "an approach to teaching in which students construct and demonstrate understanding through an art form. Students engage in a creative process, which connects an art form and another subject area and meets evolving objectives in both" (Silverstein & Layne, 2010).

The arts provide multiple ways for students to make sense of what they learn (knowledge and comprehension), use what they learn (application), and create something new based on what they learn (creative synthesis). A Common Core Anchor Standard for Reading that can readily be used to develop creativity and curiosity through integrating the arts while reading both literary and informational texts is:

Reading—Integration of Knowledge and Ideas

Integrate and evaluate content presented in diverse media and formats, including visually and quantitatively, as well as in words.

This standard can be used when students examine pictures, graphics, maps, digital media, and so on and also when they create visual displays to illustrate their understanding of written text.

One Common Core Anchor Standard for Speaking and Listening that I use frequently in lessons involving creative presentations and project-based learning, whether the students are drawing, painting, sculpting, creating digital works of art, or using multi-media is as follows:

Speaking and Listening—Presentation of Knowledge and Ideas

Make strategic use of digital media and visual displays of data to express information and enhance understanding of presentations.

This standard increases in complexity as grade levels increase, but at each grade level it lends itself to arts integration, expression, and creative production.

Some educators wonder if creativity can be taught. In their book *Curiosita Teaching*, Shade and Shade (2011) state that when appropriate tools, techniques, methods, and strategies are used and practiced regularly, students' creativity can be greatly enhanced.

Tools: Questivities, Encounter Lessons, and SCAMPER

If it is indeed possible to encourage and increase creativity and also curiosity through CCSS, what tools can teachers use to plan and implement lessons that do this? In this chapter you will find three user-friendly lesson-planning formats that contain a number of strategies, techniques, and tools to encourage creative thinking and production with your students. These are:

- Questivities
- Encounter lessons
- SCAMPER.

For each, I explain what it is, how it is structured and written, and give suggestions for how to use and implement each in a classroom setting. I have also included an example of each that can be used as a guideline or outline for writing your own.

Tool No. 1 Questivities (Questioning Activities)

Questivities, an amalgam of *Questioning* and the word *Activities*, began in the early 1990s when educators at Pieces of Learning noticed that project activities that had the potential to engage students in higher levels of thinking and the development of creativity were often conducted too quickly and with too little thought on the student's part. Students often spent more time making an attractive product than they did in thinking critically or creatively about what they were learning through the activity (Coil, 2011). The introduction of the CCSS provides even more reason to emphasize students' higher levels of thinking as they complete short as well as more sustained research projects demonstrating an understanding of the topics being studied.

Questivities provide teachers with an excellent guideline in planning instruction and learning that emphasizes higher-level thinking. The Questivities format consists of a Project Activity based on one or more of the CCSS along with a series of Thinking Questions that stimulate creative and critical thinking and give practice in research skills. The questions are starter questions in which students engage before doing the project itself.

I find that students who use Questivities before beginning the Project Activity create projects that reflect higher levels of thinking, more creativity, and increased evidence of research. Questivities take students beyond just working on a project to thinking about the project ideas in more depth and greater detail.

Questivities can be done individually by students in order to enhance and extend their work and research, or with partners and in small groups. Teachers can require all students do Questivities in conjunction with a project in a differentiated unit of study.

Additionally, Questivities are useful for students who *compact* out of the regular curriculum. Curriculum Compacting (Reis & Renzulli, 2005) is a structured process to discover and record what students know before beginning a unit of study. Students who have mastered the material compact out, that is, they do not need to do the work to learn what they already know. Instead of doing the regular classroom work, these students work on other, more advanced activities. Questivities are excellent to use with such students.

Teachers can write Questivities for a unit of study or teach their students how to write and develop them for their own research projects. Questivities are assessed using mini-rubrics (small assessment checklists) or other performance assessment criteria.

Questivities are written on a user-friendly one-or-two page form that has the following elements:

- Project Activity, which provides the focus for the Questivities
- Common Core State Standards
- Assessment mini-rubric/checklist for the Project Activity
- Project Questions (essential questions answered through the Project Activity)
- Questivities Thinking Questions
- Active Question.

The **Questivities Thinking Questions** follow the following format:

1. List
2. Compare and contrast
3. What would happen if
4. Would you rather . . . and why
5. How would you feel if
6. Why
7. How.

I generally use the "List" question as a vehicle for brainstorming and opening the students' minds to multiple possibilities. Questions two to six broaden the students' thinking even more, with questions three, four, and five having the potential for eliciting the most creative answers. On the other hand, I usually use the "How" question to focus the student on how he will actually do the project activity.

The Active Question requires that students generate creative questions and innovative answers. Some students find this very challenging, especially students who always look for the one correct answer and think no further!

The Active Question is a personification question in this form:

Make a list of questions _____ might ask _____. (There is a developed Active Question in the next section.)

The blanks can be objects, persons, places, animals, or anything else that connects in some way to the topic. It is amazing to see the amount of knowledge, understanding, and creativity that is required to generate a list of such questions!

A sample Questivities lesson on masks follows (Coil, in press). Keep in mind that students answer the Thinking Questions and the Active Question before beginning the Project Activity. This lesson generates a great deal of thinking about the topic itself and through the Thinking Questions that help students see how the invisible masks worn by people in everyday life can hide the real self.

QUESTIVITIES—MASKS

Directions

Answer the Questivities Thinking Questions and the Active Question before beginning work on the Project Activity.

Project Activity

Create a mask of an important character from a literary text or a person you understand from an informational text. Make sure your mask shows the person's physical, mental, and emotional characteristics. Include quotes from the text on an index card that provide evidence of the person's traits.

COMMON CORE STATE STANDARDS

- Reading—Integration of Knowledge and Ideas

  Integrate and evaluate content presented in diverse media and formats, including visually and quantitatively, as well as in words.

- Writing—Research to Build and Present Knowledge

  Draw evidence from literary or informational texts to support analysis, reflection, and research.

- Speaking and Listening—Presentation of Knowledge and Ideas

  Make strategic use of digital media and visual displays of data to express information and enhance understanding of presentations.

Assessment Mini-Rubric/Checklist for the Project Activity

(This can be utilized by using checkmarks, pluses, and minuses or another type of point system.)

1. _____ Originality/creativity
2. _____ Likeness of mask to selected character or person
3. _____ Shows physical, mental, and emotional characteristics
4. _____ Size of a human face with appropriate colors and details
5. _____ Evidence for traits shown in mask is quoted from the text.

This checklist format for assessment usually works well in most classrooms. These criteria could also be the basis for criteria in a larger, more complex rubric if needed or desired.

Project Questions (Essential Questions that Will Be Answered during the Questivities and the Project Activity Process)

- What purposes do masks serve?
- Can masks show more than just physical characteristics?
- Why is it important to know people in more depth beyond surface traits?

Questivities Thinking Questions

1. List at least 10 significant reasons people might wear a mask.
2. Compare/contrast a mask and a hat.

3. What would happen if everyone wore a mask and never took it off? What would life be like?
4. Would you rather have everyone wear masks or everyone show their faces? Why?
5. How would you feel if you were forced to reveal everything about yourself?
6. Why is privacy valued? Do people sometimes wear masks that aren't visible in order to protect their privacy? Give some examples.
7. How are you going to create a mask that shows feelings and emotions as well as physical characteristics?

Active Question

Make a list of questions a *Halloween mask* might ask a *mask worn by a robber*.

Tool No. 2: Encounter Lessons

A second tool to encourage and enhance creativity is called an Encounter Lesson. These lessons contain open-ended questions that help students practice good listening skills, stimulate curiosity, creativity, and higher-level thinking, and also provide motivation for all students. They are often used at the beginning of a unit of study but can also be used after students have preliminary information about the topic. At the beginning, Encounter lessons help the teacher to personalize the topic for the students and open up discussion in a nonthreatening way (Coil, 2007). At the end of a unit the Encounter Lesson is a creative way for students to review what they have learned. When done at the end of a unit, the Encounter Lesson has no differentiated extenders. Differentiated Extenders are the bulk of the unit activities and are used as the means for students to learn the material in a variety of different ways. We will discuss these in greater depth later in the chapter.

Creativity is fostered when students are forced to think differently to come up with answers to the Boundary Breaker and the Leading Questions. The Leading Questions in an Encounter Lesson generally initiate the deeper thinking because the student cannot simply answer those questions by reading the correct answer from the book. Often these are ill-structured questions and nearly always they require a creative answer using original and elaborative thinking. The CCSS used in Encounter Lessons can vary, depending on the topic and the student's choice of extenders, which range in difficulty and can be chosen or assigned according to ability or interest. Extenders often involve project and performance-based learning that has the potential to foster creativity. In general when students must do an original skit, podcast, PowerPoint, or any number of other original projects or performances, creativity is present in some form. These provide the vehicle for thinking more flexibly and openly.

Excluding the extenders, Encounter Lessons usually last from 20 to 30 minutes and are best done in small heterogeneous groups of five students per group. Encounter Lessons have open-ended questions that ask the student to pretend she is an object, a place, or a famous person and respond accordingly.

An Encounter Lesson begins with a Boundary Breaker where each student shares something about himself in response to the question being asked. There are five Leading Questions in an Encounter Lesson. Each student in the group answers one question in round-robin fashion. The answer to the second question is based upon what was said in answer to the first question. Therefore, Encounter Lessons are excellent for building listening skills and fast-paced emergent and divergent thinking (for further information about types of thinking see chapter four).

STRUCTURING AND WRITING
AN ENCOUNTER LESSON

Title:

The title should reflect the major theme or focus of the lesson.

Common Core State Standards:

List the Common Core State Standards that will be addressed by the Leading Questions and/or the extenders.

Boundary Breaker:

This is an easily answered nonthreatening question that usually reveals something about each student's interests, feelings, or opinions.

Setting the Stage:

This sets the scene for the questions. The group facilitator sets the stage, and group members decide which person, place, or object to pretend to be.

Leading Questions:

1. This is the description question. In answering this question, the person should describe something.
2. This question asks for a reason and usually begins with the word *Why*.
3. This is the storytelling question. In answering this question, the person should tell a story or relate an imaginary incident that has happened.
4. This is the motto, slogan, or message question. The answer to this question should be short—usually 10 words or less.
5. The answer to this question shows some kind of change or transformation. It may be phrased as a "*What would happen if?*" question, an "*imagine*" question, or a question that reflects a new point of view.

Differentiated Extenders:

The extenders are the activities in the unit of work itself. There is no limit to the number of extenders an Encounter Lesson may have. These activities can be required for everyone, chosen by students, or chosen by the teacher for individual students. The extenders could take anywhere from one or two days to several weeks to complete, depending upon the number each student has to do, and how extensive each is.

An example of an Encounter Lesson, Ancient Structures and Geometric Figures, follows (Coil, in press). You can use the same format and pattern to write your own.

Encounter Lesson–Ancient Structures and Geometric Figures

Title: Geometry and the Ancients

COMMON CORE STATE STANDARDS

- Geometry—reason with shapes and their attributes
- Writing—research to build and present knowledge

  Draw evidence from literary or informational texts to support analysis, reflection, and research.

- Reading—integration of knowledge and ideas

  Integrate and evaluate content presented in diverse media and formats, including visually and quantitatively, as well as in words.

- Reading—integration of knowledge and ideas

  Analyze how two or more texts address similar themes or topics in order to build knowledge or to compare the approaches the authors take.

Boundary Breaker:

Speak about a structure that you have seen in person or looked at in a book, video, or online that is unusual or unique and is at least 100 years old.

Setting the Stage:

Pretend you are an ancient (at least 2,000 years old) edifice such as Stonehenge, an Incan fortress, an Egyptian pyramid, the Great Wall of China, the library at Ephesus, the Roman Coliseum, or another such structure. (Note: To do this activity, students need some background knowledge of ancient structures. Use several appropriate informational texts to provide this knowledge.)

Leading Questions:

1. What structure are you? Describe how you looked when you were first erected. Describe some geometric figures that are a part of you.
2. Why do you think it is difficult for people living in the 21st century to determine your original purpose and/or the methods used to construct you?

3. Tell a story of something interesting, scary, or exciting that has happened to you over the years.
4. What slogan can you come up with that praises one of the geometric figures used to build you?
5. How would modern structures be different if they were constructed using the methods of the ancient culture that constructed you?

DIFFERENTIATED EXTENDERS

1. Write a short story set in ancient times at your chosen structure. Use your imagination and creative words to describe the structure. Be historically accurate but also creative as the plot unfolds.
2. Research how anthropologists study structures built by ancient peoples to determine information about these civilizations. Present what you learn in a creative way. For example, present a skit, write a blog, do a podcast, or design a PowerPoint presentation or slide show. View portions of the "Nova" Miniseries, *Secrets of Lost Empires*. Write 10 questions that are posed by this series. Select one question, and use other sources to find possible answers.
3. View the information about this program on the PBS website, www.pbs. org. Make a plan detailing how you would uncover another ancient secret if you had the funding to do it. Include maps or charts as well as writing what you would do.
4. Paint a mural featuring an ancient structure of your choice. Include as many details as you can to show the area and the people of that time. Embed descriptive phrases from informational texts into your mural that describe in words what you are showing visually.

Tool No. 3: SCAMPER

SCAMPER, a strategy originally developed by Bob Eberle in the early 1980s, is an acronym for words describing seven different-thinking techniques to spark creativity and generate ideas for problem-solving (Eberle, 1996). See chapter two for additional information about SCAMPER. In essence, SCAMPER is a general-purpose checklist with idea-spurring questions—which is both easy to use and surprisingly powerful. SCAMPER is based on the notion that most creative-thinking results in modifications of things that already exist. While many people think of creativity as being only original thinking, this is an incorrect assumption. Creativity is also the elaboration and association of existing ideas and products. In the 1950s Guilford identified four elements of creativity—fluency, flexibility, originality, and elaboration (New World Book Encyclopedia, n. d.), and SCAMPER is designed to help students think creatively in all four of these areas.

Using SCAMPER as a guide, you or your students can develop higher-level thinking questions and ideas on any topic. SCAMPER can provide teachers with the means for generating questions. It can also be used by students as a vehicle for demonstrating higher levels of thinking in their writing, discussions, and performances. Below are the letters that make up SCAMPER along with some general questions and guidelines for each. Use these questions to assist you in thinking creatively as you plan your SCAMPER lessons.

Following this list, you will find a sample SCAMPER lesson on the Trail of Tears (Coil, in press). Notice how the CCSS are combined with creative thinking throughout the lesson's activities.

SCAMPER MEANS . . .

S—SUBSTITUTE

- Who else or what else instead?
- Can you remove one thing and replace it with something or someone else?
- What other ingredients, materials, processes, places, or approaches could you use?
- Can you change the tone of voice or point of view and substitute another?
- Can the setting or time period be changed to another setting or time period?

C—COMBINE

- Can something be blended, made into an assortment, or ensemble?
- Can you combine units, shapes, sizes, or colors?
- Can two different people or groups be combined to work for the same purposes?
- Can ideas be combined?
- What new characters can be made by combining traits of two or more existing characters?

A—ADAPT

- What else is similar to this?
- How could you change this in a small way?
- Does the past offer a parallel? Can you take an idea from the past and use it now?
- Could small changes be made so that this could be used/viewed in other ways?

M—MODIFY

- How can you change the meaning, color, motion, sound, odor, form, shape, plot, characters, setting, or theme?
- What can you add to make this different?
- Can you change the timing by having more time, less time or greater frequency?
- Can it become stronger, higher, longer, thinner, thicker, larger, or smaller?
- How can you give this extra value?
- Should another ingredient or element be added?
- Can something be duplicated, multiplied or exaggerated?

P—PUT TO OTHER USE

- Can you think of new ways to use this as it is?
- Are there other potential uses if it were modified?

- Are there other places to use it?
- Could other people or groups benefit from it?

E —Eliminate

- What could be eliminated?
- What could be condensed or made smaller?
- What could be miniature instead of full size?
- Could something be lower, shorter, or lighter?
- How could something be streamlined?
- How could superfluous words be eliminated?
- Could words be eliminated and pictures or digital images used instead?

R—Rearrange/Reverse

- Could components be interchanged?
- Could there be another pattern, layout, or sequence?
- Could cause and effect be transposed?
- How could the schedule, pace, or time sequence be reversed?
- Is there a way to transpose positive and negative?
- Can you use opposites or antonyms?
- Is there a way to turn it backward or counterclockwise?

SCAMPER—TRAIL OF TEARS

COMMON CORE STATE STANDARDS

- Reading—key ideas and details

  Read closely to determine what the text says explicitly and make logical inferences from it; cite specific textual evidence when writing or speaking to support conclusions drawn from the text.

- Writing—text types and purposes

  Write narratives to develop real or imagined experiences or events using effective technique, well-chosen details, and well-structured event sequences.

- Writing—research to build and present knowledge

  Draw evidence from literary or informational texts to support analysis, reflection, and research.

- Speaking and listening—presentation of knowledge and ideas

  Make strategic use of digital media and visual displays of data to express information and enhance understanding of presentations.

Background Activity:

Students will read at least three informational texts about the Trail of Tears and take notes. Informational texts may vary and can include the grade-level textbook, Internet articles, library books on the Cherokees, paintings, maps, cartoons, information from historical markers along the Trail of Tears, and so on. Afterwards, students will discuss the information found and read.

SCAMPER Activity:

Students will work in pairs using their knowledge of the Trail of Tears and their creative imaginations to answer the SCAMPER questions about this historical event. Each pair will write their answers to share with the class. Whenever possible, students should support their creative answers with evidence from the informational texts they have read.

Materials: Informational texts, notes, pencil, paper, markers, or other drawing tools.

Substitute: What might have happened if the white settlers had walked the Trail of Tears instead of the Cherokee? Brainstorm ways history would have been different, and how attitudes might have changed.

Combine: Could the Trail of Tears have been avoided if both the Creeks and Cherokees had banded together? Why or why not?

Adapt: How might Cherokee history been different if they had adapted to the life of the white settlers and given up their Cherokee language, land, and customs?

Modify: How do you think the Trail of Tears would have ended differently if the 20 Cherokees who had signed the treaty agreeing to give up their land had not done so?

Put to Other Use: Identify an object that was important to the Cherokees during their journey on the Trail of Tears. How did they use this object? Draw a picture or diagram of five other creative ways this object could have been used.

Eliminate: Write a story, song, or poem that imagines what might have happened to the Cherokees if the Trail of Tears journey had never taken place.

Rearrange/Reverse: Even though the Cherokees were forced to leave their land, what if, instead, they had secretly devised a plan for all of them to stay? Describe in writing the details of this plan, and how this plan would be carried out.

Concluding Activity:

Divide the class into groups representing one of the SCAMPER letters. Members of each group will share the work they did during the SCAMPER activity that focused on the group's assigned letter. Each group will synthesize all of the information and present their answers, ideas and conclusions in a creative way.

For more information to teach for creativity, log onto my website (www.car olyncoil.com) and click on "Carolyn's Blogs." Scroll down to vol. 2, no. 5. for an explanation of Criteria Cards and a PDF file of some samples. In addition, in vol. 2, there is an article on Curriculum Compacting, the strategy I referenced earlier.

CONCLUSION

In this chapter, I have discussed the importance of fostering creativity and curiosity but also provided practical, standards-based lesson-planning formats teachers can use to do this. The CCSS with their emphasis on breadth, depth, and higher-level thinking skills are exemplary vehicles to creative practice in the classroom.

The three formats I have shown in this chapter can be adapted to any grade level or content area. Each is structured in such a way to make it easy to use the standards while fostering creative thinking and production. It is my hope that these formats can be used with students to develop and enhance their creative skills.

REFERENCES

Coil, C. (2007). *Successful teaching in the differentiated classroom.* Marion, IL: Pieces of Learning.

Coil, C. (2011). *Differentiated activities and assessments using the Common Core.* Marion, IL: Pieces of Learning.

Coil, C. (in press). *Creativity x 4.* Marion, IL: Pieces of Learning.

Eberle, B. (1996). *Scamper: Creative games and activities for imagination development.* Waco, TX: Prufrock Press.

Howard, B., McGee, S., Shin, N, & Shia, R (2001). The triarchic theory of intelligence and computer-based inquiry learning. *Educational technology research and development, 49*(4), 49–69.

Guilford, J.P. (n.d.). In *New World Book Encyclopedia.* Retrieved from http://www.new worldencyclopedia.org/entry/J._P._Guilford.

Meacham, J.A., & Emont, N.M. (1989). The interpersonal basis of everyday problem solving. In J.D. Sinnott (Ed.), *Everyday problem solving: Theory and applications* (pp. 7–23). New York: Praeger.

National Governors Association Center for Best Practices, Council of Chief State School Officers. (2010). *Common Core State Standards. National Governors Association Center for Best Practices.* Washington, DC: Council of Chief State School Officers.

Questivities series. (1994). Marion, IL: Pieces of Learning.

Reis, S., & Renzulli, J. (2005). *Curriculum compacting.* Austin, TX: Prufrock Press.

Shade, P., & Shade, R. (2011). *Curiosita teaching.* Marion, IL: Pieces of Learning.

Silverstein, L.B., & Layne, S. (2010). *What is arts integration?* Washington, DC: The John F. Kennedy Center for the Performing Arts.

12

THE POTENTIAL OF TECHNOLOGY TO FOSTER CREATIVITY

Brian C. Housand
East Carolina University

Let me begin by clearing up several common misconceptions. Technology by *itself* is not going to revolutionize or save education. Likewise, technology by *itself* has little chance to significantly foster creativity. That being said, emerging research from Nicholas Negroponte's One Laptop per Child (OLPC) project demonstrated that illiterate first-grade–aged children living in remote villages in Ethiopia, who had no experience with computers, or educational programs, could teach themselves the alphabet in a matter of two weeks. Over the course of five months, these children circumvented OLPC's lockdown of the computer's desktop settings and activated the camera. Ed McNierney, OLPC's chief technology officer, was astonished that these

> kids had completely customized the desktop—so every kids' tablet looked different. We had installed software to prevent them from doing that, and the fact they worked around it was clearly the kind of creativity, the kind of inquiry, the kind of discovery that we think is essential to learning. (Talbot, 2012, para. 7)

See chapter 13 to read about Migata Sutra's similar Hole-in-the-Wall experiments.

At the beginning of the 21st century, education in the United States has focused primarily on having students demonstrate minimum competency of content standards on state mastery tests. Meanwhile, the world has become increasingly complex and riddled with problems requiring the highest level of thinking, creativity, and innovation for their solution. Instead of nurturing creativity and critical thinking, educators have focused on content mastery as a measure of success. Sternberg (2007) suggested we are running the risk of creating a generation of "walking encyclopedias" unable to think creatively or critically. It is possible now to retrieve almost any fact and most information from digital information devices, or DIDs. With the advent and widespread availability of this technology the need to shift focus to the utilization of information from simple content mastery has arrived. Quite simply, if students can google answers, then teachers may be asking the wrong types of questions.

Indeed, this is not a new idea. *Taxonomy of Educational Objectives* by Bloom, Engelhart, Furst, Hill, & Krathwohl (1956) is often heralded as a sacred tome of education espousing the virtues of higher-order thinking skills that have been the subject of professional development for the past 50 years. Yet, there is a general neglect of evaluating these skills in our students.

In *Future Shock* (1970), the pioneering examination of the future effects of technology, Alvin Toffler quoted Herbert Gerjuay regarding education in the 21st century: "Tomorrow's illiterate will not be the man who can't read; he will be the man who has not learned how to learn" (p. 414). Gerjuay emphasized that education must teach the individual

> how to classify and reclassify information, how to evaluate its veracity, how to change categories when necessary, how to move from the concrete to the abstract and back, how to look at problems from a new direction—how to teach himself. (p. 414)

In the second decade of the 21st century, new standards and frameworks are emphasizing teaching and assessing critical thinking. For example, the Framework for 21st Century Learning created by the Partnership for 21st Century Skills (http://www.p21.org) emphasizes the four Cs of Learning and Innovation Skills: Critical Thinking, Communication, Collaboration, and Creativity in addition to the three Rs—reading, writing, and arithmetic

Likewise the National Educational Technology Standards for Students (NETS-S) from the International Society for Technology in Education (http://www.iste.org/standards) emphasizes the importance of skills and application rather than content. NETS-S (2007) is comprised of six strands to increase students' ability to effectively utilize technology for a variety of purposes. The six strands are as follows: Creativity and Innovation; Communication and Collaboration; Research and Information Fluency; Critical Thinking, Problem-Solving, and Decision Making; Digital Citizenship; and Technology Operations and Concepts.

By 2012, 45 states had formally adopted the Common Core State Standards (CCSS) thus signifying an important shift to the application of knowledge through higher-order thinking from content-based driven pedagogy. The primary purpose of the CCSS is to prepare American students for college and the workforce; the need to nurture creativity and critical thinking is obvious. In addition, the CCSS require students to successfully utilize a variety of technology tools to demonstrate competency of skills. For example, CCSS Anchor Standard no. 6 for writing requires students use technology, including the Internet, to produce and publish writing and to interact and collaborate with others.

Even though Marc Prensky (2001) coined the term digital natives for their willingness (for the most part) to adapt to technology that has fundamentally changed the way these natives process information, there is little to suggest they choose to use technology just because it is technology. Typically, natives use technology because it can do something for them. For example, I have witnessed students avoid *Study Island*, a computer-based test practice website because it is perceived as not helpful. A mistake educators make is thinking that if it is technology, kids will be attracted to it. Technology by itself is neither motivating to students nor educationally valuable (Housand & Housand, 2012). Instead, the value of technology to new millennium learners occurs when it is woven throughout their educational experiences (Pedro, 2006) and becomes part of normal day-to-day functioning.

While some are tempted to criticize technology and the Internet for its potential to dumb down students (Carr, 2010) and video games to zap student creativity (Kim, 2011), empirical evidence does not support these claims. Johnson (2005) believed that media and technology may actually be making us smarter by increasing intellectual demands. Before we demonize technology for the ills of this generation, perhaps a close look at the educational system and its pedagogical practices is warranted.

THE NEED TO FOSTER CREATIVITY

In 2006, Sir Ken Robinson recorded a now infamous talk at the annual TED Conference. TED began as an annual gathering of some of our generation's greatest minds who were challenged to synthesize their ideas into an 18-minute talk. Each talk is video-recorded and posted online at http://www.ted.com for the world to view. In his Ted talk, Ken Robinson blamed schools for killing creativity and suggested that schools routinely stigmatized and squelched student creativity: "We don't grow into creativity, we grow out of it. Or rather, we get educated out of it." Robinson believes we are living in an age where creativity is as important as literacy.

The previously described discovery by Ethiopian children who had never been subjected to schooling supports Robinson's TED talk statements about creativity. Perhaps we need to focus on ways to help children remain creative, curious, and open to mistakes. Perhaps we should consider how to create meaningful links between the personal proclivity of students to utilize technology and the ways in which we ask students to use technology in schools. The purpose of this chapter is to offer one potential model for uniting students, educators, and technology for the explicit purpose of promoting creative productivity.

WALLAS' FOUR STAGES OF CREATIVITY

Although there is no shortage of theories and conceptions about the creative process, technology is rarely part of these discussions. Rather than propose a new framework that integrates creativity and technology, I utilize Graham Wallas' four stages of the creative process: preparation, incubation, illumination, and verification. In *Art of Thought* (1926), Wallas was first to identify a model that identified the *process* of creativity. Each stage is discussed later with examples of how technology can be meaningfully integrated.

Preparation

In the preparation stage, the learner defines a problem and gathers necessary information. By understanding a particular subject or artistic medium, the learner prepares herself to manipulate information and possibly construct new knowledge. Teachers of reading might consider this building background knowledge whereas others might compare this stage to the teaching of methodological or how-to skills.

The Internet offers a wealth of resources and information on any topic imaginable. However, educators often mistakenly equate students' predisposition to technology with the ability to successfully navigate the Internet. Reading online is not the same experience as reading traditional texts, and students who are identified as the best class readers as measured by standardized tests may not be the best readers in online environments (Leu, et al., 2007). As a result of the digital environment in which they are situated, there exists a set of New Literacies that differ from traditional literacies (Leu, Kinzer, Coiro, & Cammack, 2004). If we expect students to successfully employ the Internet and its resources, then we must consider ways to teach these skills.

According to the New Literacies framework (Leu, et al., 2007), when using the Internet students must first *identify important questions* and generate the terms [key words] to insert into the search engine. Second, students *locate the information* they are seeking by reading the search results page, clicking on the appropriate links, and navigating a variety of websites. Third, students *critically evaluate* the information found on the Internet to verify it authenticity and reliability. Fourth, students *synthesize information* to determine whether or not the material found matches their needs. Finally, students *communicate answers* digitally and technologically to various audiences such as teachers and peers. Rather than assuming that digital natives can follow the New Literacies Framework, we should work to specifically teach Internet search skills.

One tool, I propose, is Google's free instructional modules (http://www.powersearchingwithgoogle.com) that are a series of six lessons offering specific strategies and tips to increase searching effectiveness. Google's instructional modules are appropriate for middle and high school students. In addition, Google offers a collection of resources and lessons for K–12 educators (http://www.google.com/insidesearch/searcheducation). One of the most intriguing resources is *A Google a Day* (http://www.agoogleaday.com), daily trivia questions requiring multiple-step Internet searching. This resource is engaging to students and provides educators opportunities to equip students with strategies for conducting superior searches while helping students to hone their Internet searching ability.

A second tool is Wonderopolis (http://wonderopolis.org) that offers students a daily point to ponder. Each day a question is posed, an activity provided, a set of vocabulary words presented, and further exploration suggested. These prompts spur curiosity and inspire students to pursue new areas of interest.

Preparation is a crucial first step in the creative process that allows students to explore a world of possibilities. Internet technologies, particularly mobile devices, afford us opportunities to have all of our quandaries resolved in the moment. By teaching students new literacies, they will be better prepared for creative productivity.

Incubation

While most theories of creativity focus entirely on the act or process of creating, Wallas (1926) emphasized moments when the creator is not acting or even directly thinking about the project itself. Wallas encouraged a period of incubation or detachment from the creative objective as a means of stimulating thought and reflection. No doubt you have worked on a solution to a problem, but only after stepping away from the project did the solution occur. Incubation, Wallas believed, was the stage that ultimately led to creativity. Meanwhile in schools, we are working to maximize instructional time while minimizing opportunities for student reflection and incubation.

Yet, children crave time to play. Vygotsky (1978) argued that play is an essential part of a child's psychological development. Today, many youth experience play in the form of video games. As McGonigal (2011) points out, the younger the child the more likely he is to be a gamer. Video game play is reported by 97 percent of boys and 94 percent of girls under the age of 18. It is perhaps shocking to learn that the average young person plays approximately 10,000 hours of video games by the age of 21 (McGonigal, 2011), which is the amount of time needed to develop expertise. In the *Outliers*, Malcolm Gladwell (2008) repeatedly pointed out that 10,000 hours is generally considered the amount of time one must invest in learning and serious practice to become an expert at something (Ericsson, Krampe, & Tesch-Römer, 1993). Chapter five contains further information about the 10,000-hour rule. Students need time and practice—not afforded by many schools, to become "mini-c" experts, the foundation for more significant creations.

Gee (2003) offers a compendium of 36 learning principles, and one is the benefit of playing video games. To be a successful gamer, one must exert a great deal of effort in problem-solving and devote attention to repeatedly practicing skills. Gamers learn to navigate a variety of digital environments where the meaning of signs and symbols are situated and contextualized while learning to develop multiple pathways for accomplishing very specific goals; all of this is done in the name of play. By comparison, school environments may seem too abstracted and ill defined.

In 2012, the Smithsonian American Art Museum's exhibit, The Art of Video Games, recognized video games as a viable art form. Guests entering the exhibit encountered Nolan Bushnell's, the founder of Atari, quote: "Video games foster the mindset that allows creativity to grow." This notion is supported by the Jackson et al. (2012) study of 491 12-year olds who associated increased videogame-playing with greater creativity. Interestingly, the type of video game played did not matter. Unlike videogame play, computer, Internet, and cell phone use were not statistically related to creativity.

While I am not suggesting schools be turned into arcades, a great deal can be learned from video game design. As students play games, perhaps they can dissect the experience and think about creating their own games. This is precisely the idea behind Gamestar Mechanic (http://gamestarmechanic.com). Initial development of the product was supported by a grant from the John D. and Catherine T. MacArthur Foundation and is a project of the Institute of Play. Designed for students aged seven to 14, children start out playing a game, but after learning the basics, they transition from game player to game designer. The learning experience is scaffolded to support students in their struggle to create through a wealth of resources and support materials designed for educators.

The idea of students designing their own video games is supported through the annual National STEM (science, technology, engineering, and mathematics) Video Game Challenge (http://www.stemchallenge.org/). Middle and high school students create video games that promote STEM. This challenge promotes the important skills required in game, which include creativity, critical thinking, and decision making—the very skills our country needs to succeed and compete in this global economy.

A variety of tools and resources are recommended for the National STEM Video Game Challenge. These include the previously mentioned Gamestar Mechanic as well as free programming tools such as Scratch (http://scratch.mit.edu/). Scratch is a free downloadable program that introduces students of all ages to computer programming. Developed by the Lifelong Kindergarten Group at the Massachusetts Institute of Technology, Boston, MA, Media Lab, the Scratch interface consists of blocks of instructions that programmers click together to make characters, or sprites, move on the screen and interact with one another. Programmers are encouraged to share their creations with the online community. For educators, ScratchED (http://scratched.media.mit.edu/) provides numerous resources and support materials.

While it is one thing to play a video game, it is entirely different to design a game. By offering students the opportunity to design and construct their own video games or applications, educators are building on students' seemingly inherent interest in gaming that helps them transition from incubation into illumination.

Illumination

Wallas' (1926) stage of illumination is the moment of discovery, a sudden, epiphany-like affirmation—the metaphoric light bulb of thought turning on. For our purposes, illumination represents the transition from the mental musings and meanderings of thinking represented in the preparation and incubation stages to tangible products created with technology. Rather than considering technology or computers as only information devices or word processors, Resnick (2006) suggested we think of computers as paintbrushes capable of allowing users to create new and imaginative works of art. A multitude of creative products are ripe for exploration; we will focus on three types represented by a click, a flash, and a bang.

CLICK—Interactive Posters

Perhaps as long as there have been school reports, there have been poster projects. The idea of physically using a pair of scissors and a glue stick seems like a 20th century construct in the age of online media and digital images. Glogster EDU (http://edu.glogster.com/) brings the poster project into the current century and offers students an intuitive interface for creating by dragging and dropping images and media. Glogster offers a wide variety of stock images, backgrounds, and layouts, but it also allows users to insert additional images, videos, and audio files. Consider the value of students creating bi-GLOG-raphies of historical figures or even Glog book reports or science projects that incorporate existing online media and illustrate the content being studied.

Similarly, Prezi (http://prezi.com/) allows students and teachers to escape mundane PowerPoint reports by creating interactive online presentations. Rather than PowerPoint's linear movement, Prezi provides choice in presentation order. Similar to Glogster, users insert images, audio, and video found on the Internet or uploaded to the site.

As you and your students transition from traditional to dimensional surfaces and dynamic, interactive online spaces, we should also provide instruction and emphasize the importance of design. In *A Whole New Mind* (2005), Daniel Pink identified design as one of six essentials for success in the Conceptual Age; he contends that products must be functional and well designed. Because students may not understand or practice good design, it is important that educators instruct and model good practice and design.

FLASH—Photography

In 2012, a significant shift in the world of photography occurred when the Kodak film company filed for bankruptcy and Facebook, three months later, purchased Instagram (http://instagram.com/). These events signified the death of photographic film thus establishing digital as the preferred medium for photography. Although the idea of using cameras in school is not new, their widespread availability in almost every digital device and the ability to take an almost unlimited amount of photographs has made photography a realistic product option to explore.

A basic Internet search reveals countless numbers of daily photo challenges that could be adapted easily for use with students. Building on the maxim that a picture is worth a 1,000 words, having students create narratives through photography is a liberating experience. Likewise, photography could help students capture emotions or experiences they find difficult to express linguistically. For example, teachers can ask students to use photography to portray emotions such as happiness or confusion, or capture images that represent big ideas or universal concepts such as change and power that provide a scaffold for discussing words.

One strategy for more advanced storytelling with photographs is to impose a structure, or constraint, such as to tell a story in five frames; each frame serves a specific purpose. The first frame establishes the characters and location. In the second frame students create a situation with possibilities of what might happen. Next, characters could be involved in the established situation. The fourth frame builds to a probable outcome. The fifth and final frame would have a logical, but surprising ending. To understand the five-frame concept and what can be accomplished, view the story of Humpty Dumpty in this Flickr Photo Group (http://bit.ly/hd-five).

BANG—Music

We are in the midst of a musical revolution that is allowing anyone with a computer or digital device to create, record, edit, and publish music. Although the iPod put a thousand songs in our pockets, initially the iPod was no more than a very small stereo. Resnick (1996) suggested we think of computers and technology more like pianos and less like stereos. Stereos play music created by others, but computers allow for the creation of new music as does a piano.

We have come a long way from the Casio keyboards of the 1980s. Now almost every computer device is capable of playing music. Perhaps the most widely available and powerful tool for musical creativity is Apple's GarageBand available for the Mac (http://www.apple.com/ilife/garageband/) and the iPad or iPhone (https://itunes.apple.com/us/app/garageband/id408709785?mt=8). This app comes complete with a variety of digital instruments including keyboards, guitars, and percussion, and GarageBand is equivalent to a portable recording studio capable of recording and editing multiple tracks at the same time.

For students who are musically inclined, Smule (http://www.smule.com/) offers a wide variety of musical applications to allow users to quickly and easily manipulate sounds into songs. One such app, MadPad (http://www.smule.com/

madpad) allows users to record environmental sounds and use them to create musical compositions and percussion loops.

Metaphorically, Android tablets, iPod Touches, and iPhones represent Swiss Army Knives of Creativity. Each digital device is filled with tools, gadgets, and apps designed for the purpose of promoting and supporting creativity. As educators, our job is to encourage students to explore the uses of these digital devices and provide creative purposes for doing so.

Verification

Wallas' (1926) final stage is verification, a time that the creative product or process is performed. In this Internet age, the process of sharing with a global audience has become as easy as clicking a button. At one time, students' creative products might have been seen only by teachers, presented for classes, or at best displayed in the school library. Typically with an increase in audience size, a student's motivation to create a higher-quality product increases. It is possible now for students to display their work online for the entire world to see. As a result of this incredible power, educators should encourage students to become "Googleable" by developing online digital portfolios that represent their best work and greatest accomplishments. Likewise, educators could model these behaviors by creating professional websites to highlight student accomplishments. Of course, follow the directives of your school district regarding student use of email and other tools that could become safety issues. Teach students about Internet safety.

One possible way to achieve this is to "dot com" yourself. While website creation was once a complicated process involving programming and computer languages, this is no longer the case. Weebly (http://education.weebly.com/) is one of the easiest ways to create and publish a well-designed and fully functioning website in a matter of minutes. Weebly features hundreds of templates and design layouts to choose from. The user interface utilizes a simple drag and drop functionality that requires no knowledge of coding or programming. Educators can develop a class site for their students to edit and publish individual pages. As students apply to schools and for scholarships and internships, you can be assured that someone somewhere will be googling this student's name. Should we not enable students to develop a digital portfolio that represents their capabilities and accomplishments?

Additionally, the Internet provides students opportunities to connect with others through a variety of social media. While I am not recommending that all students and teachers befriend one another on Facebook, I suggest we explore with students ways to effectively and responsibly create Personal Learning Networks. Instead of being confused or even outraged at students' online behaviors, we should provide students opportunities to develop and practice good digital citizenship in safe learning environments. One tool created specifically for educational social networks is Edmodo (http://www.edmodo.com/). With its similar look and feel to Facebook, educators create assignments, quizzes, polls, and discussion groups for students and parents that are private to the specific group and do not require email addresses.

While not designed specifically for educational purposes, sites like Shelfari (http://www.shelfari.com/) and Goodreads (http://www.goodreads.com/) are social networks built around individual's virtual bookshelves. Either tool allows students to view their classmates' reading lists while learning and practicing responsible social network participation. By promoting these virtual sandboxes of digital citizenship, students verify their ideas and creativity worldwide.

CONCLUSION

As I stated at the beginning of this chapter, technology by itself does not foster creativity or promote student learning. However, technology does offer new opportunities to explore the creative process. In this chapter, I have described particular apps and programs useful to the integration of technology into the creative process. What consistently rings true is that individuals become invested in learning and doing when it is meaningful and personal. Children have a natural curiosity and inquisitive nature that needs to be celebrated and encouraged. As John Dewey (1938) wrote, "The whole process of education should thus be conceived as the process of learning to think through the solution of real problems." What are the real problems that your students want to solve?

Perhaps education should follow the Google model whereby its employees devote 20 percent of their workweek investigating a problem or creative product of personal interest. Imagine how different schools and learning would be if this Google model were adopted.

Now that we are fully situated in the second decade of the 21st century, the question is no longer if we are going to use technology, but how to use these changing technologies. To prepare students for the future, we can no longer deny them access to technology while in school. Let us switch our focus because today's technologies are unbelievably powerful tools for educators to foster creativity through educationally relevant experiences.

The missing link is educators who understand how creativity is fostered and help students participate in today's digital society. We are in a new golden age of creative productivity, and our job is to help students stay plugged into creative outlets.

REFERENCES

Bloom, B.S., Engelhart, M.D., Furst, E.J., Hill, W.H., & Krathwohl, D.R. (1956). *Taxonomy of educational objectives: The classification of educational goals, handbook book 1: cognitive domain*. New York: David McKay.

Carr, N. (2010). *The shallows: What the Internet is doing to our brains*. New York: W.W. Norton.

Dewey, J. (1938). *Experience and education*. New York: MacMillan.

Ericsson, K.A., Krampe, R.T., & Tesch-Rômer, C. (1993). The role of deliberate practice in the acquisition of expert performance. *Psychological Review, 100*(3), 363–406.

Gee, J.P. (2003). *What video games have to teach us about learning and literacy*. New York: Palgrave Macmillan.

Gladwell, M. (2008). *Outliers: The story of success*. New York: Little, Brown, & Company.

Housand, B.C., & Housand, A.M. (2012). The role of technology in gifted students' motivation. *Psychology in the Schools, 49*, 706–715.

Jackson, L.A., Witt, E.A., Games, A.I., Fitzgerald, H.E., von Eye, A., & Zhao, Y. (2012). Information technology use and creativity: Findings from the Children and technology Project. *Computers in Human Behavior, 28*(2), 370–376.

Johnson, S. (2005). *Everything bad is good for you: How today's popular culture is actually making us smarter*. New York: Riverhead Books.

Kim, K.H. (2011). The creativity crisis: The decrease in creative thinking scores on the Torrance Tests of Creative Thinking. *Creativity Research Journal, 23*, 285–295.

Leu, D.J., Jr., Kinzer, C.K., Coiro, J., & Cammack, D. (2004). Toward a theory of new literacies emerging from the Internet and other information and communication technologies. In R.B. Ruddell & N. Unrau (Eds.), *Theoretical models and processes of reading* (5th ed., pp. 1568–1611). Newark, DE: International Reading Association.

Leu, D. J., Zawilinski, L., Castek, J., Banerjee, M., Housand, B., Liu, Y., and O'Neil. M. (2007). What is new about the new literacies of online reading comprehension? In L. Rush, J. Eakle, & A. Berger, (Eds.), *Secondary school literacy: What research reveals for classroom practices* (pp. 37–68). Urbana, IL: National Council of Teachers of English.

McGonigal, J. (2011). *Reality is broken: Why games make us better and how they can change the world*. New York: Penguin.

Pedro, F. (2006). The new millennium learners: Challenging our views on ICT and learning. OECD-CERI. Retrieved from http://www.oecd.org/dataoecd/1/1/3835 8359.pdf.

Pink, D.H. (2005). *A whole new mind: Why right-brainers will rule the future*. New York: Riverhead Books.

Prensky, M. (2001). Digital natives, digital immigrants. *On the Horizon, 9*(5), 1–6.

Resnick, M. (1996). Pianos not stereos: Creating computational construction kits. *Interactions, 3*(6), 41–50.

Resnick, M. (2006). Computer as paintbrush: Technology, play, and the creative society. In D.G. Singer, R.M. Golinkoff, & K. Hirsh-Pasek (Eds.), *Play = learning: How play motivates and enhances children's cognitive and social-emotional growth* (pp. 192–208). Oxford, UK: Oxford University Press.

Robinson, K. (2006). Ken Robinson says schools kill creativity [Video file]. Retrieved from http://www.ted.com/talks/ken_robinson_says_schools_kill_creativity.html.

Sternberg, R.J. (2007) Creativity as a habit. In A. Tan (Ed.), *Creativity: A handbook for teacher* (pp. 3–25). Singapore: World Scientific Publishing.

Talbot, D. (October 29, 2012). Given tablets but no teachers, Ethiopian children teach themselves: A bold experiment by One Laptop per Child organizations has shown "encouraging" results. *MIT Technology Review*. Retrieved from http://www.tech nologyreview.com/news/506466/given-tablets-but-no-teachers-ethiopian-chil dren-teach-themselves/.

Toffler A. (1970). *Future shock*. New York: Random House.

Vygotsky, L. (1978). *Mind in society*. Cambridge, MA: Harvard University Press.

Wallas, G. (1926). *The art of thought*. New York: Harcourt, Brace and Company.

13

FOSTERING CREATIVITY THROUGH INQUIRY

Jami Biles Jones
East Carolina University

Education is often criticized for its pendulum-like swings from one pedagogical initiative to the next. In the 1960s, America's response to the Soviet Union's launch of Sputnik, the first Earth-orbiting satellite, was New Mathematics. New Math was criticized by Morris Kline (1958), author of *Why Johnny Can't Add: The Failure of New Math*, for teaching abstract number theory before students had learned the basics. The open classroom's learning by doing and inquiry was all the rage in the 1970s, but within a decade schools went back to basics. More recently the focus on pacing guides, rote learning, and excessive testing has left many educators too exhausted to contemplate the next initiative, like the Common Core State Standards (www.corestandards.org).

Recent standards and skills, such as the Partnership for 21st-Century Skills (www.p21.org) support creativity and innovation, but is this a fad too? More importantly, if the powers to be decide that a focus on creativity is important, can this be accomplished when content and pedagogy is so politicized? Will creativity become a No Child Left Behind–type initiative replete with assessments to determine student creativity? Creativity requires openness, flexibility, and time for reflection that is likely not supported in an environment of high-stakes tests and rote learning.

Contributors to this book have defined the theories of creativity and presented its controversies. More importantly they have described the environments and learning opportunities likely to foster creativity in students and educators. Is it possible in today's educational environment to cultivate creativity? I believe the answer is yes, but practice must change and change substantially. School librarians hold the keys to the creativity kingdom through their emphasis on inquiry. This kingdom is clearly in demand. In many ways there has never been a more opportune time to open the door to it.

In this chapter I discuss three essentials for school librarians who choose to guide teachers and students to this kingdom. The first essential step is for school librarians to embrace inquiry and oppose creativity-squelching. The second is to understand the importance of the question. The third is to introduce school librarians to a process model of creativity to facilitate student's development of "mini-c" creativity (Kaufman & Beghetto, 2009).

THE AASL STANDARDS' FOCUS ON CREATIVITY

In 2007, the American Association of School Librarians (AASL), a division of the American Library Association, unveiled the Standards for the 21st-Century Learner (www.ala.org/aasl/standards) to foster high expectations for today's students through skills, dispositions, responsibilities, and self-assessment strategies. Although the focus of the AASL Standards (2007) is inquiry, creativity is reflected throughout the document.

Characteristics of creative people and their behaviors such as openness, intrinsic motivation, collaboration, problem-finding/posing/solving, knowledge acquisition, perseverance, and divergent thinking are represented as outcomes in the Standards for the 21st-Century Learner (AASL, 2007):

- Openness is represented in indicator 4.2.3 to "maintain openness to new ideas by considering divergent opinions . . ."

- Intrinsic motivation is represented in indicator 4.2.2 to "demonstrate motivation by seeking information to answer personal question and interests . . ."

- Collaboration is represented in indicators 1.1.9 to "collaborate with others to broaden and deepen understanding"; 2.1.5 to "collaborate with others to exchange ideas, develop new understandings, make decisions, and solve problems"; and 3.1.2 to "participate and collaborate as members of a social and intellectual network of learners."

- Problem-finding/posing/solving is represented in indicators 1.2.5 "to demonstrate adaptability by changing the inquiry focus, questions, resources, or strategies when necessary to achieve success" and 1.1.3 to "develop and refine a range of questions to frame the search for new understanding."

- Knowledge acquisition is represented in indicators 4.1.7 to "use social networks and information tools to gather and share information," and 1.4.1 to "monitor own information—seeking processes for effectiveness and progress, and adapt as necessary."

- Flexibility is represented in indicator 2.2.1 to "demonstrate flexibility in the use of resources by adapting information strategies to each specific resource and by seeking additional resources when clear conclusions cannot be drawn."

- Perseverance is represented in indicator 1.2.6 to "display emotional resilience by persisting in information searching despite challenges."

- Divergent thinking is represented in indicator 2.2.2 to "use both divergent and convergent thinking to formulate alternative conclusions and test them against evidence."

ESSENTIAL ONE: SCHOOL LIBRARIANS EMBRACE INQUIRY AND OPPOSE SQUELCHING

The AASL Standards for the 21st-Century Learner (2007) represented a paradigm shift for school librarians who are required now to provide learning environments supporting exploration and inquiry, instead of the conventional "locate information—cut and clip—report" model of library projects. Loertscher, Koechlin, and Zwaan (2005) referred to this old model as "bird units" (p. vii) that regrettably continue today. Gordon (1999) characterized bird units as "no-learning inquiry" that "has masqueraded as research for so long that the terms [research and inquiry] are used interchangeably" (para. 3).

Bird units are easy to identify. First, bird units are controlled by teachers who identify the topics and specify the product (oftentimes a paper). Students are told what to do, and how to do it. Second, students have little opportunity to suggest, develop, and ask questions to turn a meaningless learning opportunity into one that is engaging and memorable. Third, bird units are simplistic reports that teachers likely repeat year after year. These units are easy for teachers who may have lost their zeal to motivate and engage students. Most egregious though are the lost opportunities for students to develop habits of mind such as openness, flexibility, perseverance, as well as the motivation to collaborate and gain expertise that is so central to the creative process. Inquiry is the school librarian's surest way to foster student creativity, but she must embrace the habits of mind and behaviors of the creative personality for this to happen.

Inquiry is hindered when school librarians fail to oppose simplistic bird units—useless learning devoid of opportunities to build the habits of mind described throughout this book and identified in the AASL Standards for the 21st-Century Learner (2007). Bravery to challenge bird units is essential for school librarians who choose to embrace creativity. The school librarian's strategy for eliminating bird units hinges on building relationships with teachers, developing trusting collaborations, conducting frequent professional development about the cognitive and dispositional benefits of inquiry to foster creativity, and modeling inquiry and creativity. It is through leadership that school librarians communicate their extraordinary potential to foster creativity.

What Is Inquiry?

Jeffrey D. Wilhelm (2007) defines "inquiry" as the process of addressing problems through guiding questions. Inquiry as a way of teaching and learning can be pursued either on the unit level that could take weeks or months to accomplish or at the shorter lesson level that may involve students in posing and considering a question or two about a topic that interests them at that moment. Students can engage in activities or discussion around essential questions or problems important in the community, state, country, or world.

Wilhelm (2007) identified the six Es of inquiry as:

- Engagement with a disciplinary question
- Exploration of what is already known and thought
- Explanations and interpretations of established date, making associations, and articulating connections

- Elaboration by providing new insights into what is already known
- Extension and application by extrapolating what has been learned
- Evaluating and adapting what has been learned in new ways and transferring new understandings to other situations.

The classic definition of creativity is a novel and appropriate product or idea. Through inquiry, students can combine and associate concepts and ideas to form something novel and appropriate. Arthur Koestler (1964) proposed that creativity is the "bisociation," or blending, of two previously unrelated concepts to form a new concept. It is this new concept that is the creative product. Inquiry is creative when students have sufficient knowledge of a topic to bisociate, or blend, concepts thus creating something new. In doing this, students would want to embrace a stance of curiosity, motivation, and perseverance, but they need access to teachers and school librarians who can model these behaviors and make connections and associations themselves.

Although eminent creators (e.g., Darwin and Picasso) create at a very sophisticated level that withstands historical scrutiny, the role of educators is to prepare students to create at the "mini-c" level by asking questions, observing, searching for information, associating ideas, forming hypotheses, collecting data, and presenting findings. Inquiry is ideal for fostering "mini-c" creativity (Beghetto & Kaufman, 2007).

Inquiry requires individuals to make new associations, or "unexpected links among apparently discrepant elements of information" (Cropley & Cropley, 2008, p. 361). The challenge for school librarians practicing at the intersection of the AASL Standards for the 21st-Century Learner, Common Core State Standards, and the Partnership for 21st Century Skills (P21) is convincing educators encumbered by threatening high-stakes tests and overly prescriptive pacing guides to relinquish control and embrace inquiry—a messier, but more effective pedagogy for learning.

Some educators may balk at the messiness of inquiry, and may unknowingly squelch students' creativity by employing inhibiting phrases such as "we've always done it that way" or "we can't fight city hall" (Davis, 1999, p. 169) or "we don't have time." Cropley (2010) found that "many educators express strong approval of creativity in *theory* . . . in *practice* the situation is different" (p. 297). Novelty, questioning, and dissatisfaction with the *status quo* threatened the self-image of educators and were unwelcomed in the classroom, a condition Cropley called the "dark side of creativity" (p. 304).

The notion of curious delight [such a delicious term], which is the subtitle of Starko's (2010) book *Creativity in the Classroom: Schools of Curious Delight*, hinges on educator's support of exploration, innovation, joy, and questioning, but for some children these opportunities may be few and far between. What does curious delight look like? Following are two examples of curious delight—abundant motivation, perseverance, question posing, and joy of learning.

Examples of Curious Delight

In 2011, Angela Zhang, then a senior at Monta Vista High School in Cupertino, California, won the prestigious Siemens Competition in Math, Science, and

Technology (2011) for her research in the design of a cancer detection system that delivered personalized treatment to a tumor. Zhang's after-school inquiry began by reading doctoral-level peer-reviewed articles to learn all she could about cancer and highlighting words and concepts she did not understand. At first, almost every word was highlighted in yellow, but as her expertise grew, she highlighted less and understood these articles more quickly and completely. She synthesized these readings—some with contradictory findings— to select the questions that ultimately defined her research in the laboratory. As Zhang discovered, question posing defined her inquiry.

A second example of curious delight occurred at Georgetown University, Washington, D.C., in 2008, when Professor Phillip A. Karber showed students pictures of the geological consequences of a devastating earthquake in China's Sichuan province. Chinese news accounts reported that hundreds of radiation technicians had swarmed to the area. Karber asked students: "What do you think this means?" Students spent hours of their own time combing through a variety of documents to answer this question. Although criticized by more traditional folks for relying on Internet-based resources such as Google Earth, blogs, military journals, and a fictionalized television docudrama about the Chinese military, these students were convinced that a vast network of tunnels had been built to protect that country's missiles from nuclear attack. In 2009, Chinese military officials admitted the existence of a 3,000-mile network of tunnels for that very purpose (Wan, 2011).

These students' findings were considered controversial, which is no surprise since creativity and bisociation challenged conformity and established ways of thinking, and upset the apple cart. Their research was labeled ridiculous and its methodology questioned. Relying on the Internet and a televised docudrama was touted as dangerous, but these students connected the dots unlike others in the arms-control community.

These inquiries into medicine and military affairs led to amazing findings and discoveries. Zhang and Karber's students exhibited the habits of mind, motivation, collaboration, expertise, and curiosity that educator's desire for all students, but these qualities are unlikely when the focus is on rote learning and students have few opportunities to engage in authentic and meaningful inquiry. Traditional school libraries evolve into school libraries of curious delight when librarians choose to be creative and curious and possess the habits of mind described in this book. One student interviewed by William Wan (2011) reveled in the opportunity for curious delight provided by Karber: "Dr. Karber just tells you the objective and gives you total freedom to figure out how to get there. That level of trust can be liberating" (para. 30). Once students experience the liberation and excitement of inquiry will they settle for less?

ESSENTIAL TWO: CURIOUS DELIGHT
BEGINS WITH QUESTIONS

Creativity is often associated with the ability to solve problems, but many creative advances result when the problem is not known, but emerges from the process of the work itself (Sawyer, 2006, p. 183). Starko (2010) was fascinated with problem-finding: "the identification and framing of problems" (p. 29), which she believed to be the essence of the creative process and thinking. Question posing is the first step of inquiry, but this is a challenge when students are assigned readings and projects and given specific instructions on how to proceed—when the message is that there is only one right way and one right conclusion.

When students are denied opportunities to ask questions and discover problems, these abilities are not developed. Starko (2010) wrote: "Teaching for creativity entails creating a community of inquiry in the classroom, a place in which asking good questions is at least as important as answering them" (p. 17).

Jean Lave and Etienne Wenger (1991) proposed "learning as increased participation in communities of practice [that] concerns the whole person acting in the world" (p. 49). They considered "situated learning" ideal for learning whereby students learned by delving into practice and activities, often through apprenticeships. Knowledge separated from situated learning may become too abstracted and meaningless to students "unless they can be made specific to the situation at hand" (p. 33). This helps to explain why students ask questions such as "why do I need to learn this" or "when will I ever use algebra."

Brown, Collins, and Duguid's (1989) article on situated cognition identified knowledge as a tool, but it is the authentic activity that provides meaning, which is the key to learning. They argue that "learning and cognition . . . are fundamentally situated" (p. 32) and occur together. Inquiry allows students to simultaneously gather knowledge, collaborate, and pursue authentic activity.

Types of Questions

Helping a student find a problem is unlikely if she is presented with the problem rather than allowing her to discover it on her own. Jacob Getzels is known for bringing to the fore the importance of asking good questions. Getzels (1987) categorized three types of problems.

- Type 1 problems have a solution, and students know the method of solution, but must apply the solution to a variety of problems. These problems represent the most widely used problem type in education. For type 1 problems, the "teacher presents students with a problem and expects that they will arrive at a specific answer through a particular means" that has been presented (Starko, 2010, p. 31).
- Type 2 problems are also presented, but the method of solution is not known to students who must discover first the appropriate method to solve the problem.
- Type 3 problems represent the truest type of problem-finding because the problem as well as the solution must be discovered.

Barb Johnson's class exemplifies Getzels's type 3 problems. Johnson begins each year by asking her sixth-grade students two questions: "What questions do you have about yourself?" and "what questions do you have about the world?" (Bransford, Brown, & Cocking, 2000). Students hesitate sometimes to articulate their questions because they might seem silly, but Johnson assures them that "if they're your questions that you really want answered, they're neither silly nor little" (p. 156).

Students develop, share, and prioritize their questions, which guides the curriculum that year in Johnson's class. One student asked if she would live to be 100 years old. This question led to inquiry about genetics, family and oral history, actuarial science, statistics and probability, heart disease, cancer, and hypertension. The students sought out information from family members, friends, experts in various fields, online computer services and books, as well as from the teacher. According to Johnson,

> We decide what are the most compelling issues, devise ways to investigate those issues and start off on a learning journey. Sometimes we fall short of our goal. Sometimes we reach our goal, but most times we exceed these goals—we learn more than we initially expected. (pp. 156–157)

Johnson's focus on inquiry and authentic learning represented curious delight, but other educators could do this too if they wanted. What sets Johnson apart is her wide range of disciplinary knowledge that allows her to make connection and association, and she does not fear losing control. Johnson is curious and open to authentic learning. In short, Johnson chooses creativity.

How much can children learn by themselves? In 1999, Sugata Mitra conducted his first Hole-in-the-Wall experiment by embedding a computer with high-speed Internet in a wall in a slum area of New Delhi, India. Within mere hours, children who had never before seen a computer were working together to make films, emailing, and chatting (Mitra & Dangwal, 2010). Mitra has conducted similar experiments throughout the world since then. Mitra's 2010 TED Talk, The child-driven education, at http://www.ted.com/talks/lang/en/sugata_mitra_the_child_driven_education.html, that has been watched more than 1.5 million times, is a fascinating affirmation that "children will learn what to do what they want to do" (Mitra, 2010).

Creativity and inquiry requires that teachers and school librarians relinquish control and allow students to meet standards through question posing and projects that are compelling to them. How would this look in the school library? Kathy Gaines, a school librarian in North Carolina, who at one time was a graduate student in a class I taught about inquiry, conducted her own Mitra-type experiment with a class of third-grade students described as lacking self-motivation. Gaines and the collaborating language arts teacher decided that students would present their folktale findings using Microsoft's PowerPoint program. After a brief introduction to PowerPoint, students broke into self-selected groups and were given 30 minutes to develop their presentations. The group that worked with Gaines "had to follow my exact directions and couldn't explore (Gaines, personal communication, December 4, 2012).

Gaines found that self-selected groups learned more through their explorations, produced more slides of better quality, and were much more excited about their finished product. Gaines concluded:

> So, here is what I think I learned from this experiment. The students in my group did not exceed the learning objectives that I set. The students who did not have the boundaries of my control learned more. They were also more excited and proud of their accomplishments. I am guessing that if I give the students a choice of learning models again, they will all choose the self-driven learning group. (Gaines, personal communication, December 4, 2012)

ESSENTIAL THREE: MODELS OF CREATIVITY AND INQUIRY

I propose throughout this chapter that inquiry is the school librarian's surest way to foster student creativity. Yet, how do school librarians *do* creativity? Several models offer insight into the phases of creativity that are helpful to school librarians who bisociate inquiry and creativity to develop libraries of curious delight. Creativity is active—that is

> in real life, creative ideas often happen while you're working with your materials. Once you start executing an idea you often realize that it isn't working out like you expected, and you have to change what you had in mind. (Sawyer, 2006, p. 58)

Students who do not understand that inquiry and creativity can be frustrating at times may quit too quickly. Giving up can stunt the development of behaviors vital for future creations. Creators at all levels experience false starts, but must plow through nevertheless.

Although there are numerous process models of creativity such as John Dewey's (1910) five-phase model of reflective thinking, Graham Wallas' (1926) classic model that was described extensively in the previous chapter and E. Paul Torrance's four-stage model that is unique for including a final communication stage that implies actually doing something, in this chapter I describe Arthur Cropley's and David Cropley's seven-step extended phase model of the creative process. Cropley and Cropley (2008) believed that a seven-step phase model identified the phases more cogently than a shorter model. For instance, Cropley and Cropley subdivided Wallas' (1926) preparation phase into preparation and activation, added communication, and considered validation by others (in the case of the classroom this could be teachers, students, the school librarian, school administrators, and staff as well as community members) as the final step.

A danger with any step-by-step process is the possibility of it being viewed as simplistic if one does not realize that these are probable, not required, phases. In addition, phases could occur in different order or there might be looping, which would cause creators to return to a previous phase, or start over. Also, the more expert one becomes with a process, the more internalized the process, and the less likely she can describe it. Table 13.1 identifies the model as well as the responsibilities of teachers, school librarians, and students in the creative process. In addition, examples of inquiry based on Carolyn Coil's use of SCAMPER in chapter 11 are provided. In the right-hand column, Coil provides additional implementation suggestions.

SCHOOL LIBRARIANS OF CURIOUS DELIGHT CARE

School libraries of curious delight begin with school librarians who care. The notion of care (Dewey, 1933; Noddings, 2005) is central to learning because students who do not feel cared for and respected are likely to disengage from learning that seems meaningless. Kathleen Cushman (2006) interviewed 65 students to gather their perspectives on high school culture and climate. Students told her they wanted classes that are engaging. When "classes offer only a steady tedium, these students would just as soon forget about school and look to the media, the streets, or peer relationships for interest and stimulation" (Cushman, 2006, p. 34). Students asked for hands-on projects that combined high-interest topics with academic competencies, fair and consistent treatment, inspiring role models, and extracurricular activities such as sports and clubs that helped them express their passions, feelings, and competence.

School librarians who care will develop opportunities for inquiry and creativity. School librarians care to ask questions of students. They care to wrap the curriculum

Table 13.1 Application of the Extended Phase Model of Creativity to Inquiry

PHASE	TEACHER'S ROLE	SCHOOL LIBRARIAN'S ROLE	STUDENT'S RESPONSIBILITY	IMPLEMENTATION EXAMPLES	ADDITIONAL IDEAS AND COMMENTS
Preparation General and specific knowledge accumulated.	Content is taught so that it matters to students. Teacher checks for understanding for all students and adds background knowledge as needed.	Has knowledge about curriculum and standards. Recommends and acquires appropriate resources at various reading levels that fuel knowledge accumulation.	Perseveres to understand and gain knowledge and expertise about the topic and is engaged and motivated.	Students presented content about the Trail of Tears; students read three informational texts and other resources.	It is likely that students will have a range of knowledge about a given topic. Make sure each student learns something new during this phase.
Activation Problem awareness based on knowledge develops.	Models question-posing to support student's efforts to recognize missing links/contradictions/problems; students are challenged to pose questions.	Models and teaches question-posing; provides information literacy instruction to activate problem awareness and contradictions; models collaboration with teacher.	Increasing awareness of topic's complexity; remains curious; thinks outside and inside the box; effectively uses information; poses engaging questions that guide further activation and inquiry.	Working in collaborative groups, students activate knowledge by developing guiding questions; for example, students brainstorm ways the Trail or Tears could have been avoided.	Many students are used to giving the one correct answer but are not skilled in thinking outside the box, working in groups, or brainstorming. These skills may need to be taught before this activity can be done successfully.

(*Continued*)

Table 13.1 (*Continued*)

PHASE	TEACHER'S ROLE	SCHOOL LIBRARIAN'S ROLE	STUDENT'S RESPONSIBILITY	IMPLEMENTATION EXAMPLES	ADDITIONAL IDEAS AND COMMENTS
Cogitation Information is processed in the person's head.	Models reflection; students are provided ample time and opportunity to think about the question, topic, or problem. Models and demonstrates how to have several possible answers instead of the one correct answer.	Models reflection; teaches students about the ambiguity of inquiry. Can provide examples in other resources to show how this is done.	Reflects; remains open to new ideas; handles the frustration of not having the "one right answer." Learns to think about several possibilities instead of the one right answer.	Working in a small group, student participates in the SCAMPER process; continues to ponder questions and brainstorms ideas; creates songs or poems about this historical event.	The SCAMPER process leads students to answer questions in a creative way. The background knowledge developed in the previous phases enriches the creative thinking that occurs with SCAMPER.
Illumination The person sees a possible answer (product).	Provides appropriate feedback; makes meaningful suggestions; supports student's decisions.	Supports illumination by investigating possibilities with students.	Bisociates by considering all learning; considers all ideas; considers a possible solution to inquiry.	Working in their SCAMPER group, students combine efforts to answer a question about the Trail of Tears or develop a product.	Important that the students listen to one another during the SCAMPER process. No "put-downs" for different or unusual ideas.
Verification The product is checked out and found to be appropriate.	Provides opportunities for student's inquiry to be checked out for appropriateness, accuracy, and feasibility.	Ensures that students use information skills to verify appropriateness of inquiry. Shows students how to cite their evidence when using informational texts.	Student continues to verify inquiry that may include further information searching and revisions.	Before the concluding activity in the Trail of Tears lesson, students check their answers and review the information they will present to others.	When the SCAMPER process has been completed, students need to go back and check their work and their answers. This is similar to editing in a writing assignment.

Communication The product is revealed to knowledgeable others.	Provides opportunity for students to share solutions; supports student's courage; develops assessment instrument with student input.	Provides technology and instructional support for presentation of inquiry; creates a welcoming library environment to display and present creative products of inquiry.	Communicates the results of the inquiry using appropriate means.	Students apply the jigsaw method to share information about their inquiry with members of other groups.	Communicating ideas and solutions should be done in a creative way in order to sustain the interest of others. All students should learn new things during the communication phase.
Validation Knowledgeable others confirm product is novel, relevant, effective, etc.	Teacher and classmates provide feedback about appropriateness and value of student effort that may result in a grade; practitioners may be invited to validate answer or product.	Plans and provides opportunities for students to exhibit, demonstrate, and share answers and products of inquiry.	Welcomes confirmation; remains open to feedback; exhibits and/or demonstrates answers or products.	Each group exhibits inquiry product in the school library, in the community, or on the Internet.	Students are validated and generally motivated to do their best when their work reaches an audience larger than their teacher, parents, or classmates.

Note: Table adapted from "Resolving the Paradoxes of Creativity: An Extended Phase Model," by A. Cropley and D. Cropley (2008) *Cambridge Journal of Education,* 38(3), 364. Adapted with permission. Table 13.1 represents a collaborative effort between Jami Biles Jones and Carolyn Coil.

around these questions. Also, they care that students are engaged in learning. This is a very different pedagogical journey than rote learning, presented questions, and a staid curriculum that ignores student input. Inquiry begins with questions reflecting the interest of students, and it is blended with the curriculum to meet standards. Inquiry is child-centered learning at its creative best.

CONCLUSION

I conclude this chapter with a Manifesto of Creative Inquiry patterned after Torrance's Manifesto for Children (2002) consisting of seven guidelines gleaned from his analysis of the creative achievements of 101 children who were followed for 40 years. Torrance's (2002) longitudinal research indicated the difficulty for some creative children to find

> a kind of work that they could fall in love with, while others had fallen in love with their work in the early grades and were now pursuing it with intensity. (p. 9)

Torrance (2002) found children who had tested high in creative potential; nevertheless, they lost their creativity due to insecurity, lack of support, or inability to free

> themselves of the expectations of others and to walk away from those imposed by their parents, teachers and others. Only about half of them had found a teacher or mentor who could help them. (p. 11)

The difference for children who could hold onto their creativity was motivation, skills, and opportunities (Torrance, 2002). Robert J. Sternberg (2003) considered creativity to be a matter of decision [or choice], and that "fomenting creativity is largely a matter of fomenting a certain attitude toward problem solving and even toward life" (p. 118). Educators help students to decide for creativity when they provide students with choices and help them build self-efficacy to "believe that, ultimately, they have the ability to make a difference," (p. 124) provide time for creative thinking, and allow mistakes. Throughout this process, educators:

- Encourage creative collaborations
- Increase student's knowledge because "those with a greater knowledge base can be creative in ways that those who are still learning about the basics of the field cannot be" (p. 121)
- Support sensible risk-taking
- Help students to tolerate ambiguity because "there are a lot of grays in creative work" (p. 123).

Most importantly though, educators help students discover what they love to do. School librarians do this by providing opportunities to inquire about the world and developing rich collections thus allowing students to wonder and learn about themselves.

The Manifesto for Creative Inquiry based on Torrance's Manifesto for Children represents my effort to employ Sternberg's (2003) and Davis's (1999) notion that creativity is a choice, made one decision after another, that could lead to libraries of curious delight. Unlike the student-based outcomes of the AASL Standards for the 21st-Century Learner (2007), the Manifesto for Creative Inquiry is developed for school librarians who choose to nurture every student's creative potential through inquiry.

The Manifesto for Creative Inquiry

The joy of discovery begins with problem finding. Make sure that teachers understand this and put a stop to those "locate information—cut and clip" reports.

Inquiry begins with students' interests, desires, and hopes. If students are bored, consider your complicity and do something.

Inquiry is a flexible and dynamic journey that begins with discovered questions and calls for thoughtful and deliberate choices.

Every inquiry is different. There is no one right way to conduct inquiry no matter what you learned in library school.

Students will take creative chances when it is safe to do so. Your job is to create a joyful school library environment that nurtures exploration, innovation, and questioning.

It's all about the kids who trump everything else you do.

REFERENCES

American Association of School Librarians (2007). *Standards for the 21st-century learner.* Chicago, IL: American Library Association.

Beghetto, R. A., & Kaufman, J. C. (2007).Toward a broader conception of creativity: A case for mini-c creativity. *Psychology of Aesthetics, Creativity, and the Arts, 1*, 73–79.

Bransford, J. D., Brown, A. L., & Cocking, R. R. (2000). *How people learn: Brain, mind, experience, and school.* Washington, DC: National Academy Press.

Brown, J. S., Collins, A., & Duguid, P. (1989). Situated cognition and the culture of learning. *Educational Researcher, 18*(1), 32–42.

Collins, M. A., & Amabile, T. M. (1999). Motivation and creativity. In R. J. Sternberg (Ed.), *Handbook of creativity* (pp. 297–312). Cambridge, UK: Cambridge University Press.

Cropley, A. J. (2010). Creativity in the classroom: The dark side. In D. H. Cropley, A. J. Cropley, J. C. Kaufman, & M. A. Runco (Eds.), *The dark side of creativity.* Cambridge, UK: Cambridge University Press.

Cropley, A., & Cropley, D. (2008). Resolving the paradoxes of creativity: An extended phase model. *Cambridge Journal of Education, 38*(3), 355–373.

Cushman, K. (2006). Help us care enough to learn. *Educational Leadership, 63*(5), 35–37.

Davis, D. A. (1999). Barriers to creativity and creative attitudes. In M. A. Runco & S. R. Pritzker (Eds.), *Encyclopedia of creativity* (Vol. I, pp. 165–174). San Diego, CA: Academic Press.

Dewey, J. (1910). *How we think.* Boston, MA: Heath.

Dewey, J. (1933). *How we think: A restatement of the relation of reflective thinking to the educative process.* Boston: D.C. Heath.

Getzels, J. W. (1987). Problem finding and creative achievement. *Gifted Students Institute Quarterly, 12*(4), B1–B4.

Gordon, C. (1999). Students as authentic researchers: A new prescription for the high school research assignment. *School Library Media Research, 21*(9). Retrieved from http://www.ala.org/ala/mgrps/divs/aasl/aaslpubsandjournals/slmrb/slmrcontents/volume21999/vol2gordon.cfm.

Guilford, J. P. (1975). Creativity: A quarter century of progress. In I. A. Taylor & J. W. Getzels (Eds.), *Perspectives in creativity* (pp. 37–59). Chicago, IL: Aldine.

Kaufman, J.C., & Beghetto, R.A. (2009). Beyond big and little: The Four C Model of Creativity. *Review of General Psychology, 13*(1), 1-12.

Kline, M. (1958). *Why Johnny can't add: The failure of new math.* New York: Random House.

Koestler, A. (1964). *The act of creation.* New York: Macmillan.

Kuhlthau, C. C. (2004). *Seeking meaning: A process approach to library and information services.* Westport, CT: Libraries Unlimited.

Lave, J., & Wenger, Etienne (1991). *Situated learning: Legitimate peripheral participation.* New York: Cambridge University Press.

Loertscher, D., Koechlin, C., & Zwaan, S. (2005). *Ban those bird units: 15 models for teaching and learning in information-rich and technology-rich environments.* Salt Lake City, UT: Hi Willow.

Mitra, S. (2010, July). *TED: The child-driven education* [video file]. Retrieved from http://www.ted.com/talks/lang/en/sugata_mitra_the_child_driven_education.html.

Mitra, S., & Dangwal, R. (2010). Limits to self-organising systems of learning—the Kalikuppam experiment. *British Journal of Educational Technology, 41*(5), 672–688.

Noddings, N. (2005). *The challenge to care in schools: An alternative approach to education* (2nd ed.). New York: Teachers College Press.

Plsek, P. (1996). *Working paper: Models for the creative process.* Retrieved from http://www.directedcreativity.com/pages/WPModels.html.

Runco, M. A. (2007). *Creativity: Theories and themes: Research, development, and practice.* Amsterdam, NL: Elsevier.

Sawyer, R. K. (2006). *Explaining creativity: The science of human innovation.* Oxford, UK: Oxford University.

Siemens Competition in Math, Science and Technology (2011). Retrieved from http://www.siemens-foundation.org/en/competition/2011_winners.htm.

Starko, A. J. (2010). *Creativity in the classroom: Schools of curious delight* (4th ed.). New York,: Routledge.

Sternberg, R. J. (2003). The development of creativity as a decision-making process. In R. K. Sawyer, V. John-Steiner, S. Moran, R. J. Sternberg, D. H. Feldman, J. Nakamura & M. Csikszentmihalyi (Eds.), *Creativity and development* (pp. 91–137). New York: Oxford University Press.

Sternberg, R. J., & Lubart, T. I. (1999). The concept of creativity: Prospects and paradigms. In R. J. Sternberg (Ed.), *Handbook of creativity* (pp. 3–15). New York: Cambridge University Press.

Torrance, E. P. (1995). *Why fly?* Norwood, NJ: Ablex.

Torrance, E. P. (2002). *The manifesto: A guide to developing a creative career.* Westport, CT: Ablex.

Wallas, G. (1926) *The art of thought.* New York: Harcourt Brace.

Wan, William (2011, November 29). Georgetown students shed light on china's tunnel system for nuclear weapons. The *Washington Post.* Retrieved from http://www.washingtonpost.com/world/national-security/georgetown-students-shed-light-on-chinas-tunnel-system-for-nuclear-weapons/2011/11/16/gIQA6AmKAO_story.html.

Wilhelm, J. D. (2007). *Engaging readers & writers with inquiry: Promoting deep understandings in language arts and the content areas with guiding questions.* New York: Scholastic.

THE ROLE OF THE SCHOOL LIBRARIAN IN DEVELOPING CREATIVITY THROUGH FUTURE PROBLEM SOLVING

Bonnie L. Cramond
The University of Georgia, Athens

Suehyeon Paek
The University of Georgia

At one time keeping tidy shelves and hushing students to be quiet were viewed as major duties of the school librarian. Although school librarianship has changed, and continues to evolve, tidying and hushing stereotypes are difficult to shake. In the April 2012 issue of *School Library Journal*, Linda W. Braun interviewed Sarah Ludwig who had taken a job as technology coordinator, but she still maintained many school library duties. The title of the article, Next Year's Model, caused a flurry of blog activity about the role of the school librarian. Although Ludwig felt "limited by the title [of school librarian] and the expectations of the job," Buffy Hamilton (2012) in her *The Unquiet Librarian* blog of April 2 moved the conversation from technology to instructional leader and learning mentor. In this book, school librarians are presented yet another challenge—nurturers of creativity.

One way that school librarians fulfill their evolving instructional role as nurturers of creativity is by introducing the Future Problem Solving Program International (FPSPI) (http://www.fpspi.org) and using the Future Problem Solving (FPS) method with teachers and students. Because the FPS requires such skills as problem-finding, communication, teamwork, inquiry, and research for proposing solutions to real open-ended problems, it is in line with core curriculum standards (Cramond, 2009) and 21st-Century Skills (Trilling & Fadel, 2012). More importantly, the structure of the FPSPI requires that students, regardless of grade level, work on the same set of four to five topics sequentially throughout the year. Students are assigned to the following levels according to their grade level in school: juniors, grades four to six; intermediates, grades seven to nine; and seniors, grades 10 to 12. The topics describe problem areas that are expected to be of continued or increasing difficulty in the future.

For example, the first topic of 2012–2013 is "culture of celebrity." The description of the topic discusses "celebrity-worship syndrome," which is defined as all-consuming idolatry of celebrities. The topic includes information on how the ubiquitous images of famous people causes some young people to consider celebrities as role models and emulate their destructive behaviors. Although celebrity may bring attention to worthwhile causes, it may also lead to loss of privacy and even stalking. The trend, which seems to be escalating, has resulted in the creation of magazines, websites, fan fiction, and other media to follow celebrity's every move. Students are urged to consider the positive and negative ramifications of celebrity at http://www.fpspi.org/topics.html.

A school librarian working with students throughout a school could help students through the processes of the FPSPI program at whatever levels they are on, but with some common resources and background knowledge. In order for this to be clearer, it is necessary to explain more about the program.

THEORETICAL FOUNDATION OF FUTURE PROBLEM SOLVING

Why Creativity Education?

As our world becomes more and more complex, the problems we face become more complex and interconnected, too (Friedman, 2005). We have always depended upon creative people in our society to solve problems in many domains. Creativity, which is commonly defined as the generation of novel and valuable, or useful, ideas (Runco & Jaeger, 2012) is the impetus for moving our societies forward in all domains, in the sciences and industry as well as in the arts. Although people may believe creative thinking in the sciences is significantly different from creative thinking in the arts, Michele Root-Bernstein and Robert Root-Bernstein (1999) found through interviews with eminent creators and some Nobel Prize winners from mathematics and science to the arts that similar thinking strategies are employed. Therefore, it is reasonable to think that helping students learn to use these strategies can be helpful in varied creative ventures.

Schools all over the world are emphasizing creativity. For example, 2009 was declared the European Year of Creativity. The European Commission (2009) presented the results of the first-ever survey on creativity and innovation in schools, which show that 94 percent of European teachers believe creativity is a fundamental competence to be developed at school. In addition, the majority of teachers expressed the belief that everyone can be creative, and creativity can be applied to every school subject. Also, the Far East nations, such as China, Korea, Japan, Singapore, and Taiwan, have looked to the West for help in adding an emphasis on creativity into their schools (Voice of America, 2011; Lim, 2012; Barber, 2012). Don't we owe our students the opportunity to learn the skills that will better prepare them to be the problem solvers and creators of the future?

How Can We Teach Creative Thinking through the Future Problem Solving Program International?

The mission of the Future Problem Solving Program is to teach students creative problem solving processes through competitive and non-competitive instructional programs so that they learn to work with others in designing positive futures

—Future Problem Solving Program's Mission
Statement (FPSP coach's handbook, 2001).

Torrance created the Future Problem Solving Program, based on the Osborn-Parnes Creative Problem-Solving (CPS) method (Osborn, 1953; Parnes, 1967; Cramond, 2009) to encourage students to employ creative methods to address authentic and real-world problems. What began in 1974 as a single unit at one high school in Athens, GA (Cramond, 2009), the Future Problem Solving program has expanded into a year-long opportunity for more than 250,000 students in 18 countries to think creatively and solve problems. Future Problem Solving Program International, (FPSPI) is the nonprofit entity that oversees the organization and worldwide competition, creates and distributes diverse resources for students and educators, provides training for educators, and offers mentoring for new affiliate programs (http://www.fpspi.org/index.html).

In contrast to the traditional format of many classes, FPS is designed for students to engage in authentic learning through solving problems creatively in the real world. Thus, FPSPI has been a popular program for gifted students as an enrichment activity of a pullout program, resource center, special class, and Saturday program (Davis, Rimm, & Siegle, 2011). FPS helps students: 1) practice how to solve problems, which might be expected in the future in their community and worldwide society creatively; 2) use critical and creative thinking abilities to identify problems for themselves; 3) learn to collect and select information appropriately; 4) cooperate with others and learn teamwork skills; 5) learn about topics in an authentic way; 6) communicate persuasively with audiences (Torrance, 1978; *Future Problem Solving Program Coach's Handbook*, 2001; Rogalla, 2003; Davis, Rimm, & Siegle, 2011).

How to Teach FPS

The process of FPS is basically the same as Creative Problem Solving (Osborn, 1953; Parnes, 1967). The differences are that FPS addresses topics that emphasize current and future societal problems we face in the real world; the topic includes a research component; emphasizes finding problems; and promotes convincing others of the solution for implementation. FPS consists of six steps, which offer techniques and perspectives for constructively looking at a topic. The steps and descriptions that follow are taken from the 2001 edition of the *Future Problem Solving Program Coach's Handbook*.

1. Identify challenges related to the topic or future scene
2. Select an underlying problem
3. Produce solution ideas to the underlying problem
4. Generate and select criteria to evaluate solution ideas
5. Evaluate solution ideas to determine the better action plan
6. Develop the action plan.

The first step, "identify challenges related to the topic or future scene" aims at identifying problems that can be addressed within fuzzy situations. Fuzzy situations can be drawn from global issues, community issues, and the curriculum. Teachers and affiliates should refer to the topics lists provided by FPSI's online website to find appropriate fuzzy situations.

During this first step, students ask clarifying questions and brainstorm challenges issues, concerns, or problems that they see in the fuzzy situation given by instructors.

Thereafter, students focus and elaborate on the 20 most promising challenges in the format of complete statements, including what the challenge is, why it is a challenge, and how it connects to the fuzzy situation. Through this step, students learn how to expand their fluency and flexibility by using brainstorming, forced relationships, and categories. In particular, most challenges students find would be described as hypothetical occurrences, and they should be discussed within the boundaries of the given situation.

The second step, "select an underlying problem" involves identifying and stating the important underlying problem of the fuzzy situation in order to solve it. In this step, students select the key challenges and underlying problems among those they generated. They state the key underlying problem in the standard FPS format, "In What Ways Might We (IWWMW)." Students break the fuzzy situation down into a smaller challenge to make it feasible for research. Therefore, students learn to identify and clarify a key underlying problem. Depending on the age and ability of the students, instructors facilitate this process by offering the basic components of problem statements, action verb lists, and techniques for honing in on the most important or basic problem.

The third step, "produce solution ideas to the underlying problem" aims at having students generate many and unusual ideas that respond to the underlying problems. In particular, instructors should encourage students to employ diverse ways of thinking about solutions in terms of who, where, when, what, and how. The emphasis is on producing many ideas and getting beyond the most obvious.

The fourth step, "generate and select criteria to evaluate solution ideas" has students develop yardsticks by which students can measure how they will select the creative solution ideas. In this step, students consider diverse criteria for evaluating solutions identified in step 3 that may include measures of efficiency—such as cost, time, and availability of resources—and measures of effectiveness—such as likelihood of success and acceptability.

The fifth step, "evaluate solution ideas to determine the better action plan" is the point at which students select the most 10 appealing solutions and apply the criteria from step four. An evaluation grid, as illustrated in table 14.1, is used to rank solutions according to the five criteria to identify the best solution. With increasing sophistication, students weigh criteria to select the most appropriate solution.

In the last step, "develop the action plan" students develop a practical application to enact the solution with the highest score in the previous step. To do so, students elaborate an authentic and detailed plan and project it recursively into the underlying problem. Thereafter, students must create a persuasive argument for a real audience in order to sell the best solution.

The FPS method may be used within the curriculum for instructional purposes, but FPSPI is a program that provides students opportunities to participate in creative problem-solving with others across the globe (Cramond, 2009). It also provides various types of problem-solving activities to meet different needs: competitive/noncompetitive; individual/group; community/global; action-based/curriculum-based; and scenario writing (Cramond, 2009; *Future Problem Solving Program Coach's Handbook*, 2001; Rogalla, 2003). In the competitive problem-solving track, students work individually or collaboratively in teams of four to practice problem-solving, which is sent to the affiliate for judging. The individual, or

Table 14.1   Grid for Evaluating Top Solution by Chosen Criteria (Cramond, 2009)

CRITERIA/ IDEAS	AFFORDABLE	PROTECTION	ACCEPTABLE	AESTHETICS	TIME	TOTAL
Solution 1	5	1	3	2	1	12
Solution 2	3	8	7	10	9	37 (√)
Solution 3	4	5	2	1	3	15
.						
.						
.						
Solution 10	2	3	4	5	7	21

Note: 10 = best (This number should be the same as the number of solutions being considered), 1 = worst, (√) means the selected solution by the score. Used with author's permission.

team, receives constructive feedback from judges. Thereafter, they get the second practice problem and more feedback. Third, they get a qualifying problem, which is used to qualify teams for the first round of competition at the affiliate level. Fourth, there is a problem for all affiliates to use at the competition, and the winners from this level go on to the international competition. The problem topic used at the international competition is one of the four topics students have studied that year. See appendix B for a list of FPSPI topics.

The topics are selected from three categories: business/economics; science/technology; social/political issues. The specific topics for the group competition are selected each year through voting of participants. Those who engage in community problem-solving choose problems from their own or other communities. Those who choose to write future scenarios may choose to write about any of the topics for the year.

PRACTICAL APPLICATION OF FPSPI IN SCHOOLS

Even excellent education programs, like FPSPI, or methods, such as FPS, require adaptation to meet the needs of students in a particular context. The following section describes what school librarians and teachers should consider to implement FPS or FPSPI.

Application I: Facilitating FPSPI in the School Library

Creativity requires that school librarians teach students the processes of inquiry; however, inquiry begins with a question or topic meaningful to students. In this case, FPS is an appropriate way for student inquiry about real-world problems and knowledge creations that may include a solution.

Above all, this requires school librarians to develop various levels and complexity of research lessons for students. Although topics across grades may be the same, the problems identified and accompanying research will be different for learners at different levels. For students in lower grades, research on the culture of celebrity may be very different from that for students in higher grades. The juniors, grades 4–6, could investigate how hero worship leads to fan emulation. Students in grades 7–9 could investigate how fan fiction impacts literature. Students in grades 10–12 could explore the cost of loss of privacy for celebrity personalities. School librarians help students identify questions of interest to them and teach inquiry and research.

In the first step "identify challenges related to the topic or future scene," the school librarians could help students find a variety of information sources related to the topic. In this step, students need to think divergently, and sensitively, about societal challenges across the domains of literature, science, history, mathematics, music, and art using resources such as fiction, newspapers, critiques, cartoons, websites, videos, and podcasts. By using various media, students in Professor Karber's class at Georgetown University identified a series of tunnels in China before the red arms-control experts. See chapter 13 (Fostering Creativity through Inquiry).

In the second step, "select an underlying problem," a school librarian should play one of the most critical roles in students' creativity. This step is very distinct from other creativity education programs in terms of problem-finding. Einstein and Infeld (1938) once wrote that a problem once recognized and well defined was already half solved. Unfortunately, most school lessons focus on solving presented problems, not how to find problems. Yet, in the real world, problems are not typically presented so clearly, and innovators must find and clarify problems for themselves. Even if they are presented with a problem by a client, the problem may not be the real problem, the underlying problem, or the most urgent problem.

In the Maker and Schiever model (2005), illustrated at http://discover.arizona.edu/problem_solving.htm, problem-solving situations are categorized into six levels according to whether the problem, method, or solution is known by the presenter or the solver. The six levels are described in the following text.

1. Type I problems are the most common type of problem encountered by students in schools. The student's task is to apply a particular method to reach the one correct answer known to the teacher. An example is, "What is the sum of 15 plus 18?"

2. Type II problems are similar, but this time the student must figure out both the method and the solution although both are known to the teacher. An example is, "The students had 15 cupcakes to sell at the sale, then Evan's father brought 18 more. How many cupcakes did they have to sell?

3. Type III problems have multiple solution methods, but there is only one correct answer. A simple example is, "Three students contributed five cupcakes each to the sale, and Evan's family contributed three more than the other contributions put together. How many cupcakes did the class have to sell?" The students might add and subtract, or they might multiply and add, but whatever way they choose to solve the problem, there is one correct answer.

4. Type IV problems have multiple methods as well as multiple possible solutions. For example, students may be asked to use the numbers 15, 18, 3, and write correct addition and subtraction equations using only these numbers. They can create several different equations and can reach several different solutions.

5. Type V problems are presented, but an almost unlimited number of solution methods and possible solutions exist. For example, if the student is given the number 18 and told to write as many equations as possible with that number as the answer, the student may generate any number of possible equations and methods to solve them.

6. Type VI problems are discovered by both the teacher and students. A math problem of this type might be to ask students to choose a method of representing mathematical concepts other than Arabic numbers and solve an equation in their system. Type VI problem situations require the most creativity and are the most real because the problem solver must define the problem before attempting to solve it.

Thus, the FPSPI is different from most educational programs in its emphasis on problem-finding as well as problem-solving (Torrance, 1976). In this problem-finding step, students must become familiar with the topic in order to readily utilize both divergent thinking for finding many possible issues and convergent thinking for finding the best most relevant issues. In a research lesson, a school librarian could help the students to access resources and communicate with practitioners and experts. In addition, the school librarian can help students understand how to evaluate the veracity of the information that they find from various sources.

It is in the "produce solution ideas" step that students think most divergently to produce their ideas for problem-solving. Thus, a school librarian should lead them to think flexibly across discipline borders. In this respect, a library should be an intellectual playground where students think, imagine, and perform flexibly, and in this playground the main plaything is knowledge. They might attain a flow state when handling intellectual challenges at the appropriate curiosity level (Csikszentmihalyi, 1990). When they perceive this process as play, this perception helps make their experience enjoyable, which increases their motivation and encourages them to continue playing. While imagining, thinking about, and experimenting with diverse solutions, they will probably seek increasingly greater challenges, which can finally provoke creative shifts in their thinking (Csikszentmihalyi, Abuhamdeh, & Nakamura, 2005).

In order to enhance their flow, a school library can provide nontraditional physical spaces, which allow students to reconfigure tables and chairs so that they can think in different ways as the design firm IDEO does (Kaufman & Sternberg, 2010). A school librarian can give students free areas for capturing ideas such as a thinking cave or other atypical structures. However, it would be more important for them to have autonomy and an open atmosphere, which boosts their creativity while allowing them to feel emotionally safe. When trying something new, the school librarian is a mentor who supports students every step of the way. In this way, school librarians become creative facilitators.

For instance, the thought experiment was Albert Einstein's novel way for exploring light beams, leading to Special Relativity because it was impossible for him to conduct the idea through normal physical experiments (Root-Bernstein & Root-Bernstein, 1999). Alexander Fleming discovered penicillin by accident while playing around with culture mediums (Root-Bernstein & Root-Bernstein, 1999). These cases indicate that creative products can come out unexpectedly as a result of exploration, which is a form of play. Thus, in this step a school librarian facilitates divergent thinking while immersing students in play that leads to finding creative solutions.

In steps four and five, "generate and select criteria" and "apply criteria to solution idea," students sharpen communication, evaluative thinking, and collaboration skills. It is better for the students to take an objective stance as evaluator for realistic solutions, and communication with others helps them to have a balanced perspective. A school librarian can provide discussion boards and tables in various places in the library in order to facilitate students' interactions with one another, or create blogs.

In step six, "develop an action plan," students learn that public recognition is necessary for creativity because creativity is strongly associated with social acknowledgment (Kaufman & Sternberg, 2010). Students are required to proficiently sell their ideas and persuade the audience to approve the value of their creative solutions. Presentation modes can include figural formats, movie clips, computer presentations, booklets, brochures, graphs, simulations, and so forth. A school librarian can provide students access to a variety of equipment and teach them to use these platforms and technologies effectively.

Application II: How to Facilitate Creativity in a Class

School librarians can work cooperatively with classroom teachers to use FPS in classroom environments. Classroom teachers may think that school librarians are not responsible for teaching curriculum and domain-specific knowledge, but the Common Core State Standards (CCSS) changed this expectation—teaching (no matter the content) is the responsibility of every educator in the school. One can argue that this was true previously. However, in many cases it is still true. That is one of the ways that CCSS is being sold to librarians.

An interdisciplinary approach is necessary for a successful transit toward creative classes, which may lead to a reconstructed curriculum based on flexibility. FPS is also a good teaching strategy to help students understand the CCSS standards more effectively. These benefits come about because many objects and topics of the CCSS overlap with those of FPS. The many educational standards that can be acquired by FPS in school are in cited in the following text (Cramond, 2009). The FPSI website also provides topics and content-specific standards; therefore, it would be a good resource for teachers. In addition, the next sections describe respectively how to apply FPS in specific subjects: mathematics, science, and social studies.

Some Curriculum Standards and the FPSPI (Cramond, 2009)

LIFE SKILLS

THINKING AND REASONING

- Understands and applies basic principles of logic and reasoning
- Understands and applies the basic principles of presenting an argument
- Effectively uses mental processes that are based on identifying similarities and differences (compares, contrasts, and classifies)
- Applies basic problem-solving techniques
- Applies decision-making techniques.

WORKING WITH OTHERS

- Uses conflict–resolution techniques when disagreements occur
- Works well with diverse individuals and in diverse situations
- Displays effective interpersonal communication skills
- Contributes to the overall effort of a group
- Demonstrates leadership skills when making decisions.

TECHNOLOGY

- Understands the nature and uses of different forms of technology to obtain topic research
- Understands the relationship among science, technology, society, and the individual
- Understands the nature and operation of systems
- Understands the nature and uses of different forms of technology.

BEHAVIORAL STUDIES

- Understands conflict, cooperation, and interdependence among individuals, groups, and institutions
- Understands that group and cultural influences contribute to human development, identity, and behavior when working on a project in a multicultural community
- Understands various meanings of social group, general implications of group membership and different ways groups function to involve various groups in a project
- Understands that interactions among learning, inheritance, and physical development affect human behavior in order to respond appropriately to a variety of situations.

Mathematics

According to a recent AP-AOL Poll (Willis, 2010, p. 5), mathematics is one of the least popular subjects among U.S. students. For many students the dislike for mathematics begins in elementary school with the memorization of math facts, and this negative attitude is continued throughout their schooling as they are taught for tests (Willis, 2010).

Through FPS, students can apply mathematical thinking to meaningful problems closely connected with their lives. In other words, they learn how to think mathematically while solving future problems, which offers them a meaningful context for learning.

Here is an example topic about the problem of energy in the future. In a mathematics class, students draw a graph, which illustrates the tendency of population change to show population growth. They might need to learn differentiation to calculate the change rate of the consumption of resources based on one unit growth of population. They also can calculate, via algebra, how long the population will be able to depend on fossil fuels. In addition, they can create a matrix in order to consider multiple variables in the real world because a matrix can help students handle complicated functions, which include many variables. They may also apply a Venn diagram to figure out common features and the distinction between two competitive future energies. In this respect, utilizing mathematics concepts would not be tedious for students; rather, it would involve meaningful problem-solving processes as well as meet CCSS.

Science

Science is a systematic entity of knowledge demanding rigorous inquiry to acquire reliable knowledge. Thus, when it comes to science, not only domain-specific knowledge but also scientific inquiry skills are emphasized in science education. Accordingly, the core standard of science addresses the how-to-do inquiry along with domain-specific knowledge in science classes. For inquiry learning, problem-based learning is frequently used as a teaching strategy. Therefore, in science classes, teachers need to encourage students to conduct inquiry in a creative manner as if they were scientists. Moreover, science education should also focus on ethics because science has greater influence on society and people's lives than many other subjects. The objective of science is not to create proficient technicians but produce creative problem solvers who can meet the needs of society. In this respect, FPS would show how to enhance ethical awareness and civic consciousness in students' learning through problem-solving based on their community and future problems for humankind.

Most scientific inquiry skills can be learned through FPS. Examples of inquiry skills included in the core standards of science for elementary grades include classifying, communicating, comparing and contrasting, creating models, gathering and organizing data, generalizing, identifying variables, inferring, interpreting data, making decisions, manipulating materials, measuring, observing, predicting (New York State Education Department, 2012). During this first step of FPSP, students might gather scattered facts about the depletion of fossil fuel and several issues about sustainable development, which would enhance their understanding by gathering and organizing information. In the second step, students question each other and analyze the relationship between the problems, which would lead them to compare, contrast, and identify the main variables. In the third step, students produce ideas for solutions through divergent discussion, which would provide experiences in communicating and classifying. In the fourth step, students generate as many criteria as possible and select critical criteria, which would require them to predict the corresponding results. In the fifth step, students evaluate the appropriateness of solutions using criteria to rank the order of the ideas for solutions, which would assist them in making decisions, predicting, and creating models. In the final step, students suggest a convincing action plan to develop a specific future energy that can substitute for fossil fuel and meet their own criteria, which would help them to communicate and to generalize.

In many cases, science teachers can use FPS in an abbreviated form to enhance the school's curriculum and differentiate instruction and learning. Future scenarios can make science more palatable for students. For example, when teaching about heat energy, teachers can introduce the topic of depletion of fossil fuels, pollution, and alternative future energy sources as a fuzzy situation. Alternative future energy sources might be too broad for students to produce their own solutions in a unit class, and therefore the teachers will need to break it down into specific problem-based activities, which students can handle in a series of classes such as inventing their own solar cookers and kinetically powered motors.

Social studies

FPS is usually applied to topics in social studies, and therefore it would be easy for social studies teachers to apply FPS. More importantly, FPS topics are based

Table 14.2   Curriculum Reconstructing Example Based on an Interdisciplinary Approach

	TOPIC: DEVELOPING A FUTURE ENERGY		
SUBJECT / FPS PROCESS	MATHEMATICS	SCIENCE	SOCIAL STUDIES
1. Identify the challenge	Drawing a graph on the remaining fossil fuels	Gathering scientific evidence of problems	Gathering the social problem
2. Select an underlying idea		Analyzing the scientific principles and selecting the fundamental problems	
3. Produce ideas for solutions			Finding similar cases from history
4. Generate and select criteria	Classifying strengths and weaknesses with a Venn diagram		Discussion with team members to select criteria
5. Apply criteria to solution ideas		Predicting or anticipating results when applying solutions	
6. Develop an action plan		Manipulating an alternative energy in a lab	Predicting and synthesizing social changes after applying action plans

Note: Created by Suehyeon Paek.

on social issues closely associated with government, civic life, and politics. Thus, students begin to understand governmental and political topics as part of the big picture while completing FPS. In particular, community problem-solving focuses on where they live, which is central to civic consciousness and social studies.

In conclusion, FPS can be applied meaningfully in individual subjects; however, an interdisciplinary approach to specific topics through FPS is also recommended. Table 14.2 shows the example of interdisciplinary reconstruction of curriculum. There might be a few teachers who have difficulties following the steps of FPS. Thus, teachers can modify FPS depending on the level of the students, the school curriculum, and the readiness of teachers themselves. For instance, many students struggle when they are required to represent their ideas via well-organized writing. One of the flexible transformations could be added into the last step of FPS, which allows diverse creative substitutions for writing. This could be a basic step for a teacher to easily adapt the FPS in his class. In particular, in the case of students in the lower grades who are not proficient at writing, a teacher can switch the final step of FPS into a classroom activity that shows students' different methods of presenting information, depending on the learners' readiness and concerns: drawings, crafts, graphs, dramas, PowerPoint, oral presentations, movie clips, or decision-making activities that don't need to be represented in writing. These additional activities can help those in the lower grades and learners who might have difficulties with written language as a final report format. Thus, a teacher can flexibly combine diverse symbolic representations.

CONCLUSION

FPS is a systematic way for school librarians and teachers to develop students' creative and collaborative skills. Educators who are uncomfortable with the open-endedness of teaching for creativity may find the structure and proven effectiveness of FPS reassuring. An added benefit of FPS is the many resources, both free and at minimum expense, that support every step of the process. As illustrated, FPS supports teacher and school librarian collaboration. Through the use of FPS and FPSPI, students can learn knowledge (develop expertise), skills, and dispositions that are necessary for innovation and successful cooperation in the modern workplace (Cramond & Fairweather, in press).

REFERENCES

Barber, M. (August 22, 2012). Lessons on education from Singapore. *The Guardian.* Retrieved from http://www.guardian.co.uk/commentisfree/2012/aug/22/lessons-education-singapore-gove.

Baron, D. E. (2009). *Inventing the wheel. A better pencil: Readers, writers, and the digital revolution.* New York: Oxford University Press.

Cramond, B. (2009). Future problem solving in gifted education. In L. Shavinina (Ed.), *Handbook on giftedness* (pp. 1143–1156). New York: Springer.

Cramond, B.L., & Fairweather, E.C. (in press) Future problem solving as education for innovation. In L. Shavinnia (Ed.), *The international handbook of innovation education* (pp. 215–226). New York: Routledge.

Csikszentmihalyi, M. (1990). *Flow: The psychology of optimal experience.* New York: Harper & Row.

Csikszentmihalyi, M., Abuhamdeh, S., & Nakamura, J. (2005). Flow. In A. Elliot & C.S. Dweck (Eds.), *Handbook of competence and motivation* (pp. 598–608). New York: Guilford Publications.

Davis, G.A., Rimm, S.B., & Siegle, D. (2011). *Education of the gifted and talented.* Boston, MA: Pearson.

Einstein, A., & Infeld, L. (1938). *The evolution of physics: The growth of ideas from early concept to relativity and quanta.* New York: Simon and Schuster.

European Commission. (2009). *Creativity in schools in Europe: A survey of teachers.* A report by the European Schoolnet (EUN) and the Institute for Prospective Technological Studies (JRC-IPTS). Retrieved from http://ftp.jrc.es/EURdoc/JRC55645_Creativity%20Survey%20Brochure.pdf.

Friedman, T. (2005). *The world is flat.* New York: Farrar, Straus, & Giroux.

Future Problem Solving Problem International (FPSPI) (n.d.). Retrieved from http://www.fpspi.org.

Future Problem Solving Program. *Future Problem Solving program coach's handbook* (2001). Lexington, KY: Future Problem Solving Program.

Hamilton, B. (April 2, 2012). Do I really have to leave the role of school librarian to do the work of a school librarian? [Web lot comment]. *The unquiet librarian.* Retrieved from http://theunquietlibrarian.wordpress.com/2012/04/02/do-i-really-have-to-leave-the-school-library-to-do-the-work-of-a-school-librarian/.

Kaufman, J.C., & Sternberg, R.J. (2010). *Cambridge handbook of creativity.* New York: Cambridge University Press.

Lim, R. (May 22, 2012). *Singapore wants creativity, not cramming.* BBC News, Singapore. Retrieved from http://www.bbc.co.uk/news/business-17891211.

Maker, C.J. DISCOVER problem continuum. Retrieved from http://discover.arizona.edu/problem_solving.htm.

Maker, C.J. (2005). *The DISCOVER project: Improving assessment and curriculum for diverse gifted learners. Senior Scholars Series.* Storrs, CT: The National Research Center for the Gifted and Talented. RM05206. Retrieved from http://www.gifted.uconn.edu/nrcgt/reports/rm05206/rm05206.pdf.

Maker, C.J., & Schiever, S.W. (2005). *Teaching models in education of the gifted* (3rd ed.). Austin, TX: PRO-ED.

New York State Education Department (2012). *New York State learning standards and science resource guide with core curriculum.* Retrieved from http://www.p12.nysed.gov/ciai/cores.html.

Osborn, A.F. (1953). *Applied imagination.* New York: Scribner.

Parnes, S.J. (1967). *Creative behavior guidebook.* New York: Scribner.

Rogalla, M. (2003). *Future problem solving program coaches' efficacy in teaching for successful intelligence and their patterns of successful behavior* (doctoral dissertation). Retrieved from OAIster (edsoai.729302593).

Root-Bernstein, R., & Root-Bernstein, M. (1999). *Sparks of genius: The 13 thinking tools of the world's most creative people.* Boston, MA: Houghton Mifflin.

Runco, M., & Jaeger, G. (2012). The standard definition of creativity. *Creativity Research Journal, 24(1),* 92–96.

The Creative Economy 2010—Creative economy: A feasible development option (2010). New York: United Nations Conference on Trade and Development and United Nations Development Program. Retrieved from http://www.unctad.org/creative-economy.

Torrance, E.P. (1976). *Future problem solving and career education.* Athens, GA: Pre-Service Training in Career Education Project, College of Education, University of Georgia.

Torrance, E.P. (1978). Giftedness in solving future problems. *Journal of Creative Behavior, 12,* 75–86.

Trilling, B., & Fadel, C. (2012). *21st century skills: Learning for life in our times.* New York: Jossey-Bass.

Voice of America (September 18, 2011). *Seeking creativity, Asian educators look to US programs* [Audio podcast]. Retrieved from http://www.voanews.com/content/seeking-creativity-asian-educators-look-to-us-programs-130115718/168004.html.

Willis, J. (2010). *Learning to love math: Teaching strategies that change student attitudes and get results.* Alexandria, VA: Association for Supervision & Curriculum Development.

15

BIBLIOCREATIVITY: HOW BOOKS AND STORIES DEVELOP CREATIVITY

Brian Sturm
University of North Carolina, Chapel Hill

While the idea that written language and books can exert a powerful influence on people and society has existed for at least 2,000 years—Socrates, for example, is well-known for his belief that writing would erode memory—the concept of "bibliotherapy," the purposeful use of books to help readers cope with specific problems, is much more recent. The first English language use of "bibliotherapy" (from *biblio* meaning "book" and *theraps* meaning "healing") is attributed to novelist Christopher Morley in 1920 (Bibliotherapy, 2010). The basic premise underlying bibliotherapy is one of similarity. A reader who is experiencing a dilemma or problem finds a story character in a similar situation, and the reader can then vicariously experiment with coping strategies by watching the character struggle through the problem. Though there is ongoing discussion as to whether the power to affect the reader occurs during the reading process or during the ensuing conversation with a trained therapist, there is general consensus that reading about others' lives and situations in texts has the power to change us. While bibliotherapy explores the ability of books to augment healing, "bibliocreativity" explores the power of books to promote creativity.

Ross Mooney (1963) identifies four approaches to creativity that warrant exploration:

- The creative product
- The creative person
- The creative process
- The environment (context) in which the creation takes place (p. 331).

A product-centric approach focuses on the identification of objects that match certain criteria of creativity; the person-centric approach seeks to identify discernible signs of creativity or personality traits common to people considered creative; the process-centric approach seeks to understand how creative people think, feel, and conduct their lives during the act of creation; and the environmental approach explores the various influences of the context in which creation occurs. Taken to-gether, these are the what, who, how/why, and where of creativity.

All of these stances are pertinent to the reading experience, as an author (*person*) writes a book (*product*) that is read (*process*) by a reader (*person*) in a setting (*environment*), and each one could be the focus of legitimate study. A study of the creative book might explore creativity in telling the story, such as elements of style, word selection, figurative language, illustration, plot devices, or other authorial techniques; alternatively, it could focus on the book as object and ex-amine creativity evident in the layout, overall shape, typography, or binding. A study of the creative person in the reading transaction could seek to divulge the creative characteristics of the author that helped him to write the book, or it could examine the creativity needed by the reader to understand the book, such as the ability to immerse oneself in an alternate world (Nell, 1988; Sturm, 2001). Studying the environment of reading might lead to an examination of the influ-ence of location (i.e., fireside, bedroom, or library) on the reading experience, or the impact of other contextual factors (i.e., physical comfort, lighting, or space) on reading. This chapter, however, seeks to address primarily the creative process of reading: how people's interactions with texts and pictures may evoke their creative potentials.

CREATIVITY?

The *Oxford English Dictionary Online* traces the etymology of the word "create" back to the Latin *creāre* meaning "to procreate or give birth or to bring into being, to produce, to bring about, cause," and it offers, among others, the comparison words of *creer, crier* (Anglo-Norman meaning "to create from nothing, to pro-duce") and *criar* (Spanish meaning "to bring up, to raise"). Current conceptions of creativity find their origin in these words. For example, creativity has been de-fined as the ability to "produce where nothing was before" (Create, 2010) or the ability to form "novel combinations of old ideas" (Boden, 1994, p. 75).

Arthur Koestler (1964) calls this combination of disparate ideas to form some-thing new "bisociation." When a concept understood in one context is suddenly seen from a second, typically incompatible perspective, and these two association matrices collide, creativity is the result. Imagine a room in which the floor rep-resents an idea in its usual frame of reference (i.e., rain on the sidewalk), and the wall represents a different idea in *its* usual frame of reference (i.e., a person cry-ing). When these two frames of reference intersect (at the corner of the wall and the floor), a creative juxtaposition occurs, as in "his tears darkened the sidewalk." Another classic example of bisociation at work is the trucker who invented the concept of the container ship by merging his understanding of the convenience of containers on semitrucks with the inefficiency of dockside loading and unloading of cargo; why not ship the container as well so as to avoid packing and unpacking its contents?

Both the "something from nothing" and the "new connections" definitions hearken back to their etymological roots and the idea of childbirth, the union of two unrelated people to create something new. However, the act of creation is not enough for creativity because—to continue the metaphor—that which is cre-ated must then be nourished, tended, and grown-up. As R. Keith Sawyer (2012) comments, "Creativity is a new mental combination that is *expressed in the world*"

(p. 7, emphasis added). Herbert Simon (2001) concurs, claiming, "We judge thought to be creative when it produces something that is both novel and interesting and valuable" (p. 208). Creativity involves both a unique idea or synthesis and the dissemination of that idea to others.

HOW BOOKS FOSTER CREATIVITY

Something from Nothing

If creativity can be considered the ability to make something from nothing and new connections, reading is a highly creative process. When a reader engages a text, she must draw information from at least two different sources: the text itself, and the reader's background, experience, and associations that enlighten the reader and flesh out the details left out by the author. No author can possibly include all of the details of a story; indeed, to do so would create a tale that would be unmanageably long and utterly boring because the reader would be left with little to do other than to watch passively as the story evolved.

Few readers want that experience; instead, they want to be involved in the creation of the story, to be coauthors, as it were, of the unfolding narrative. The author provides enough stimulation to begin the visualization process and then leaves many of the details to the imagination of the reader. A fantasy writer might describe a dragon as being as tall as a house, covered in black scales, and with large fangs, blood-red eyes, and fiery breath. This is enough to sketch the outline, but the rest of the details are left to the reader to supply based on her previous exposure to images or descriptions of dragons (two or four legs? wings? spiked tail? etc.). Thackeray (1945) proclaimed, "I have said somewhere it is the unwritten part of books that would be the most interesting" (p. 391), or as Wolfgang Iser (1972) explained, "it is only through inevitable omissions that a story will gain its dynamism" (p. 284). The reader must fill in the gaps in any story, creating something where the author has provided nothing.

This holds true in graphic novels and comics as well. Scott McCloud (1993) drew attention to the "space between panels" that required readers to fill in missing details in the action and story line.

> Comics is often thought of as the joining of two art forms, writing and drawing, *but what happens between panels isn't about either, it's about the audience's imagination.* (p. 50, emphasis added)

To get from one panel, showing a speeding car racing across a bridge to the next showing a pile of burning wreckage in the stream below, readers would need to supply the intervening action, imagining the car spinning out of control, crashing through the barricade, and plunging through space to crumple and explode on the rocky floor below. We are given the initiating action, and its result, but the space between is left to each reader to construct independently and creatively.

How much of the world is provided by the author, and how much is envisioned by the reader depends on the moment of the reading experience as different readers bring different backgrounds to bear on any particular text, and any individual reader will experience a text differently if she is rereading it instead of encountering it for the first time.

> There will always be a trade-off between a world that is more given (more authored from the outside and therefore imbued with the magic of external-ized fantasy) and a world that is more improvised (and therefore closer to individual fantasies). The area of immersive enchantment lies in the overlap between these two domains. (Murray, 1997, p. 267)

The ability to fill in details of a story not addressed by the words is one to which we are exposed early in our reading lives. Picture books teach pre-readers this no-tion as the pictures and text interweave, each telling a slightly different story. A picture book is a book in which "the visual and the verbal aspects are both essential for full communication" (Nikolajeva & Scott, 2000, p. 226). Each relies on the other, and neither tells the complete story.

As the child encounters a picture book text and struggles to fill in the gaps left by the words, the pictures come to her aid and help fill in some of those missing details. This scaffolding bolsters the child's limited knowledge of story structure, and it provides options for creating meaning if she cannot fill the gaps effectively from her own prior experiences and associations. The unique dance of picture books, however, is that myriad relationships can exist between the pictures and the text, forcing the reader to remain open to many possible interpretations. Nikolajeva & Scott (2000) mentioned five such possibilities: *symmetrical* (pictures and text tell the same story through different media); *enhancing* (pictures amplify words); *complementary* (pictures and text work interdependently, supplying a lot of the missing information in the other); *counterpointing* (images and text move beyond what either can do alone); and *contradictory* (words and text seem to offer different and opposing stories) (p. 225–226). The child who encounters a picture book, then, must figure out the relationship between the pictures and the text, and she uses each to comprehend the other. This requires flexibility of thought and a willingness to take interpretive risks.

There are also gaps in stories due to their being experienced over time, so the reader lacks information necessary to understand the series of events that comprise the plot of the story. Readers engage with fictional text to find out what happens in the story, and this knowledge gap keeps readers constantly formulating and re-formulating their expectations of what might happen. Describing the re-creation of the fictional world by the reader, Iser (1972) explains that "we look forward, we look back, we decide, we change our decisions, we form expectations, we are shocked by their nonfulfillment, we question, we muse, we accept, we reject" (p. 293). This constant revision requires flexibility, openness to new situations and interpretations, and a proclivity to knowledge acquisition and problem-finding and problem-solving, all of which are fundamental to creativity.

Vicarious Experience

One of the most profoundly creative processes in the reading experience is the way in which we associate what has happened in the text to our own lives as readers. As the world of the story "bisociates" with the world of the reader, new connec-tions are forged between previously discrete frames of reference (story and reality).

When a suburban child reads a realistic fiction novel set in the inner city, or when a child reads an historical fiction novel or a science fiction novel set in the past or future, respectively, the reader must stretch beyond what she previously knew to accommodate this new information. The child finds similarities between "that world" and "my world" that broaden and deepen the child's experiential base, and since the story encounter is vicarious, it can be experienced *as if* real without the threat of real-world consequences. "This is why we recognize in literature so many elements that play a part of our own experience. They are simply put together in a different way—in other words, they constitute a familiar world reproduced in an unfamiliar form" (Iser, 1971, pp. 7–8).

This creative association happens on the character level as well. While there is an ongoing discussion as to the exact nature of the reader's relationship to fictional characters (Inglis, 1971; Oatley, 1995; Zillman, 1995), there is general agreement that readers *must* relate to story characters in some fashion if they are to engage in the fictional reading experience. The reader allies herself with a character's perspective and experiences the fictional world in ways similar to how the character would do so. This relationship may be fairly distant (i.e., the distinction between the reader and the character remains strong) resulting in the reader taking the stance of a bystander or spectator of the events and emotions in the story. The reader then watches the story character explore the story world but does not feel involved in it or particularly moved by it. If the reader allies herself more closely with the story character, she may begin to sympathize with that character, or *feel for* the character; this implies an investment of emotional energy in the character's world, but a refusal to enter deeply into partnership with that character. One can feel sympathy for another's pain without feeling it oneself. A reader in this stance might say, "I see you are in pain, and I am sorry."

On a deeper level, readers may feel empathy, or *feeling with*, the story character, such that the emotions of the character are understood by the reader as a result of prior experience with similar emotions. A reader in this stance might say, "I understand your pain because I have experienced similar pain in my life." Arguably the deepest level of alliance with a story character is identification, in which the reader transposes herself into the story and experiences the character's emotions as if they were her own. This reader might say, "I feel the pain of this story situation." While readers always seem to know that their experience is fictional (i.e., not real), the most immersed readers experience texts as if they were real, using such descriptions as, "I was just there; I'm just part of it," or "it [the story] was happening all around me" (Sturm, 1998, p. 106). Patrick Dust (1981) explained this transition into a story character's world:

> One way of describing this transition is to say that he [the reader] assumes a special state of mind in which he makes himself empty in order to fill himself with the reality portrayed by the text. In other words his imagination enters into such a deep and perfect rapport with the symbol [the text] that the reader *becomes* that particular reality. (p. 146)

While Dust acknowledged that this is an exaggeration (as no one can completely erase all personal experience), the way readers experience this transition is one of complete presence in the story and identification with story characters.

The reader's relationship with story characters is deepened any time that character speaks due to the multiple possible referents for the word "I," known in some circles as the "deictic shift" (Duchan, Bruder, & Hewitt, 1995). Deixis is a linguistic term referring to words that have no meaning unless the context is included. Words such as "there" or "here" mean nothing until the environment is included, but the word "I" has a special function. When a character says, "I went to the inn," the reader translates this into "the character went to the inn," but the reader also hears "I went to the inn." Because "I" requires context for meaning, the reader can understand this word in two different contexts: 1) in the story world, the "I" refers to the character, but 2) in the reading experience, the "I" can refer to the reader as well. The spoken word "I" then ends up referring to the character in one context *and* to the reader in another. When these two contexts are bisociated in the reading experience, the reader's identification with that character is heightened. The reader may then experience the words, "I went to the inn," as if she were the character and went, herself, to the inn.

The reader's vicarious experience of the story is furthered by other relationships as well. Some stories include symbols that resonate across cultures. These archetypes are behavioral patterns, emotional undertones, or prototypical characterizations that seem universally understood because they are, in Jungian terms, part of the "collective unconscious" or "the whole spiritual heritage of mankind's evolution, born anew in the brain structure of every individual" (Campbell, 1976, p. 45). Folktales and fairy tales are replete with these archetypical symbols. As Marie-Louise von Franz (1996) stated:

> Fairy tales are the purest and simplest expression of collective unconscious psychic processes . . . [and] they represent the archetypes in their simplest, barest, and most concise form. . . . In myths or legends, or any other more elaborate mythological material, we get at the basic patterns of the human psyche through an overlay of cultural material. (p. 1)

Archetypes, then, serve as fundamental, creative bridges between people and other cultures, encouraging listeners or readers to forge personal connections to unfamiliar content and contexts and easing the synergies needed for creativity.

Figurative Language

Although there have been many different ways of describing the essential process at work in a creative act . . . perhaps the simplest and most direct description has been offered by Gordon (1961); make the strange familiar and the familiar strange. As he and others point out, one aspect of human language that seems ideally suited to this dual function is that of figurative language (Pollio & Pollio, 1971, p. 1).

Metaphor, one kind of figurative language, is a linguistic bisociation. Terms that are linked metaphorically are not meant to be interpreted literally; indeed, a literal interpretation is usually impossible, as metaphors are used to express ideas that are difficult to state explicitly. "Understanding the figurative meaning of a metaphor requires mental linkage of different category domains normally not related to each other" (Rapp, Leube, Erb, Grodd, & Kircher, 2004, p. 395). In other words, a term understood in one context is associated with another context that requires the reader to merge the two in order to make meaning of the association. The Alfred Noyes (1907) poem, *The Highwayman*, is a classic example of metaphoric language:

> The wind was a torrent of darkness among the gusty trees,
> The moon was a ghostly galleon tossed upon cloudy seas,
> The road was a ribbon of moonlight over the purple moor. . . . (p. 35)

The moon, appearing and disappearing behind clouds, is compared to a ship rising and falling in a heaving ocean swell, and the result is the creative association of the tempestuous quality of these two contexts that adds the imminent danger of the ship at sea to the more benign experience of the cloudy sky. Similarly, the first line adds the reader's visual and visceral associations with "darkness" to the typically aural and tactile experience of wind. The word "torrent" adds a further layer of physicality as it is usually associated with water (either a turbulent stream or a heavy downpour). Metaphor, then, forces the reader to form creative associations between terms where none existed before.

The ambiguity inherent in other forms of figurative language works in similar ways, requiring readers to be creative as they explore meaning beyond the literal and obvious. An *oxymoron* unites two contradictory words for emphasis ("living death"), whereas *hyperbole* exaggerates a situation beyond reason ("he was so hungry he could eat an elephant"). *Verbal irony* forces the reader to differentiate between what is said and what is meant: ("That's great!" when the speaker means, "that's horrible!"); *personification* attributes human characteristics to inanimate objects ("the sky wept"); and *onomatopoeia* makes readers experience the sound of the object described ("the car vroomed past"). For readers to make sense of figurative language in narrative, they must combine disparate domains of knowledge to form new synergies, a fundamentally creative act.

Beyond Story Worlds

Readers make meaning of story by decoding what the author (and/or illustrator) provides and filling in the gaps from personal experience and associations, through a recursive process of creating and re-creating scenarios for what might happen next, establishing relationships with story characters, interpreting figurative language, experiencing the story world vicariously, and connecting the story world experience to real life. Judith Langer (1990) described this interpretive process as one of building an "envisionment . . . what a reader understands at a particular time, the questions she has, as well as her hunches about how the piece will unfold" (p. 812) that consists of four stances:

1. Being out and stepping in
2. Being in and moving through
3. Being in and stepping out
4. Stepping out and objectifying the experience (p. 813).

These stances correspond to: 1) beginning to read and encounter the structures of language, content, and genre, 2) becoming immersed in the story world, 3) drawing connection between the story world and the reader's own reality, and 4) reflecting on and evaluating the reading experience.

This last stance is one that can lead to a further creative endeavor for those who wish to remain in the story world longer than the author has allowed. As readers step out of the storyline provided by the author, they begin to realize that the story they have encountered is only one of myriad stories that *could* have been told. The author has presented some of the characters and some of the events that might take place in any fictional world, but, just as a biography is the story of one person on a planet of billions, so, too, is the author's story just one of many possibilities. Readers respond and fill this gap with their own fan fiction, telling other stories about other characters in a given story world. Avid followers of such series as *Star Trek, Harry Potter, Twilight,* and *The Lord of the Rings* have created their own stories to expand the ones written by the original authors. Margaret Mackey (1999, 2003) has explored the ways in which texts cross the boundaries of the *diegesis*—the story as told by the text—to delve into the "phase space"—the myriad potential stories that are not told by the author. The concept of transmedia storytelling is also gaining prominence in today's world of technological proliferation, as the way one particular story, organization, or brand, is shared across media.

As they step out and begin to objectify their experience, moving beyond the world-as-provided to develop their own narrative worlds, readers are being creative in the second aspect of the definition of creativity—sharing their new ideas with the world. While the reading act is often a solitary one, the reading experience, broadly construed, is a social one. Readers talk about the texts they read (whether in book, magazine, newspaper, or digital format) in casual conversation, book clubs, book reviews, wikis and blogs, and online social networks. Fictional stories become inextricably entangled with real-world experiences as readers cocreate them, and each affects the other. Readers, then, are continually negotiating the bisociation between narrative worlds and reality, and this is a process that demands a high degree of creativity.

USING BOOKS CREATIVELY WITH CHILDREN

While reading itself is a creative act, there are ways of sharing texts that can increase their creative potential. Many of these techniques are used primarily with children, but all readers can engage in these practices.

Dialogic Reading

Dialogic reading—as developed by Whitehurst and his colleagues—is a process most often used with preschool children that turns the typical parent-reading–child-listening experience into a conversation (Whitehurst, et. al., 1988). The technique involves encouraging the child to interact with the text through a PEER process:

- Prompting the child to make a comment on the text or pictures
- Evaluating that response
- Expanding the response through rephrasing and additional information
- Repeating the expanded response.

Whitehurst (n.d.) gives the following example of how this might unfold:

> Imagine that the parent and the child are looking at the page of a book that has a picture of a fire engine on it. The parent says, "What is this?" (the prompt) while pointing to the fire truck. The child says, *truck*, and the parent follows with "That's right (the evaluation); it's a red fire truck (the expansion); can you say *fire truck?*" (the repetition).

While the listening involved in the read-aloud experience is certainly creative (the pre-reading child is visualizing and filling in the gaps in the story as best he can), dialogic reading pushes the child to interact with the story in ways that are behavioral and observable (hence more readily researched) and that model thoughtful reading practices. More importantly, however, some of the prompts a parent can use encourage creativity as defined in this chapter. For example, while completion prompts and recall prompts focus more on memory and story recall, open-ended prompts encourage children to use their own words and develop their own ideas to answer questions (i.e., "What might the character do next?"), and distancing prompts ask children to relate the story world to their own lives ("Has something like this ever happened to you?"). These last two types of prompts ask children to project future possibilities based on existing evidence and to bisociate the story world and reality.

Storytelling

Storytelling and story retelling are marvelous complements to story reading, as they not only provide children (and adults) with the chance to internalize and solidify in memory the story structure and content—research shows that knowledge of story structure increases reading comprehension, reading, and writing ability in children (Haven, 2007)—they also encourage readers to take risks in reframing the heard or read story by adding their own performance touches or altering the storyline details to match their internal representations. Harold Rosen (1986), while denouncing the ubiquity of memorization in education, describes "the ways in which we [storytellers] at one and the same time repeat words and stories of others and transform them. . . . We elaborate, compress, innovate, and discard, take shocking liberties, [and] delicately shift nuances" (p. 235). As Mikhail Bakhtin (1981) states, retelling is "no simple act of reproduction, but rather a further creative development of another's [. . .] discourse in a new context and under new conditions" (p. 347). When we tell stories we have heard or read, we integrate our personal associations and experiences into the story and, thereby, personalize our performance of it; we add our own creative interpretation, using the text as a springboard.

Creative Dramatics

When readers hear or read story and turn it into theater, they engage in many of the creative behaviors that storytelling enables (personalizing, elaborating, and interpreting), but they add the element of collaboration with others. Drama adds a level of complexity to storytelling, as performers rely on each other to accomplish the story task. This requires flexibility, social poise, and an added level of risk-taking that are all hallmarks of creative individuals (Dacey, 1989; Dellas & Gaier, 1970). Theater also facilitates identification with character as the actor develops the persona of the character he is portraying, filling in subtle details in performance that were left out in the text. The improvisational possibilities of certain types of drama also open the door to inventing new storylines and characters beyond the diegesis, as the interpretive process unfolds.

Book Trailers

Creating book trailers—short movies that offer glimpses of book story lines while trying to entice potential readers to pick up the book—offers another creative outlet for engaging with texts, story, and digital technology. Making an effective book trailer entails deciding what to include and what to exclude (most trailers last no more than 40–80 seconds) to capture the viewer's interest; the creator of a book trailer must critically evaluate what is missing, as the process of condensing a novel into an extremely short, teaser video involves leaving much to the viewer's imagination. Telling the story in movie format also forces readers to confront the issue of transmedia storytelling and evaluate the strengths and weaknesses of different media for telling a particular story.

CONCLUSION

The experience of reading is an actively creative process involving synthesizing new ideas from given experiences (texts) with personal experiences and associations. As readers fill in the gaps left in stories, as they build scenarios of possible story endings, as they make imaginative leaps when interpreting figurative language, as their unconscious resonates with archetypal symbols, as they integrate their reality and their lives with those of the story world and its characters, and as they move beyond the diegesis of a particular text to create new stories or new performances, they explore and develop their creative potential. Reading is, indeed, an extraordinarily creative endeavor!

REFERENCES

Bakhtin, M. (1981). Discourse in the novel. In M. Holquist (Ed.), *The dialogic imagination: Four essays* (pp. 259–422). Austin, TX: University of Texas Press.

Bibliotherapy. (2010). In *Oxford English dictionary online*. Retrieved August 8, 2012, from http://www.oed.com/view/Entry/18658.

Boden, M. A. (1994). What is creativity? In M. A. Boden (Ed.), *Dimensions of creativity* (pp. 75–118). Cambridge, MA: MIT Press.

Campbell, J. (1976). *The portable Jung* (F. C. Hull, Trans.). New York: Viking Press.

Create. (2010). In *Oxford English dictionary online*. Retrieved, from http://www.oed .com/view/Entry/44061.

Dacey, J. S. (1989). *Fundamentals of creative thinking*. Lexington, MA: Lexington Press.

Dellas, M., & Gaier, E. L. (1970). Identification of creativity: The individual. *Psychological Bulletin, 73*, 55–73.

Duchan, J. F., Bruder, G. A., & Hewitt, L. E. (Eds.). (1995). *Deixis in narrative: A cognitive science perspective*. Hillsdale, NJ: Lawrence Erlbaum Associates.

Dust, P. H. (1981). Literature and vicarious experience: The imagination as trickster and midwife. *Journal of Mental Imagery, 5*,143–156.

Gordon, W.J.J. (1961). *Synectics: The development of creative capacity*. New York: Harper & Row.

Haven, K. (2007). *Story proof: The science behind the startling power of story*. Westport, CT: Libraries Unlimited.

Inglis, F. (1971). Reading children's novels: Notes on the politics of literature. *Children's Literature in Education, 2*, 2, 60–75. DOI: 10.1007/BF01262765.

Iser, W. (1971). Indeterminacy and the reader's response. In J. H. Miller (Ed.), *Aspects of narrative* (pp. 1–45). New York: Columbia University Press.

Iser, W. (1972). The reading process: A phenomenological approach. *New Literary History, 3*, 2, 279–299.

Koestler, A. (1964). *The act of creation*. London, England: Hutchinson and Co.

Langer, J. A. (1990). Understanding literature. *Language Arts, 67*, 812–816.

Mackey, M. (1999). Playing in the phase space: Contemporary forms of fictional pleasure. *Signal: Approaches to Children's Books, 88*, 16–33.

Mackey, M. (2003). At play on the borders of the diegetic: Story boundaries and narrative interpretation. *Journal of Literary Research, 35*, 591–632.

McCloud, S. (1993). Comics and the visual revolution. *Publishers Weekly* (October 11), 47–53.

Mooney, R. (1963). A conceptual model for integrating four approaches to the identification of creative talent. In C. W. Taylor & F. Barron (Eds.), *Scientific creativity: Its recognition and development* (pp. 331–340). New York: Wiley.

Murray, J. H. (1997). *Hamlet on the holodeck: The future of narrative in cyberspace*. New York: Free Press.

Nell, V. (1988). *Lost in a book: The psychology of reading for pleasure*. New Haven, CT: Yale University Press.

Nikolajeva, M., & Scott, C. (2000). The dynamics of picturebook communication. *Children's Literature in Education, 31*, 225–239.

Noyes, A. (1907). The highwayman. In *Forty singing seamen and other poems* (pp. 35–43). Edinburgh, Scotland: William Blackwood and Sons.

Oatley, K. (1995). A taxonomy of the emotions of literary response and a theory of identification in fictional narrative. *Poetics, 23*, 53–74.

Pollio, M. R., & Pollio, H. R. (1971). The development of figurative language in school children. Knoxville, TN: Tennessee University. (ERIC Document Reproduction Service No. 087 525).

Rapp, A.M., Leube, D. T., Erb, M. Grodd, W., & Kircher, T. T. J. (2004). Neural correlates of metaphor processing. *Cognitive Brain Research, 20*, 395–402.

Rosen, H. (1986). The importance of story. *Language Arts, 63*, 226–237.

Sawyer, R. K. (2012). *Explaining creativity: The science of human innovation* (2nd ed.). Oxford, England: Oxford University Press.

Simon, H. A. (2001). Creativity in the arts and the sciences. *The Kenyon Review, New Series, 23*, 203–220.

Sturm, B. W. (1998). *The entrancing power of storytelling: A systems approach to the storylistening discrete altered state of consciousness*. PhD dissertation, School of Library and Information Science, Indiana University, Bloomington, IN.

Sturm, B.W. (2001). The reader's altered state of consciousness. In K. Shearer & R. Burgin (Eds.), *The readers' advisor's companion* (pp. 97–117). Englewood, CO: Libraries Unlimited.

Thackeray, W.M. (1945). *The letters and private papers of William Makepeace Thackeray.* Cambridge, MA: Harvard University Press.

von Franz, M.L. (1996). *The interpretation of fairy tales* (Rev. ed.). Boston, MA: Shambhala.

Whitehurst, G.J. (n.d.). Dialogic reading: An effective way to read to preschoolers. Retrieved from http://www.readingrockets.org/article/400/.

Whitehurst, G.J., Falco, F.I., Lonigan, C.J., Fischel, J.E., DeBaryshe, B.D., Valdez-Menchaca, M.C., & Caulfield, M. (1988). Accelerating language development through picture book reading. *Developmental Psychology, 24,* 552–559.

Zillman, D. (1995). Mechanisms of emotional involvement with drama. *Poetics, 23,* 33–51.

Appendix A

CREATIVE SOLUTION AND DIAGNOSIS SCALE (CSDS)

CRITERION OF CREATIVITY	PROPERTY OF THE SOLUTION	INDICATOR
Relevance and effectiveness	Knowledge of existing facts and principles	CORRECTNESS (the solution accurately reflects conventional knowledge and/or techniques)
		PERFORMANCE (the solution does what it is supposed to do)
		APPROPRIATENESS (the solution fits within task constraints)
		OPERABILITY (the solution is easy to use)
		SAFETY (the solution is safe to use)
		DURABILITY (the solution is reasonably strong)
Novelty	Problematization	DIAGNOSIS (the solution draws attention to shortcomings in other existing solutions)
		PRESCRIPTION (the solution shows how existing solutions could be improved)
		PROGNOSIS (the solution helps the beholder to anticipate likely effects of changes)

(*Continued*)

CRITERION OF CREATIVITY	PROPERTY OF THE SOLUTION	INDICATOR
Novelty (*Continued*)	Existing knowledge	REPLICATION (the solution uses existing knowledge to generate novelty)
		COMBINATION (the solution makes use of new mixture(s) of existing elements)
		INCREMENTATION (the solution extends the known in an existing direction)
	New knowledge	REDIRECTION (the solution shows how to extend the known in a new direction)
		RECONSTRUCTION (the solution shows that an approach previously abandoned is still useful)
		REINITIATION (the solution indicates a radically new approach)
		REDEFINITION (the solution helps the beholder see new and different ways of using the solution)
		GENERATION (the solution offers a fundamentally new perspective on possible solutions)
Elegance	External elegance	RECOGNITION (the beholder sees at once that the solution makes sense)
		CONVINCINGNESS (the beholder sees the solution as skillfully executed, well-finished)
		PLEASINGNESS (the beholder finds the solution neat, well done)
	Internal elegance	COMPLETENESS (the solution is well worked out and "rounded")
		GRACEFULNESS (the solution well-proportioned, nicely formed)
		HARMONIOUSNESS (the elements of the solution fit together in a consistent way)
		SUSTAINABILITY (the solution is environmentally friendly)

(*Continued*)

CRITERION OF CREATIVITY	PROPERTY OF THE SOLUTION	INDICATOR
Genesis	Forward looking	FOUNDATIONALITY (the solution suggests a novel basis for further work)
		TRANSFERABILITY (the solution offers ideas for solving apparently unrelated problems)
		GERMINALITY (the solution suggests new ways of looking at existing problems)
		SEMINALITY (the solution draws attention to previously unnoticed problems)
		VISION (the solution suggests new norms for judging other solutions—existing or new)
		PATHFINDING (the solution opens up a new conceptualization of the issues)

Note: D. H. Cropley and A. J. Cropley proposed a system for rating the creativity of classroom products in "Recognizing and Fostering Creativity in Design Education," 2010, *International Journal of Technology and Design Education, 20.* The proposed system was named the Creative Solution Diagnosis Scale by D. H. Cropley, J. C. Kaufman, and A. J. Cropley in "Measuring Creativity for Innovation Management," 2011, *Journal of Technology Management and Innovation, 6(3).* Reprinted with permission.

Appendix B

FUTURE PROBLEM SOLVING INTERNATIONAL TOPIC LISTS

2012–2013 Topic Order

TYPE OF PROBLEM	TOPIC
Practice problem # 1	Culture of celebrity
Practice problem # 2	Robotic age
Qualifying problem	Megacities
Affiliate competition	Ocean soup

2015–2016 Topic Vote

CATEGORY	TOPIC CANDIDATES
Business/economics	Consumerism
	Currency
	The global workplace
	Product stewardship
	Social insurance
Science/technology	Biosecurity
	Electronic waste
	Energy of the future
	Insects
	Sleep patterns
Social/political	Climate refugees
	Demographic shifts
	Disappearing languages
	Recovering from disaster
	Treatment of animals

RESOURCES

ARTICLES

Please be sure to peruse the reference sections at the end of each chapter for extensive coverage of the topic highlighted in each.

ASSOCIATIONS

American Creativity Association: http://www.aca.cloverpad.org/
>	An interdisciplinary organization where members learn and apply creative and also innovative theory, tool, and techniques.

American Educational Research Association (AERA) Research on Giftedness, Creativity, and Talent SIG: http://www.aeragifted.org/
>	A special interest group of AERA dedicated to research on creativity and giftedness and talent development. Publishes a quarterly journal.

American Psychological Association, Division 10: http://www.apa.org/divisions/div10/
>	*The Society for Psychology and the Arts (APA Division 10)* is dedicated to interdisciplinary scholarship, of both a theoretical and empirical nature, which covers the encompassing the visual, literary, and performing arts.

Destination Imagination: http://www.idodi.org/
>	An offshoot from Odyssey of the Mind, DI is an educational program for teams of students to solve open-ended problems and present creative solutions at tournaments. In solving challenges, students learn important life skills, such as time management, collaboration, conflict resolution, creative and critical thinking.

European Association for Creativity and Innovation (EACI): http://www.eaci.net/EACI/EACI_-_European_Association_for_Creativity_and_Innovation.html
>	The EACI is a not-for-profit, interdisciplinary association, focused on disseminating information and knowledge about innovation and creativity throughout Europe.

Future Problem Solving Program International (FPSPI): http://www.fpspi.org
>	FPSPI engages students in creative problem-solving within the curriculum and provides competitive opportunities. See chapter 14 for more information.

National Association for Gifted Children: www.nagc.org
>   As named, a national advocacy organization dedicated to research and education
>   about gifted and creative children.

Odyssey of the Mind: www.odysseyofthemind.org
>   An international program that develops creative problem-solving skills in students
>   K–12. Can operate as a curricular element directed by teachers or librarians or as an
>   enrichment program directed by trained volunteers.

BOOKS

This eclectic collection of titles was chosen for a variety of reasons: some for their importance in the field, others for their unique observations, and still others for their usefulness to practitioners or students of creativity.

Amabile, T. (1992). *Growing up creative: Nurturing a lifetime of creativity.* Amherst, MA: Creative Education Foundation.
>   A seminal, research-based work about creativity that explains how to foster creativity
>   in children.

Arden, A. (2012). *The book of doing: Everyday activities to unlock your creativity and joy.* New York: Perigee.
>   If we want to encourage creativity in children, we need to discover or rediscover it in
>   ourselves. A practical book of suggestions for doing just that.

Ayan, J. (1996). *Aha! 10 ways to free your creative spirit and find your great ideas.* New York: Clarkson Potter.
>   An inspiring and practical guide to enhancing creativity in all of us.

Bender, W. (2012). *Project-based learning: Differentiating instruction for the 21st century.* Thousand Oaks, CA: Corwin.
>   Strategies and methods for designing, differentiating, and implementing meaningful
>   inquiry-based or project-based learning in classrooms and libraries.

Benke, K. (2010). *Rip the page! Adventures in creative writing.* Boston, MA: Roost Books.
>   An out-of-the-box collection of ideas to inspire a variety of creative writing in people
>   aged nine and above.

Coil, C. (2011). *Differentiated activities and assessments using the common core standards.* Marion, IL: Pieces of Learning.
>   Includes over 50 topics for use in classroom or library that differentiate instruction
>   for diverse students while simultaneously meeting Common Core State Standards.

Costa, A. (2001). *Developing minds: A resource book for teaching thinking.* Alexandria, VA: Association for Supervision and Curriculum Development.
>   The content of this book, a collection of articles, helps all educators understand how
>   a shared vision for thinking creates thinkers.

Costa, A. (2008). *Learning and leading with habits of mind: 16 essential characteristics for success.* Alexandria, VA: Association for Supervision and Curriculum Development.
>   A compilation of the four original Habits of Mind books, this strives to teach us how
>   to encourage the use of habits of mind by our students.

Cropley, D., Cropley, A., Kaufman, J., & Runco, M. (eds). (2010). *The dark side of creativity.* West Nyack, NY: Cambridge University Press.
>   Creative students whose needs are not met can sometimes turn to their darker side;
>   this book examines how this happens, who is affected, and how we can prevent these
>   problems.

Csikszentmihalyi, M. (1997). *Creativity: Flow and the psychology of discovery and invention.* New York: Harper Perennial.

A must-read for those who wish to understand how to achieve those large and small creative moments that make life worthwhile.

DeBono, E. (2008). *Creativity workout: 62 exercises to unlock your most creative ideas.* Berkeley, CA: Ulysses Press.

DeBono, an expert on thinking, has pulled together exercises that show us that we don't have to be born creative, that we can grow our own and students' creativity.

Gardner, H. (2011). *The unschooled mind: How children think and how schools should teach* (2nd ed). New York: Basic Books.

As relevant as ever in this age of standards-based education, Gardner teaches us why must first teach for understanding and how if we are to help students meet standards.

Kaufman, J. (2009). *Creativity 101.* New York: Springer Publishing.

A friendly primer on creativity, further explaining many of the concepts covered in the Creative Imperative.

MacLeod, H. (2009). *Ignore everybody: And 39 other keys to creativity.* New York: Portfolio Hardcover.

Forty keys to creativity and how we can use these to help uncover, explore our own and students' creative sides.

Michalko, M. (2006). *Thinkertoys: A handbook of creative-thinking techniques* (2nd ed.). Berkeley, CA: Ten Speed Press.

Being playful is a part of the creative process. The author helps us approach problems in innovative and interesting ways.

Osborn, A.F., & Osborn, A. (1999). *Your creative power.* Mansfield, MA: Motorola University Press.

A reissue of an old favorite by one of the fathers of creativity—Alex Osborn. Through anecdotes, we learn how to unleash the imagination on a variety of topics/problems.

Piirto, J. (2004). *Understanding creativity.* Tuscon, AZ: Great Potential Press.

This world-renowned author and researcher of creativity offers practical direction on how to create learning opportunities, value work without grading it, create a friendly place for creativity to occur, and incorporate it into our homes and schools.

Piirto, J. (2011). *Creativity for 21st century skills: How to embed creativity into the curriculum.* Boston, MA: Sense Publishers.

Simple tried-and-true techniques for integrating creativity into one's curriculum, whether classroom or library.

Pink, D. (2006). *A whole new mind: Why right-brainers will rule the future.* New York: Riverhead Trade.

A very readable book about what skills and habits we need to cultivate in ourselves and our children to meet the needs of a future that is already here.

Randel, J. (2010). *The skinny on creativity.* Westport. CT: Rand Media Co.

A quick read to understand creativity, and how to do it.

Robinson, K. (2009). *The element: How finding your passion changes everything.* New York: Penguin Books.

When people are in the "element" they feel like they are at their personal best. This book discusses how talent, passion, and achievement combine to help us achieve our element.

Robinson, K. (2011). *Out of our minds: Learning to be creative.* North Mankato, MN: Capstone.

A compelling argument for why we need to integrate creativity with education and training to have the best life and world we want.

Root-Bernstein, R., & Root-Bernstein, M. (2001). *Sparks of genius: The thirteen thinking tools of the world's most creative people.* New York: Mariner Books.
   A set of tools we can use with students to encourage creative and innovative thinking.

Starko, A. (2009). *Creativity in the classroom: Schools of curious delight.* New York: Routledge.
   Targeted to educators of all types, this volume links everyday teaching to research in creativity in a very accessible way.

Sternberg, R., Kaufman, J., & Grigorenko, E. (2008). *Applied intelligence.* West Nyack, NY: Cambridge University Press.
   Going far beyond the IQ notion of intelligence, this text helps prepare students of all ages for the challenges they face in the real world.

Van Oech, R. (2008). *A whack on the side of the head: How you can be more creative.* New York: Business Plus.
   This is the 25th anniversary version of the book that helps readers unlearn rigid thinking and stretch their minds to break down mental blocks and unlock creativity.

Wagner, T. (2012). *Creating innovators: The making of young people who will change the world.* New York: Scribner.
   Wagner describes how play, passion, and purpose drive innovation in this innovative book that has more than 60 accompanying videos (accessed through QR codes or website).

Wallace, V., & Husid, W. (2011). *Collaborating for inquiry-based learning: School librarians and teachers partner for student achievement.* Santa Barbara, CA: Libraries Unlimited.
   A step-by-step guide to how collaboration between librarians and classroom teachers can promote inquiry learning in students.

Wujec, T. (1995). *Five star mind: Games and puzzles to stimulate your creativity and imagination.* Jackson, TN: Main Street Books.
   Using a variety of techniques, this book teaches us how to unlock and build upon the creative potential we already possess.

Zhao, Y. (2012). *World class learners: Educating creative and entrepreneurial students.* Thousand Oaks, CA: Corwin.
   In this book, we learn why competition for higher test scores is counterproductive to what we really need in our schools and world today: creative and innovative thinking and ability.

CATALOGS: BOOKS AND MATERIALS FOR TEACHING CREATIVITY/CREATIVELY

Free Spirit Publishing: http://www.freespirit.com/
Great Potential Press: http://www.greatpotentialpress.com/
Mindware: http://www.prufrock.com/
Pieces of Learning: http://www.piecesoflearning.com/index.php?route=common/home
Prufrock Press: http://www.prufrock.com/

MAGAZINES AND JOURNALS

Creativity Research Journal, Taylor & Francis _____
Gifted Child Quarterly, SAGE Publications

Gifted Child Today, SAGE Publications

The Journal of Creative Behavior, Wiley

Journal of Creativity in Mental Health, Routledge, The Taylor & Francis Group

Journal for the Education of the Gifted, SAGE Publications

Parenting for High Potential, National Association for Gifted Children

Psychology of Aesthetics, Creativity, and the Arts, American Psychological Association (APA)

Teaching for High Potential, National Association for Gifted Children

Thinking Skills and Creativity, ELSEVIER

VIDEOS

An interesting selection of videos on creativity and inquiry.

29 Ways to Stay Creative: http://vimeo.com/24302498
> A captivating little video to inspire us to be more creative in our everyday lives!

Art of Teaching: Engaging Students in Inquiry Learning: http://www.viu.ca/iel/teachlearn/art_of_teaching_2/index.asp
> This video has a good discussion of inquiry and shows examples of inquiry occurring.

Creating Innovators: http://creatinginnovators.com/videos/
> Education expert Tony Wagner and filmmaker Robert Compton created a new book (featured in our book list) about what educators and parents need to do to encourage creative innovation in today's students. This site has over 60 videos that accompany the book.

The Creativity Crisis: http://www.creativitypost.com/education/yes_there_is_a_creativity_crisis
> See author Kyung Hee Kim discuss the creativity crisis in the United States.

David Kelley: How to Build Your Creative Confidence: http://www.ted.com/talks/david_kelley_how_to_build_your_creative_confidence.html
> This video offers advice on how to help members of your own feel more confident in their own creativity

Dan Pink: The Puzzle of Motivation: http://www.ted.com/talks/dan_pink_on_motivation.html
> A must see talk on what we really need to know about motivation, and how schools don't always (or usually) get it right.

Elizabeth Gilbert on Creative Genius: http://www.ted.com/talks/elizabeth_gilbert_on_genius.html
> An inspiring, witty, and insightful video on the genius within each of us.

The Essence of Creativity: http://www.ted.com/tedx/events/1899
> Author and scholar Bonnie Cramond discusses the essence of creativity with other panelists.

Harald's 10 Best Videos on Creativity: http://creativity.trainings.ee/best-videos-on-creativity/
> Ten diverse videos on creativity and being more creative.

How Creativity Happens: http://vimeo.com/38798735
> An entertaining and very brief on how creativity really works.

Inquiry Videos: http://www.ed.psu.edu/englishpds/inquiryvideos
> Five years of videos on inquiry from interns at Penn State University.

Ken Robinson Says Schools Kill Creativity: http://www.ted.com/talks/ken_robinson_ says_schools_kill_creativity.html
> What we need to do to create creativity-friendly schools and other institutions.

Tim Brown: Tales of Creativity and Play: http://www.ted.com/talks/tim_brown_on_ creativity_and_play.html
> An interesting and engaging talk about the importance of play to creativity.

Workshop: Inquiry-Based Learning: http://www.thirteen.org/edonline/concept2class/ inquiry/index.html
> Free award-winning modules on a variety of topics related to inquiry and creativity.

Why Work Doesn't Happen at Work: http://www.ted.com/talks/jason_fried_why_ work_doesn_t_happen_at_work.html
> In this video we see why creative work doesn't usually happen at work; it is really all about incubation.

WEBSITES

Each of these websites contains a wealth of information about creativity—everything from theory to practice. Happy browsing!

http://www.creativity-portal.com/
> Explore and express your creativity.

http://www.coe.uga.edu/torrance
> The Torrance Center for Creativity at the University of Georgia.

http://www.creativeeducationfoundation.org/
> The place where brainstorming began and whose purpose is to engage and develop the next generation of creative thinkers and innovators.

http://www.creativityday.org/
> Connecting creative minds around the globe.

http://enchantedmind.com/
> This site was designed to help anyone, from age 5 to 105, develop their latent creativity and have fun in the process.

http://members.optusnet.com.au/charles57/Creative/index2.html
> A wide-ranging collection of resources for creativity and innovation.

http://www.creax.net/
> 843 Handpicked websites on creativity and innovation.

http://workingcreativity.com/activities/index.html
> Creative activities to attain deeper understandings and insights about people and their stuff, about culture and the media.

http://www.bdance.com/en/
> Brain dance to help us work smarter, learn faster, and manage more information more easily.

http://www.hoagiesgifted.org
> This quintessential site on all things gifted and creative contains over 3,000 pages.

http://www.teachthought.com/learning/30-ideas-to-promote-creativity-in-learning/
> How to train your brain.

http://www.creativitycultureeducation.org/
   A UK-based charity, which works internationally to unlock the creativity of young
   people in and out of formal education.

http://www.celt.iastate.edu/creativity/techniques.html
   Iowa State Center for Excellence in Teaching and Learning supplies various techniques for creative teaching.

INDEX

ABOUT THE EDITORS AND CONTRIBUTORS

MARILYN P. ARNONE is a research associate professor and associate professor of practice in the School of Information Studies at Syracuse University. She also serves as co-director of the Center for Digital Literacy. Her research focuses on motivational factors contributing to information and digital literacies in formal and informal online learning environments including curiosity, interest, and engagement. She has authored or co-authored a number of professional books including most recently *Teaching for Inquiry: Engaging the Learner Within* with Ruth Small, Barbara Stripling, and Pam Berger. She embraces the inclusion of curiosity and creativity as important dispositions in the AASL Standards for the 21st-Century Learner and incorporates them into the print and web-based projects she has designed to inspire inquiry and imagination in young children.

GAIL BUSH is professor emerita of education, National Louis University in Chicago, Illinois. Gail's academic background includes a bachelor's degree in anthropology, master's degree in library science, and doctorate in educational psychology. Her research includes educator collaboration and the development of professional dispositions; areas of engagement are poetry, social justice, the transliterate learner, and the library state of mind.

CAROLYN COIL is an internationally known speaker, author, trainer, consultant, and educator who has worked in the field of education for over 30 years. Carolyn is known for her energy, enthusiasm, practical knowledge, and down-to-earth presentation style. She works with teachers, parents, and administrators and presents workshops offering realistic and user-friendly strategies for raising student achievement, using the Common Core Standards, motivating underachievers, differentiating curriculum, and assessing student performance. She has taught at all grade levels and has been an adjunct professor at several different universities since 1989. Carolyn has presented workshops throughout the United States and in Australia, New Zealand, Bermuda, the Marshall Islands, Spain, Germany, Ecuador, Croatia,

Hong Kong, Abu Dhabi, Mexico, Canada, China, and South Korea. She is the author of many journal articles and a number of best-selling educational books published by Pieces of Learning.

STEPHEN V. COXON is a veteran public school teacher who now serves as assistant professor of gifted education at Maryville University in St. Louis. He directs Maryville's programs in gifted education including the graduate program, several grant-funded projects, and the Maryville Summer Science and Robotics Program for high-ability students. Steve's primary interest is in illuminating means by which schools can develop spatial ability, creativity, and other important STEM talents in children. He conducts experimental research on these topics and has published and presented widely on them, including the book *Serving Spatially-Able Learners*. He is the book review editor for *Roeper Review* and writes the column Scientifically Speaking in Teaching for High Potential. Steve was the 2010 recipient of the Joyce VanTassel-Baska Award for Excellence in Gifted Education.

BONNIE L. CRAMOND is the director of the Torrance Center for Creativity and Talent Development at the University of Georgia and a professor of educational psychology. She has been a member of the board of directors of the National Association for Gifted Children, editor of the *Journal of Secondary Gifted Education*, and a schoolteacher. She is on the review board for several journals and has survived parenting two gifted and creative children. An international and national speaker, she has published numerous articles, chapters, and a book on creativity research and teaches classes on giftedness and creativity. Bonnie is particularly interested in the identification and nurturance of creativity, especially among students considered at risk because of their different way of thinking, such as those misdiagnosed with ADHD, emotional problems, or those who drop out.

ARTHUR CROPLEY was born in Australia in 1935. He graduated with a PhD from the University of Alberta in 1965 and taught at the Universities of Regina and Hamburg (with brief stints in Australia). After retiring in 1998 he became visiting professor at the University of Latvia. He has published extensively on creativity. Arthur was founding editor of *High Ability Studies* and is on the board of *Creativity Research Journal*. He has received awards and fellowships and an honorary doctorate from the University of Latvia. In 2004, he received the Order of the Three Stars from the President of Latvia.

DAVID CROPLEY is an associate professor of engineering innovation at the University of South Australia's Mawson Lakes Campus. He is deputy director of the Defence and Systems Institute (DASI). David's research interest center on creativity and innovation in engineering—measurement of product creativity and the process of innovation form two key focal points. David edited *The Dark Side of Creativity* (Cambridge University Press, 2010) with Arthur Cropley, James Kaufman, and Mark Runco. He holds one current indoor-rowing world record (tandem, 100 km) and one past record (tandem, 24 hrs).

LORI J. FLINT is an associate professor in the Department of Special Education, Foundations, and Research, College of Education, at East Carolina University, who has taught students around the country from preschool through graduate school ages, and has a wide range of experience in both private industry and educational areas. She holds a MEd in talent development/curriculum and instruction, and a PhD in educational psychology/gifted and creative education from the University of Georgia, Athens. Lori has an irrepressible curiosity about student achievement and motivation, especially the specific teaching of skills needed for school and real-life survival; gender; social and emotional areas; and individual differences such as gifted students with learning disabilities. She writes about and consults with educators, community groups, students and their families on a wide range of topics surrounding gifted education and student achievement.

MICHAEL HANCHETT HANSON is director of the Masters Concentration in Creativity and Cognition in the Department of Human Development at Teachers College, Columbia University in New York City. He has a BA from Yale University and his PhD in developmental psychology from Columbia University. Michael has studied and written about practical guidelines for creativity in education; creativity as an emerging social construction; use of ironic thinking in creative work and existential implications of systems theories. Michael sees creativity as one of the defining ideas of our times, a relatively new, and still emerging, concept about the value and processes of change. He encourages his students to participate in the ongoing construction of this idea by studying, evaluating, and applying a variety of theories and practices. His pragmatic approach is informed by his research, as well as decades of firsthand experience, working in curriculum development and program evaluation for educational institutions, youth development programs, and museums.

BETH A. HENNESSEY is a professor of psychology at Wellesley College in Massachusetts, where she has been a member of the psychology department since 1985. She served as the faculty director of Wellesley's Pforzheimer Learning and Teaching Center from 2007 to 2011. A former elementary school teacher and social psychologist by training, Beth has carried out numerous studies showing a powerful link between intrinsic task motivation and creativity of performance. This relation holds for everyone from preschoolers to seasoned research and development scientists. Yet, most classrooms and workplaces are set up to kill intrinsic motivation . . . with the imposition of extrinsic constraints like reward systems, evaluations, and competitions. At present, Beth is involved with a number of cross-cultural investigations of this phenomenon, and she is also collaborating with colleagues at the Massachusetts Institute of Technology International Design Center and in Singapore at the new University of Technology and Design to develop a cutting-edge university environment dedicated to promotion of student and faculty members' motivation and creativity.

BRIAN C. HOUSAND is an assistant professor and co-coordinator of the Academically and Intellectually Gifted Program at East Carolina University. Brian earned a PhD in educational psychology at the University of Connecticut's National Research Center on the Gifted and Talented with an emphasis in both gifted education and instructional technology. In 2008, the National Association for Gifted Children (NAGC) recognized him as doctoral student of the year. His column,

Technology Untangled, appears in the NAGC publication *Teaching for High Potential*. He currently serves on the NAGC Board of Directors as a member-at-large. Brian frequently presents and works as an educational consultant on the integration of technology and enrichment into the curriculum. He is currently researching ways in which technology can enhance the learning environment and is striving to define creative-productive giftedness in a digital age.

GARRETT J. JAEGER is a doctoral student and E. Paul Torrance Endowed Student Scholar of Gifted and Creative Education at the University of Georgia, Athens. Prior to arriving at the university, he received an MA in developmental psychology at San Francisco State University. His research on play and the creative process has been influenced by preschool teaching experience, along with continued scholarly investigations of Eastern philosophical traditions and the values that both perspectives place on play throughout the lifespan. Ongoing research under the guidance of Dr. Mark A. Runco has cultivated proficient skills and experience with the advancement of creativity psychometrics. Measurements of creative potential and performance are some of the many contributions—not unlike the contents of this book—which elevate exposure to the potent contributions that creativity research has to offer librarians, along with those whose minds and imagination they influence every day.

VERA JOHN-STEINER, Regents' professor emerita of language, literacy, and sociocultural studies and linguistics, has been engaged in interdisciplinary teaching and research at the University of New Mexico and as a visiting lecturer. She has published in psycholinguistics, cultural historical theory, creativity, collaboration, and bilingualism. John-Steiner co-edited Vygotsky's *Mind in Society*, a text that has been very influential in educational, psychological, linguistic theory, and practice. In *Notebooks of the Mind* she explores the development and diversity of thought processes and creative endeavors. The book received the William James Award in 1990. In *Creative Collaboration,* Vera documents the impact of working partnerships in the human sciences. Her most recent publication, *Loving and Hating Mathematics* is coauthored with Reuben Hersh. Her honors include a fellowship at the Center for Advanced Study in the Behavioral Sciences, a lifetime achievement award from the American Educational Research Association, and a Sussman Distinguished Visiting Professorship at Teacher's College, Columbia University. She has taught and lectured in Latin America, Europe, and the United States.

JAMI BILES JONES is an associate professor in the Department of Information and Library Science at East Carolina University, Greenville, North Carolina. She has published numerous articles in scholarly and popular professional journals and written or coauthored five books on topics rarely or never addressed in school library literature, such as resiliency, dropout prevention, dispositions, caring, and creativity. She is author of the Florida Association of Media in Education's *Amanda Award* presented annually to secondary school librarians who develop programs and services that strengthen and build students' resilience. A graduate student's comment, "I am not creative," led Jami to explore creativity at Teachers College, Columbia University, during the 2010–2011 academic year and is the genesis for this book. Her goal is to unsettle conventional ways of thinking about and practicing school librarianship.

KYUNG HEE KIM is an associate professor of educational psychology at The College of William and Mary. In July 2010, her study "the Creativity Crisis" featured in Newsweek along with her written assessments of sample creativity tests, "How Creative Are You?" opened a national and international dialogue, which indicated that the United States has experienced a general overall decline in creativity since 1990. Kyung Hee is regularly featured in national and international news outlets including *The Washington Post*, the *U.S. News & World Report*, *The Wall Street Journal*, *Time*, and others. She serves on the editorial board of the *International Journal of Creativity and Problem Solving* and the *Psychology of Aesthetics, Creativity, and the Arts*, and on the advisory board of *The Creativity Post*. She is the Chair Elect of the Creativity Network of NAGC. She is the first editor of the book *Creatively Gifted Students Are Not Like Other Gifted Students: Research, Theory, and Practice*. Kyung Hee has received many honors and distinctions that recognize her scholarly contributions including the following: The 2012 Torrance Lecturer; in 2011, The Early Scholar Award from the National Association of Gifted Children (NAGC); in 2009, The Berlyne Award from the American Psychological Association and The New Voice in Intelligence and Creativity Award; in 2008, The Hollingworth Research Award from NAGC; and others. She trains parents and teachers around the world to foster creativity in children.

SUEHYEON PAEK is a doctoral student in the Department of Educational Psychology and Instructional Technology at the University of Georgia, Athens. She has conducted research about strength, intrinsic goals, resiliency, and subjective well-being. Currently, Suehyeon is concentrating on creativity, gifted education, and problem finding. She taught elementary school students for seven years and was an assistant administrator for the Positive Psychology Association of Korea.

RUTH V. SMALL is the Laura J. & L. Douglas Meredith Professor of Information Studies at Syracuse University. She is also founding director of the Center for Digital Literacy and director of the school media program. Her research focuses on the motivational aspects of information use by both children and adults in a variety of contexts; she has authored or coauthored more than 100 publications, including seven books, and served on the editorial boards of three professional journals. For her work, she received the 1997 Highsmith Research Award from the American Association of School Librarians and the 2001 Carroll Preston Baber Research Award from the American Library Association. In addition, Ruth was recognized for outstanding teaching performance with her school's 1996 "Professor of the Year" award and "Teacher of the Year" award in 2004 by the Syracuse University Alumni Association. In 2006, Ruth was named a Meredith Professorship for Teaching Excellence, Syracuse University's highest teaching honor.

ALANE JORDAN STARKO is a professor in the Department of Teacher Education of Eastern Michigan University. A former elementary classroom teacher, teacher of the gifted, college department head and interim dean, she is enjoying her return to faculty life, particularly the new adventures of blogging (*creativiteach. me*) and teaching online classes. Alane is the author of *Creativity in the Classroom: Schools of Curious Delight* and other publications on creativity, gifted education, teaching research to children, and curriculum development.

BRIAN STURM is an associate professor and director of the Masters of Science in Library Science degree at the School of Information and Library Science at the University of North Carolina at Chapel Hill. Brian is also a professional storyteller, performing folktales from around the world with children and adults and offering workshops on storytelling theory and practice. His research interests gravitate toward the experience of immersion—or trance-like engagement—in various contexts such as reading, storytelling, and video games, and he teaches graduate classes in storytelling, children's literature, and children's public library services.

SARAH E. SUMNERS is an assistant research scientist and the assistant director of the Torrance Center for Creativity and Talent Development at the University of Georgia, Athens. Before joining the Torrance Center, Sarah served as the principal investigator for the CHAMPS Mathematics and Science Partnership and Project Citizen grants for the state of Mississippi. In this capacity, she provided considerable experiences and success in providing professional development opportunities for teachers in the state. Prior to working for the Center for Creative Learning at Mississippi University for Women, Sarah served as the project manager for the Jacob K. Javits grant for gifted and talented education at the Mississippi School for Mathematics and Science, where she taught high school social studies. Sarah has a wide range of experience in grant writing, teaching, and professional development. She holds a MEd in gifted studies from Mississippi University for Women and a PhD in curriculum and instruction from Mississippi State University.

ROBERT W. WEISBERG is professor of psychology and director of graduate studies at Temple University. A cognitive psychologist, Robert's area of interest is creative thinking, the cognitive processes involved in the intentional production of novelty: solutions to problems, works of art, scientific discoveries, and inventions. He has published papers investigating cognitive mechanisms underlying problem-solving and has published papers and books examining cognitive processes underlying creative thinking. Robert and his students have carried out laboratory studies of undergraduates solving problems of various sorts, in order to gain understanding of the mechanisms underlying leaps of insight and Aha! experiences in problem-solving. He and his students have also examined "real-world" creative thinking at the highest levels through case studies of people such as Edison, Picasso, Frank Lloyd Wright, and jazz great Charlie Parker. In those studies, attempts are made to apply scientific methods to historical data, in order to derive conclusions concerning how the creative process functions at the highest levels.